ON
COLD
MOUNTAIN

ON COLD MOUNTAIN

A Buddhist Reading of the Hanshan Poems

PAUL ROUZER

A China Program Book

UNIVERSITY OF WASHINGTON PRESS
Seattle and London

On Cold Mountain was made possible in part by a grant from the University of Minnesota's Imagine Fund, awarded through the College of Liberal Arts.

This book also was supported by the China Studies Program, a division of the Henry M. Jackson School of International Studies at the University of Washington.

Printed and bound in the United States of America
Design by Thomas Eykemans
Composed in Minion, typeface designed by Robert Slimbach
18 17 16 15 5 4 3 2 1

"Self-Portrait in a Borrowed Cabin," "On the Beach," "Bees," "Light House" (from "Seventeen Pebbles"), "Against Certainty," and "The Adamantine Perfection of Desire" (three-line excerpt) were also published in Jane Hirschfield, *Each Happiness Ringed by Lions: Selected Poems* (Hexham, UK: Bloodaxe Books, 2005). "The Promise" was published in *Come, Thief* (Hexham, UK: Bloodaxe Books, 2012).

UNIVERSITY OF WASHINGTON PRESS
www.washington.edu/uwpress

LIBRARY OF CONGRESS CATALOGING-IN-PUBLICATION DATA
Rouzer, Paul F.
On cold mountain : a Buddhist reading of the Hanshan poems / Paul Rouzer.
pages cm
Includes bibliographical references and index.
ISBN 978-0-295-99499-4 (hardcover : alk. paper)
1. Hanshan, active 627–649—Criticism and interpretation. 2. Chinese poetry—Tang dynasty, 618–907—History and criticism. 3. Buddhism in literature. I. Title.
PL2677.H3Z83 2015
895.11′3—dc23 2015012274

The paper used in this publication is acid-free and meets the minimum requirements of American National Standard for Information Sciences—Permanence of Paper for Printed Library Materials, ANSI Z39.48–1984. ∞

Spoken words and written text all are Marks of Liberation. Why is that? Liberation is neither internal, external, nor in between. Written text is also neither internal, external, nor in between. And so, Śāriputra, you may speak of Liberation without transcending written text. Why is that? All dharmas are Marks of Liberation.

—The Vimalakīrti Sutra

Now when people like us select a teacher, it's no good to pick a Buddha or a Zen patriarch—only Master Cold Mountain can serve as a teacher.

—Hakuin Ekaku

CONTENTS

PREFACE AND ACKNOWLEDGMENTS

I should mention from the first that the following does not purport to be a biography of Hanshan (Cold Mountain), nor does it argue that the Hanshan poems are meant to represent the personal experience of their author(s). Nor is this a history of the reception of the Hanshan poems—worthy though such a project would be. This is a work of literary criticism and close reading from a Buddhist perspective, taking the Hanshan poems as its focus.

In recent decades, scholars in East Asia and in the West have immensely expanded their understanding of East Asian literature, not only in terms of basic literary history (broader knowledge of the tradition, greater familiarity with minor works, and increased sensitivity to historical factors), but also in terms of theoretical tools (literary and cultural theory most obviously). As a result, interested readers in English-speaking countries now have available to them an increasing number of translations and studies that can grant them a more sophisticated sense of the Chinese tradition. And yet in that same period, academic specialization has tended to demand more from its readership as well, making this scholarship inaccessible at times to anyone without a considerable background in history and language. Certainly it would be to the benefit of everyone if the scholars among us spent time demonstrating why East Asian literature is just as worth reading as anything produced by the Western tradition, and that its worth is tied not to an antiquarian historicism but rather to broader matters of aesthetic appreciation as well as personal cultivation (whether one counts the latter as specifically Buddhist or as more broadly "humanist"). This book tries to do just that, walking a path between a specialist monograph on the one hand and a popular introduction on the other, proposing what I hope are novel arguments about the poems while also making them more accessible to a general reader. I have deliberately conceived of this book (especially its middle chapters) as a sort of "appreciation" of Hanshan.

Another feature of this study is that it attempts to root its method in a specifically Buddhist approach to poetry. This is not new, especially in Japanese literary scholarship, where a Buddhist perspective has played a vital role in textual close reading at least since William R. LaFleur's *The Karma of Words* (1983); this tendency has continued in the work of Rajyashree Pandey and Stephen D. Miller, among others. However, this has been much less the case in the Chinese field, particularly in the study of poetry. The Buddhist "way of reading" I am interested in here does not include, for example, the work of scholars who have analyzed the influence of Buddhist concepts on mainstream Chinese poetics (as in Xiaofei Tian's recent work on Chinese early medieval culture), nor the explication of concrete Buddhist details as they occur in verse specifically tailored to believers (as in Mary Anne Cartelli's discussion of Wutai poetry from Dunhuang). Rather, I wish to consider a way of interpreting and appreciating verse that is governed by Buddhist beliefs. The difference should become clear in the course of my discussion.

I also argue for the radical "presentness" of the poems themselves in close readings and interpretations of a number of modern texts by Jack Kerouac, Gary Snyder, and Jane Hirshfield, who respond in their own ways to the East Asian Buddhist tradition. This is not out of disregard for historical and cultural difference, but rather to demonstrate how different writers have responded to the same religious discourse over the centuries. Historical and cultural difference is part of the story, but it operates against the awareness in all of these writers of some basic Buddhist assumptions about the way the world operates.

Special acknowledgements are due to Lorri Hagman, my editor at the University of Washington Press, and the UWP manuscript reviewers; to my production editor and copyeditor, Jacqueline Volin and Caroline Knapp; to Tim Zimmermann, who provided invaluable help in obtaining permissions; to Jane Hirshfield, who generously looked at my discussion of her poems; and to my colleagues in the Department of Asian Languages and Literatures at the University of Minnesota, especially Joseph Allen. I am also grateful to the College of Liberal Arts at the University of Minnesota, which granted me a sabbatical leave for Spring 2014, enabling me to complete the manuscript, and which provided a subvention through the Imagine Fund to aid in the publication. A very special thanks also to Jennifer Carpenter, who has proved my most sympathetic and critical reader.

Conventions

As readers will likely know, the legendary author of the Hanshan poems named himself after his place of reclusion, Cold Mountain. This can cause some confusion (sometimes intentional) in differentiating man from place. For the sake of clarity I will use the Chinese *Hanshan* when talking about the supposed author, and *Cold Mountain* when talking about the location. However, readers should keep in mind that in Chinese the terms are the same.

I have left a number of common Buddhist terms unitalicized and without diacritical marks: Mahayana, Hinayana, samsara, nirvana, tripitaka, Dharma, kalpa, sutra, sangha, satori, koan, roshi. I assume that my readers will have a general knowledge of the basic principles of Buddhism, and so I have not felt it necessary to explain the fundamental points of Buddhist doctrine. I have tried to explain any concepts that occur beyond that level, however. Occasionally I will capitalize English-language terms when I emphasize their equivalent to a Buddhist doctrinal concept: Impermanence, Mind.

I have made some attempt to use the terms *Chan* and *Zen* in a consistent manner. When I use *Chan* (the original Chinese designation), I refer specifically to the early development of the Chan movement in Tang dynasty China (618–907) until its relative stabilization during the Song (960–1279). After that, I use *Zen* (the Japanese designation) for any aspects of the movement, no matter what country or tradition is being discussed. This is not meant to suggest a preference for the Japanese form of the movement; it is merely the term with which the average English-speaking reader is most familiar.

Citations to the *Taishō Tripitaka* (the standard edition of the East Asian Buddhist canon, published in Japan from 1913 to 1921) follow this format: volume number (T), text number (no.), page number, range (a, b, c), and line number(s). For example: T. 40, no. 2012, 382, b11–27. A complete list of the cited Taishō texts may be found in the bibliography.

I have used pinyin romanization for Chinese terms throughout; however, I occasionally quote scholars who use the older Wade-Giles system. In such cases, I have changed the Wade-Giles rendering to pinyin and have indicated this in the notes.

Neither the Hanshan poems nor the poems attributed to Shide have titles. Consequently, many scholars use numbers when identifying them. Unfortunately, two factors lead to inconsistent numbering: there are two textual traditions for the Hanshan collection, with somewhat different sequencing of the poems, and there is some disagreement among scholars about whether certain groups of verse are one poem or more than one poem. In this study, I number the poems based on the Xiang Chu edition, also used in the *Complete Tang Poems* (Quan Tang shi). Xiang Chu uses the earliest Song dynasty textual transmission line, whose earliest surviving text dates to the early 1100s. The other tradition, the so-called Guoqing Temple edition, dates from the 1180s; this is followed, for example, by Red Pine's English translation.

Xiang Chu also differs slightly from other editors in assigning numbers. First, he holds that the poem elsewhere numbered HS 159, consisting of forty-four lines, is actually two poems (consisting of lines 1–36 and lines 37–44). He consequently numbers lines 37–44 of this poem as HS 160, and the numbers that follow are thus displaced. A similar case occurs in what other editions have as the forty-four-line poem HS 275, a lengthy satire on monastic malfeasance. Xiang Chu assumes that this is two poems, lines 1–18 (HS 276 in his system) and lines 19–44 (HS 277 in his system). In the end, he concludes that there are 313 poems in the collection, as opposed to 311.

The texts in my discussion are based on the Sibu Congkan (SBCK) edition, a reprint of the early Song edition, which in turn serves as the basis of Xiang's edition. There are five or six variant readings that have been accepted by all scholars working with Hanshan; I have accepted these as well without making a note of it.

ON
COLD
MOUNTAIN

INTRODUCTION

WHO GETS TO CLIMB COLD MOUNTAIN?

EARLY in Jack Kerouac's novel *The Dharma Bums*, the narrator, Ray Smith, goes to visit Japhy Rider, a young man who has grown up amid the forests of the Pacific Northwest. He is currently living a double life as a UC Berkeley student of East Asian culture and as a bohemian intellectual:

> A peacefuller scene I never saw than when, in that rather nippy late red afternoon, I simply opened his little door and looked in and saw him at the end of the little shack, sitting crosslegged on a Paisley pillow on a straw mat, with his spectacles on, making him look old and scholarly and wise, with book on lap and the little tin teapot and porcelain cup steaming at his side. He looked up very peacefully, saw who it was, said, "Ray, come in," and bent his eyes again to the script.
>
> "What you doing?"
>
> "Translating Han Shan's great poem called 'Cold Mountain' written a thousand years ago some of it scribbled on the sides of cliffs hundreds of miles away from any other living beings."
>
> "Wow." . . .
>
> "Want me to read you parts of this Han Shan poem? Want me to tell you about Han Shan?"
>
> "Yeah."
>
> "Han Shan you see was a Chinese scholar who got sick of the big city and the world and took off to hide in the mountains."
>
> "Say, that sounds like you."[1]

As with most of Kerouac's fiction, the scene is largely autobiographical. Smith is Kerouac himself, while Ryder is the American poet Gary Snyder at the beginning of his career. In the same year that *The Dharma Bums* appeared, 1958, Snyder published his first translations of Hanshan (whose name actually means "Cold Mountain," from his supposed place of residence) in the *Evergreen Review*. The following year they would appear in book form, along with Snyder's first poetry collection, *Riprap*. Hanshan thus became known to a community of avant-garde poetry readers.

For Snyder and Kerouac, Hanshan was exactly as Japhy describes him: "a Chinese scholar who got sick of the big city and the world and took off to hide in the mountains." They drew this conclusion from the content of some of the poems, as well as from the biographical preface appended to the collection, which has been familiar to readers since the eleventh century at least. It recounts a seventh-century official's encounter with the eccentric poet-recluse at the Guoqing Temple in the Tiantai Mountains, in Zhejiang province. The preface introduces Hanshan's companions, the equally mysterious monks Fenggan and Shide, and describes how later monks assembled the Hanshan collection from poems the recluse had inscribed on cliffs, walls of houses, and other surfaces. Though the poet is portrayed as a layman, this biographical account identifies him as a hermit concerned with the cultivation of Buddhist enlightenment. Beats took this narrative as a portrayal of the ideal poet, someone who lived the poems he wrote; for them, the verses were autobiographical, confessional, and paradigmatic. In *The Dharma Bums*, Kerouac goes out of his way to have Ray identify Japhy with this idealized Hanshan, who represents for him a supremely self-confident sage, someone who embodies the spontaneous qualities revered in a Buddhist master (especially a Zen master), at least from the perspective of the Beats. Meanwhile, since Hanshan is thus made an honorary Beat, his poetry is understood to have a similar purpose to that of the Beats themselves, protesting everything they hate: conventionality, hypocrisy, materialism. It is also telling that Kerouac has Japhy refer to the Hanshan verses as one "great poem": he has turned a disparate collection of three hundred quite independent poems into a sustained and complex countercultural confession, like Whitman's *Song of Myself* or Ginsberg's *Howl*.

While Snyder's own translations are usually faithful to the originals, he too sometimes indicates that he sees Hanshan as a fellow Beat bent on self-confession and protest, most famously when he translates the last couplet of the second poem as: "Go tell families with silverware and cars / 'What's the use of all that noise and money?'" More literally it would read: "I send word to households with bells and tripods / No benefit at all from your empty fame."[2]

The Hanshan of the Beats is thus identified largely by his adversarial position to modern American society—the way that he, like the Beats, is opposed to everything establishment. This manifests itself at the level of translation: slightly later in the same scene between Japhy and Ray, the two discuss how to render Chinese poetry in English. When Ray suggests that Japhy should translate using one English word for each Chinese character (resulting in a radically imagistic and syntax-free version), Ray replies, "Well yeah, I thought of that, but I have to have this pass the approval of Chinese scholars here at the university and have it clear in English."[3]

This is a central tenet in the idealization of Chinese verse among many modern American poets: The more "essential" nature of the Chinese poetic language (which disdains grammatical function words such as prepositions and articles) allows itself to be translated in a way that would appeal to Ray and Japhy. It is only the demands of "Chinese scholars" that forbid Japhy from capturing the true spirit of the text—a spirit the two of them instinctually understand because their empathic connection to Hanshan is more intense than that possessed by academics, even those who might be native speakers of Chinese.[4] The bond between themselves and Hanshan transcends cultural or historical difference.

In looking over the poems attributed to Hanshan, it is easy to see why he would seem a kindred spirit to the Beat writers. There is a polemical grandness to the poems that can turn to angry satire, to evangelizing, and even to a sort of hectoring. In his narrative voice Hanshan is very sure of himself, and very convinced that the people around him need to be cured of their wrong views. Many of the poems are told from the perspective of a mountain recluse and borrow images from Chinese landscape poetry; this aspect of the poems would prove particularly important to Snyder, who became increasingly attracted to how the teachings of Buddhism could resonate with modern environmentalism. Though medieval Chinese Buddhists would not necessarily recognize that the relationship between the appreciation of nature and Buddhist belief was important, for Snyder (and for most North American Buddhists) it has proved essential.[5]

Of course, this was hardly the first time in the history of literature that readers had interpreted a writer in line with their own preoccupations. And if Kerouac and Snyder saw Hanshan as a fellow Beat, that at least had the benefit of drawing Western attention to a figure whom Chinese literary criticism has tended to ignore. There are a number of reasons for this neglect. For one, the canonical tradition of Chinese poetry has been defined in large part by the works of a Confucian-educated gentry who saw the Hanshan poems more as a sort of religious text than as literary work. As a result, the poems had little impact on the historical development of Chinese poetry. Second, until recently, modern Chinese intellectuals have tended to dismiss the products of Chinese Buddhist culture as superstition pernicious to the development of a rational nation-state. Japanese scholars have paid somewhat more attention to the Hanshan poems, which reflects the acknowledged role they have played in the more openly Buddhist culture of premodern Japan. At the same time, however, those scholars have been concerned mostly with linguistic and ideological issues, attempting to examine the texts for what they say about the development of Chan Buddhism during the Tang dynasty and for their usefulness as a storehouse of Tang vernacular speech.[6] Western scholars also have tended to look at the collection from an antiquarian and historical perspective. Most of them consider the poems popular doggerel composed by a number of individuals, none of them gifted with a particularly sophisticated education. A good example of this view is evident in Victor Mair's review of Robert Henricks's scholarly Hanshan translations. After a meticulous discussion of the use of vernacular in the collection, Mair says in passing that interest in the poems "is out of all proportion to the literary merits."[7] Certainly the elevation of the supposed (and largely legendary) author to the status of a charismatic Beat poet is viewed by many academics as the manifestation of a misconceived and naive "New Age" Buddhism.

Yet beyond these two views of the poems (as products of a charismatic nonconformist or as products of a group of marginal and semiliterate folk poets), there is a third view. Starting in the eleventh century, as the collection circulated among Buddhist believers (accompanied by its supposedly biographical preface), it came to be read as a serious expression of Buddhist values and as a source of wisdom for conventional practitioners. It was closely analyzed by the Song dynasty masters of the Chan movement, who based sermons on quotations from it. When Chan moved to Japan in the twelfth and thirteenth centuries and turned into a significant institutional force in Japanese Buddhism, the Cold Mountain poems became part of the canon of Chinese classics that the monk-poets of the Gozan movement embraced and imitated. In Edo Japan, the great Zen master Hakuin Ekaku (1686–1768) preached on the Hanshan texts and provided detailed commentary regarding the deeper doctrinal significance of many of the verses. All of this runs counter to a Beat vision that would see the poet as contemptuous of ordinary religious pieties. The Beats, after all, had learned Zen at the feet of D. T. Suzuki, who, in order to "modernize" it, had attempted to turn Zen into a philosophical critique of mainstream Buddhist faith and belief.[8]

This modern distaste for traditional religious practice can result in uncomfortable contradictions, especially when transnational factors come into play. For example, in Mike Hazard's and Deb Wallwork's half-hour documentary *Cold Mountain: Han Shan*, four Americans are interviewed about the poems: the translator Burton Watson, Gary Snyder, Red Pine (the pen name of Bill Porter, a translator of the complete Hanshan corpus and of many other Buddhist texts), and the Minnesota poet James P. Lenfestey (author of a volume of witty Hanshan imitations).[9] No scholars or writers from East Asia are interviewed. In the end, Hazard and Wallwork do not provide a portrait of the "real" Hanshan, as they perhaps intended, but rather of a poet who exists in the imagination of enthusiasts committed to a Suzuki vision of Buddhism. This becomes strongly evident when Red Pine guides the filmmakers on a trip to Cold Mountain's legendary abode in the Tiantai mountains—a site of pilgrimage for Buddhist believers. Red Pine brings the cameraman into a cave temple reputed to have been the home of Hanshan. As he looks at the statue on the altar, he comments wryly on Hanshan's deification: "No matter how disreputable you are, when you die, you always get kicked upstairs." Then he comments: "In the local villagers' minds, this is a Buddhist temple." Entering deeper into the cave, the translator confronts three figures, which he identifies as Hanshan, Shide, and Fenggan. Looking at the statues, he says, "Usually they're so refined. If Cold Mountain were here today, he would laugh himself to death." An off-camera voice asks him why. Red Pine pauses for a moment, then finally replies: "Because Cold Mountain loved to laugh. And no matter how they depicted him, he would have found a way . . . a reason to laugh."[10]

It should be said that Red Pine is a knowledgeable scholar of Chinese culture and Buddhism, as well as a highly gifted translator. Here, his mockery of the worship of Hanshan comes not from a sense of arrogant Western superiority but from his own belief about the nature of Zen: it is meant to make fun of religious conventions, not embrace them. The hesitation in his final comment suggests that he realizes that his dismissal might look patronizing, coming as it does from an American critically observing Chinese religious customs from the outside. But of course the rhetoric of Zen has often embraced the very attitude that Red Pine displays here: Zen masters are typically shown emphasizing to believers that piety, ritual, and even alms-giving are ultimately useless compared to the effort of personal cultivation one must make to achieve enlightenment. And as we shall see, Red Pine's comment about Hanshan's tendency to laugh—especially at the spiritually benighted—is not so inaccurate.

What *does* lie behind this uncomfortable moment, however, is the contradiction some moderns believe exists between the rhetorical strategies of Zen texts on the one hand and mainstream Buddhist faith on the other. Yet for all of its textual critique of conventional Buddhism, the Zen tradition in East Asia has certainly not divorced itself from it in *practice*: ritual, ceremony, conventional piety, and acknowledgement of the power of "supernatural" forces have all manifested themselves in Zen circles over the centuries.[11] It is easy enough to find examples of Zen monks doing obeisance to bodhisattvas, invoking Amitābha and the Pure Land, proclaiming the power of the Lotus Sutra, or warning each other about the dangers of an unfortunate rebirth. Zen texts' seeming dismissal of traditional ritual is rooted in their critique of dualism and their emphasis on the usefulness of meditation and other techniques as a way to obtain enlightenment. But as a knowledgeable practitioner of Mahayana Buddhism might say, our immersion in the illusory realm of samsara causes us to make ultimately unjustified distinctions between one form of practice and another; consequently, an intellectual rejection of some rituals and beliefs as representing conventional or plebian forms of the faith can be only a temporary expediency. The Pure Land may only exist in the mind, as Huineng states in the Platform Sutra[12]—but then the very mind that either trusts in a Pure Land or critiques belief in it is illusory as well. To put it another way, the Pure Land does not exist, but it also does not *not* exist. It is important to keep this seemingly paradoxical nature of premodern Buddhism in mind, so that we avoid committing the ahistorical fault of assuming that the only "real" Buddhists in earlier times must have been those who inclined towards the sublime philosophical aspects of the faith and who dismissed the supposedly superstitious elements. In this sense, seeing Hanshan primarily as a countercultural figure in revolt against religious conventions is sustainable only while we see him through Beat (or Suzuki-influenced) eyes.

This Beat vision has had a further negative consequence: by reducing the poems to the expression of a charismatic way of life, it has rendered them exclusively about *the poet*. As a result, no one in the West talks about them except to the degree that they represent the confessions of a spiritual hero.

How they work as poems, why they have been important for East Asian believers for so many centuries, and why anyone (except those who want to become Beats) should read them now at all—these questions tend to be ignored. As a result, we have many translations of the Hanshan poems, but very few attempts to examine what they actually say. In fact, many modern readers would revolt at the very idea that one should talk about them: since the poems embody the personality of a spiritually inspired nonconformist, adding any commentary would be superfluous. The Cold Mountain poems simply *are*, and to talk about what they say is a sign that one is a pedant who doesn't "get it." Ultimately, this does as great a disservice to the poems as dismissing them as curious examples of Tang folk poetry would do.

Such a perspective also puts a peculiar pressure on the reader to project from the poems to what Hanshan must have been like as a person, and to make value judgments on that basis. In this light, the Beat Hanshan can inspire antipathy as well as approval. When I have taught Hanshan in poetry classes, many students have reacted quite negatively to the poems. They find the poetic voice arrogant and selfish, often indifferent to the sufferings of others and hostile to his societal obligations. Is this what a Buddhist is supposed to be? No doubt these same students would find the Beats objectionable too, for many of the same reasons (and the Beats would have welcomed their objections). The translator Burton Watson is more sympathetic, but he still emphasizes the human being behind the poems; he complains that earlier Japanese commentators have given the texts too religious a reading:

> On a larger and more serious scale, the commentators have been forced to resort to some drastic wrenching in their interpretations of the poems by the fact that Han-shan, though at times speaking from a pinnacle of calm and enlightenment, just as often seems to be profoundly involved in the misgivings and anxieties that enlightenment is supposed to dispel. Christian saints may be permitted their lapses of faith, but in Zen, with its strong emphasis on individual effort and self-reliance, a man, once enlightened, is expected to stay that way. Zen commentators have therefore been forced to regard Han-shan's professions of loneliness, doubt, and discouragement not as revelations of his own feelings but as vicarious recitals of the ills of unenlightened men which he can still sympathize with, though he himself has transcended them. He thus becomes in effect the traditional bodhisattva figure—compassionate, in the world, but not of it.[13]

This critique is unfair to the tradition, because it is posited on a theoretical assumption about the poems that is not obviously justified: that the poems represent the autobiographical confessions of an actual human being. The commentators Watson critiques here have not been forced into their readings; they are simply making the most obvious conclusions, granted what they assume the poems are doing. And what they are doing most definitely is *not* autobiographical confession.

Reading as a Buddhist

The following study tries to shift our attention during the act of reading from the empirical study of the motivations of a poet to the assumptions of the reader—which, when reinforced by complex traditions of rhetoric, vocabulary, and imagery, produce poetic meaning in a way that may not be immediately obvious to anyone outside Buddhism. This is a modern reading of Hanshan that justifies what Watson's maligned commentators were attempting to do—to see the Hanshan poems as essentially religious poems. Such a perspective may at first produce objections from those familiar with modern tendencies in the faith. A large part of North American Buddhism (the part that did not arrive with immigrant communities) has sprung out of a dissenting spirituality that rejects the pieties of conventional Protestantism, particularly those aspects that embrace capitalism and the regulation of moral behavior.[14] For members of this counterculture, religious literature is often seen as "preachy," created to enforce doctrinal uniformity and simplistic morality, rather than to allow for creative self-expression. Yet in other contexts we admit that religious literature can be profound and meaningful, even for those who do not profess the faith of the authors. I would argue that the Hanshan poems become far more compelling and interesting through a religious Buddhist lens than through an autobiographical one.

This does not preclude acknowledging that the Hanshan poems were probably a body of anonymous verse by multiple authors that have come to be attributed to a semimythical Tang-era recluse. I do not disagree with this opinion, but it does not really allow for what these poems meant to later readers, especially to devout Buddhists. As will become clear in the second chapter, traditional readers were justified in treating the poems as coming from one specific (and greater-than-human) source. Because of this, I often speak of the poems as having been authored by "Hanshan," though this "Hanshan" is a posited identity that implies a certain perspective in the *reader,* not the existence of the human poet conjured by the Beats or by Watson. Moreover, this perspective is a Buddhist one, though not because all of the Hanshan poems are "originally" Buddhist (as if it were possible to determine the exact origin of these poems). Rather, it is the product of a Buddhist way of reading.[15] This type of reading *does* create a special relationship between the reader and the poems' source, one that is influenced by traditional, secular Chinese poetics, but which also makes special unique religious claims.

Ultimately, I acknowledge that I am engaging in literary critical readings of the poems, from the perspective of a twenty-first century scholar writing in North America. I am not interested in performing literary archaeology, or in simply providing a history of Hanshan reception, but rather in exploring how knowledge of Chinese Buddhist rhetoric combined with modern interpretive techniques might grant the poems a new interest that is neither antiquarian nor Beat-era Buddhist in nature. In the final section of the book, I employ this Buddhist orientation in discussing a number of works by American Beat and post-Beat writers. Though I may disagree with the Beats' conscious vision of Hanshan the Poet, I argue that there are resonances between their work and the Cold Mountain poems at the level of Buddhist rhetoric, imagery, and themes that are shared across the centuries.

An example of this sort of reading may be demonstrated by looking at Hanshan (HS) 9, a fairly famous poem that emphasizes the deeper meaning of reclusion, one that transcends any conventional sense of place:

人問寒山道，	I'm asked the way to Cold Mountain:
寒山路不通。	You can't get to Cold Mountain by road.
夏天冰未釋，	In summer the ice never melts;
日出霧朦朧。	Sun comes out, but fog settles thick.
似我何由屆，	How did someone like me get here?
與君心不同。	This mind is not the same as yours.
君心若似我，	If your mind came to be like mine,
還得到其中。	You'd get right to the center of things.

We can obtain a sense of how a serious Buddhist reader might have interpreted the poem by looking at a premodern perspective—in this case, a most distinguished one. A disciple of Hakuin Ekaku took notes on his master's lectures on the Hanshan poems, and these in turn became the most important of the Hanshan commentaries, due to Hakuin's eminent position in the history of Japanese Zen.[16] Hakuin says of HS 9:

This poem tells of the lofty beauties of Cold Mountain, and in this way laments that no one else is able to enter there. Even if you were to imitate the exterior form of Cold Mountain—drinking from creeks and nesting on cliffs, drifting about with tattered clothing, tousled hair and a dirty face, worn away, withered and dried up, still, how would you dare enter into such a place? And why should that be? Because your mind is not the same.

What you make of your mind is a spirit of discrimination that chases after sensual attractions and choices; it is a reckless mind that pursues the beautiful and the ugly, love and hatred. This is called a mind of production and annihilation. It creates the fundamental roots of life and death. How could such a mind be able to see Cold Mountain, even in its dreams?

What I call "mind" is not like this. The mind of the Buddha and of all living things are the same and are not two. The Buddha realms, the demon realms, Buddhist temples or polluted ground, sentient beings or nonsentient ones, grass and trees growing in thick profusion—all of this is a single Buddha Mind. There is no place that is not Cold Mountain, so it is not necessary to enter there; you already *are* there. This then is a stretch of land beyond the cycles of change; in summer the ice never melts. It is called the solitary peak of Mount Sumeru;[17] it is called the land of Constant and Calm Illumination;[18] and sometimes it is called Cold Mountain. Above, below, in all directions—it has no contact with the minutest dust. Saints and sages have come here without entering; Buddhas and Patriarchs have come here without showing themselves. This is why it is said: no road goes through. What *is* a shame though, is that you incline toward a mind that adheres to the gate of production and annihilation, while I incline toward a mind that wanders about in the gate of True Suchness *(bhūtatathatā)*. That's why our minds are not the same, and why you cannot get there.[19]

It is fairly obvious that Hakuin is taking the poem as an allegory: Cold Mountain is a state of mind. Most readers would agree with this interpretation, since the poem itself plays upon the idea that entrance to the mountain is impossible unless one makes mental preparations. However, Hakuin goes further, extending that reading into the realm of Mahayana rhetoric and its interest in nonduality. It is the "spirit of discrimination" that keeps the poet's interlocutor from entering Cold Mountain. Once this discrimination is eliminated, one finds oneself on Cold Mountain spontaneously; in this, Hakuin emphasizes, Cold Mountain is like other peak-metaphors in Buddhist literature that exemplify the enlightened state. Most significantly, perhaps, Hakuin relates this breakthrough in terms of movement, but not that of conventional travel: rather, it is the movement of "a mind that wanders about in the gate of True Suchness." The highly suggestive Chinese verb *you* ("to wander," "to ramble"), with its connotations of true freedom in early Daoist texts like the *Zhuangzi*, is reenvisioned here to represent the nonpurposive freedom supposedly attained when one breaks completely free from duality and no longer has direction or purpose.

Hakuin tends not to look closely at the specifics of imagery, language, and structure. If he had, he could have reinforced his interpretation in other ways. For example, the poem begins with an uninformed interlocutor seeking knowledge from the poet. Though the poem hinges partly on the comic disjunction between a lost man asking for directions on the one hand and Hanshan's interpretation of the question in a nonliteral way on the other ("you can't get there from here"), this implied dialogue also suggests the often playfully antagonistic relationship between pupil and master in Zen literature, in which the master often replies to direct questions with riddles or similarly ambiguous speech. In his reply, Hanshan mentions the impossibility of reaching the mountain by ordinary means (a pedestrian progress that would move by stages along a road already in existence), suggesting that no two individuals' paths to Cold Mountain can be the same. He then adds a couplet describing the landscape of Cold Mountain as daunting, demanding an ascetic rigor from its residents. The couplet also suggests nondiscrimination through its images of ice and mist, which linger perpetually in spite of sunlight and summer, and which blur and conceal the distinctive elements of the scene. Such uncanny images of nature and weather are employed frequently throughout the Hanshan poems to suggest the sort of unease (or even fear) experienced by practitioners as they seek enlightenment.[20] In the second half of the poem, which abandons imagery for straightforward argument, the poet balances "me" against "you." Here, as is typical of the rhetoric of Madhyamaka texts (the branch of Mahayana philosophy most concerned with exposing the dangers of certainty), duality is emphasized in order to undermine it: what prevents you from entering Cold Mountain is the very fact that you remain trapped in an existence where "you" and "I" still exist as separate entities that are "not the same." The poet frequently employs the rhythms and structures of the Chinese poetic couplet precisely to stress (and undermine) duality in this way. The pronoun "I" occurs in line 5, "you" in line 6, and both occur in line 7, to suggest the listener's potential breakthrough. As a result of transcending Self and Other, the reader will reach "the middle,"—in this case, the center of the mountain, the balance between "you" and "I" that eliminates both categories, and the major principle of a transcendent truth.

Finally, behind the entire poem is the deliberate confusion between the location called Cold Mountain and the poet who takes a name from it: when one *enters* Cold Mountain, one in turn *becomes* Hanshan. By the end of the poem, the clueless interlocutor has entered into a special relationship with Hanshan and with Cold Mountain; to understand on a deeper level what the poet is saying (and to follow the poem's directions) eliminates the division that separates poet from reader. As we shall see later, this is perhaps the most important lesson one can learn from any of Hanshan's works.

Overview of This Book

This study is divided into three sections. The first deals with many of the technical and historical issues surrounding the Hanshan poems, looking closely at the biographical preface, its narrative strategies, the later debates surrounding its authenticity, and the complex arguments in Chinese scholarship surrounding attempts to provide a timeframe for the poet. It then turns to what the poems themselves say about their supposed author. Finally, it makes some suggestions about what might constitute a "Buddhist poetics."

Part 2 looks closely at many individual poems in order to examine their overarching themes and rhetoric. It first considers the poems' typical structure, what they borrow from mainstream Chinese poetry (including devices like parallelism), and how they employ certain strategies that make them amenable for the explication of Buddhist ideas. It then explores some of the poems' most common themes—quiescence and movement, constraint and freedom, residence and travel—and the recurring use of a series of images and motifs throughout the corpus of poems: blasted trees, jewels, the moon, and beautiful women. Finally, it looks at the poems' critiques of society through the use of animal fables and through parodies of scholars, the rich, and monks.

Part 3 consists of a single chapter, "Who Gets to Climb the Matterhorn?" It applies the lessons of part 2 by examining a series of modern American texts that show a Buddhist influence. In the process, it suggests ways in which Buddhist tropes and rhetoric make up a specific way of constructing meaning. The direction of the study is thus brought to a conclusion: from defining Hanshan and a Buddhist poetics, to recognizing how such a poetics functions in the poems, to the application of it to modern letters.

PART ONE

The Poet

CHAPTER 1

WHO WAS HANSHAN?

The vague scholarly consensus concerning Hanshan's identity is that he was a recluse who lived in the seventh, eighth, or ninth centuries, during the Tang dynasty (618–907). He dwelled alone on a place called Cold Mountain (Hanshan) or Cold Cliff (Hanyan), near the Guoqing Buddhist monastery at the famous religious center of Tiantai, in Zhejiang. We have only this location for his name; his personal name is not recorded in any source. He was by most accounts a Buddhist, though some have cited an anecdote to claim that he was predominantly Daoist in his attitude. He was an eccentric loner and may never have lived as a monk in an organized religious community, though he may have made friends with two monks from the Guoqing monastery, Fenggan and Shide. He may or may not have been connected with the developing Chan meditation school of Tang China, and he may or may not have had contact with significant early Chan teachers. One account claims (as do two of the poems attributed to him) that he wrote his poems on any available surface—on walls of houses and temples, on cliffs, on trees. We are told that a Buddhist follower (or, in the only other significant account concerning him, a Daoist follower) collected these poems after Hanshan's death or disappearance, and that they were circulated in manuscript form along with a few poems attributed to Fenggan and about sixty attributed to Shide. We don't have any conclusive testimony as to when his poems became popular; an increasing number of allusions to them and to the poet appear starting in the ninth century,[1] but the earliest surviving printed copy of the poems probably dates from the mid-twelfth century, coinciding with the rise of inexpensive commercial printing.

The poems won a following among Buddhist monks and lay believers following the eleventh century. No one read them as canonical literary texts that belonged to the mainstream of Chinese poetic production; they were, it seems, always seen as examples of religious literature. As a result, Hanshan himself became a Chan saint of sorts, and popular representations of him and his friends Fenggan and Shide became part of Buddhist iconography. The poems traveled to Japan and Korea with the Chan movement, where they circulated among medieval monks and were frequently imitated. In recent decades, his influence has become global: since the Snyder translations of the 1950s, Hanshan has come to have significant impact on Buddhist-inspired American poets.

Even this brief account should tell us how complicated it is to read Hanshan's poems today. Their very history is intimately entwined with that of East Asian religion. Their meaning and significance shift as beliefs change and as each generation of believers sees something new in them. Moreover, we cannot know what it was like to read or hear Hanshan's poems at their time of composition—even our earliest surviving edition of the text was printed three to five hundred years after they were written. In fact, we might say that even if we are working with the original texts rather than translations, which are inevitably limited interpretations, we are not so much reading as we are "reading." I mean this not as a facile postmodern gesture (every reading is a misreading; no act of reading arrives at a stable meaning that conveys knowledge to the reading subject), nor as an equally facile pop-Zen gesture (reading is an illusion—why are you immersed in illusory texts when the only true knowledge is acquired through direct experience?). I refer to a "reading" that bears no similarity to anything we remotely consider reading in everyday life.

Scholars at present are likely to read Hanshan in the best edition currently available: Xiang Chu's *Hanshan's Poems Annotated* (Hanshan shi zhu, 2000), which contains more than one thousand pages of commentary, variant readings, and supplementary material. General data about the texts is available in Chen Yaodong's *Research on the Editions of Hanshan's Poetry* (Hanshan shi ji banben yanjiu, 2007). The scholar can turn to the massive *Comprehensive Dictionary of the Chinese Language* (Hanyu da cidian), the Chinese equivalent of the OED, to check meanings, or to the *Buddha's Light Comprehensive Dictionary* (Fo guang da cidian), an eight-volume dictionary of Buddhist usage, for specialized religious usages. Sutra quotations can be checked online at the website of the Chinese Buddhist Electronic Text Association (cbeta.org) and in their electronic edition of the *Taishō Tripitaka* (the standard edition of Chinese Buddhist texts, compiled in Japan from 1913 to

1921). To check how other English-language poets and scholars have translated (and interpreted) a given poem, a reader might consult Gary Snyder's renderings in *Riprap and Cold Mountain Poems* (1965); Burton Watson's selection of about a third of the corpus (1962), heavily dependent on modern Japanese commentaries; or Robert Henricks's scholarly, annotated translation of the entire collection (1990); or Red Pine's more creative rendering (second edition, 2000), not to mention the scattering of other poets who have put their hands to translating them. This double-checking and consultation of disparate sources is not so much an act of reading as a scholar's attempt to think through what each poem means in as thorough and as historically thoughtful a way as possible.

But what sort of "meaning" can be discovered? Can we reconstitute the intentions of the poet (whoever he was—a problematic issue in itself)? Or is the meaning what some sort of ideal reader would derive from the poem? And how likely is the existence of such an ideal reader? Would a monk know more than an educated layperson? How erudite would a tenth-century reader of Hanshan's poetry be? Would a tenth-century reader be any different from a twelfth-century reader? A seventeenth-century reader? A reader in nineteenth-century Japan? A graduate student in a religious studies program at a North American university? A Beat-inspired poet?

Imagine for a moment an interested reader from the twelfth century, that is, the Song dynasty (960–1279) (I will call her Ms. Chen), purchasing a copy of an early printed edition of Hanshan's poems. Ms. Chen comes from an educated gentry family, and she has received a basic mainstream education: she knows the Confucian classics, the classic literary anthologies, the major poets. Her family has strong sympathies with Buddhism and a good relationship with the local Chan monastery: they have given substantial gifts for the monastery's upkeep, and her father is close friends with the abbot, who prides himself on his own poetic abilities. She visits the monastery fairly often on festivals and has heard sermons on major aspects of Buddhist and Chan doctrine. She recognizes a substantial amount of Buddhist terminology and knows the content of the most famous of the sutras. What sort of reading experience can she expect upon opening her new purchase?

Reading the Preface

Before she even arrives at the poems, Ms. Chen sees a preface to the collection, written by an official named Lüqiu Yin. Ms. Chen may not recognize the name, though if she consults the official history of the Tang dynasty she will find listed a moderately prominent bureaucrat by that name active in the 630s and 640s. The preface's existence would be unlikely to surprise her: by the time the Hanshan collection was circulated in print form, prefaces to collected literary works were commonplace and acted as guarantees of literary worth. Literary men wrote them for the collected works of their friends and acquaintances or sometimes were commissioned to write them by the author's next of kin. Prefaces could contain literary criticism, evaluations of what made the author interesting or distinctive, or biographical reminiscences. In the twelfth century it was not unusual for Chan monks to publish their literary works as well, and in such cases, it was typical for their secular literati associates to write the preface. For example, in 1043 the prominent writer and statesman Ouyang Xiu (1007–1072) composed a preface for the monk Miyan's collection. The resulting work is one of Ouyang's most famous, and it also tells us about how laypeople (especially Confucian gentry) might evaluate monk-poets.[2]

Ouyang begins his preface by positing the existence of recluses, men who do not participate in the world of officialdom because they find no use for their talents there. Instead, they form a mysterious, semi-invisible class of men, men who have turned to hermit life and to occupations well beneath their class and breeding. Of course, the trope of the recluse had been a convention of traditional Chinese culture for at least a millennium, as many members of the elite in the post-Han era chose self-consciously to refuse a role in society or government. By literary convention, the mark of such men is their deep frustration: unable to fulfill their very reason for existence, they express themselves in other ways, most typically through drinking and composing poetry. Ouyang comes to realize this through his friendship with Shi Yannian (courtesy name Manqing), who is just such a frustrated poet-recluse. Like many Confucian writers, Ouyang portrays himself as a sort of connoisseur of friendship: on the lookout for extraordinary men and hoping to benefit intangibly through associating with them. He sees Manqing as his entrée into the secret society of recluses. Having befriended Manqing, he meets the monk Miyan, whom Ouyang understands as Manqing's fellow recluse and close friend:

> The Buddhist monk Miyan was Manqing's oldest associate. He too was able to transcend the vulgar customs around him and had a natural eminence that resulted from the strength of his personality. The two of

them delighted in each other and nothing could come between them. Manqing hid himself in his drinking, while Miyan hid himself in his Buddhism; and both of them were amazing men. They also delighted in entertaining themselves with poetry. When they reached the height of their drinking, they would sing, chant, laugh, and shout, and so they would experience all of the pleasures of the world—how vigorous they were! All of the worthy men of the age wished to befriend them, and I too from time to time would visit them at their homes. . . . Miyan was also manly and imposing of aspect, overflowing with noble aspirations; and yet because he was a practitioner of Buddhism, these qualities had no use. Only his poems could circulate in the world, and yet he was negligent in preserving them.

It may seem to be trivializing Buddhism to compare it to drinking—and indeed Ouyang may be deliberately blasphemous here, poking fun at Buddhist injunctions against intoxication. However, that is not his main point. Heavy drinking had been acknowledged at least since the times of the bucolic poet Tao Qian (365–427) as a sanctioned way for hermits to act. Drinking could provide a vital way of releasing the hermit's frustration and stress; such men could be acknowledged as true artists of the cup. Yet this text *is* co-opting Buddhism as a sort of personal response to frustration, a deliberate hobby or art adopted by Miyan through which he chooses to express himself in the private world of recluses. It also ultimately places drinking and Buddhism on the same level as a third occupation: poetry composition.

Ultimately, Ouyang wishes to emphasize the role of poetry as a form of expressing the self. In doing so, he is participating in the most venerable tradition of Chinese poetics: poetry as a form of personal lament, composed through emotional compulsion and appreciated by close friends. In this situation, Manqing's and Miyan's poetry would be pointless if they did not have each other. Even Ouyang is an outsider here: he can visit occasionally and join in their celebrations, but he acknowledges that their poetry-writing is a demonstration of the deep friendship between them. Moreover, Miyan's position as a monk has prohibited the fullest expression of his noblest aspirations (presumably because of the ascetic demands of his order). Only poetry can grant him the full release he should have been allowed as a man of the world. And because it allows this liberty, poetry runs afoul of Buddhism itself. Though becoming a monk might serve as a gesture to reveal one's frustration with the world, being a monk ultimately interferes with the ideal of self-expression manifested through poetry and drinking. In fact, Buddhism is meant to problematize the very idea of "self," vital to the act of self-expression. Most poet-monks had to confront this dilemma, because they composed verse through their dealings with elite society: they exchanged poems with literati friends, attended their parties, and shared in their aesthetic (not ascetic) worldview.

In the preface to the Hanshan collection, Ms. Chen will find a text very different from that of Ouyang—and a poet very different from the typical monk-poet. She will first of all see that the preface is purportedly written by Hanshan's Tang contemporary, the government official Lüqiu Yin, listed with his full official title: "Grand Master for Court Discussion, Commissioned with Extraordinary Powers as Taizhou Prefect of Military Affairs, Supreme Pillar of State, Recipient of the Crimson Fish Sack." That seems typical enough—as we have seen with Ouyang's piece, a preface by a member of the Confucian elite gives a certain cachet to a work by a Buddhist. But she has also been transported back to the Tang dynasty, when elites were less likely to see a conflict between Buddhist beliefs and Confucian culture. As she continues to read, she realizes that this preface is quite outside her usual expectations for literary prefaces. True, it includes some biographical descriptions of the poet, and it also incorporates the author's own relationship with its subject. But the tone very quickly becomes fantastic and hagiographical.

First, we have a distanced third-person description of Hanshan:[3]

> When I look into the matter of this "Master Cold Mountain," I find that I do not know where he came from. In the view of certain elders, he was assumed to be an impoverished man, a demented scholar. He dwelt in reclusion at Tiantai, seventy *li* west of the county seat of Tangxing, at a place referred to as "Cold Cliff."[4] He always lived there, though he would come back to Guoqing Monastery from time to time. There was a certain Shide who oversaw the monastery refectory. Often Shide would save some leftover scraps, which he would store in a bamboo tube. If Cold Mountain would happen by, he would take off with the tube carried on his back. Sometimes he would stroll the long corridors of the monastery, shouting with delight, or talking or laughing to himself. Occasionally a monk would chase after him and try to drive him off with curses and beatings. He would then stand stock-still, rubbing his hands and laughing. Then, after some time, he would finally leave.

He looked like a pauper, withered and haggard in appearance. But with every word and breath he communicated thoughts quite in keeping with reason; after profound reflection, one found them subtly reflective of the nature of the Way—words that penetrated deeply into the profound and mysterious. He wore a cap made of birch-bark, a tattered robe of hemp, and walked about in wooden clogs. In this way, a perfected man will conceal his traces, acting in accordance with the transformation of things. Sometimes he would sing and chant on the temple veranda, saying only: "Pah! The turning wheel of the three realms!"[5] Sometimes he would sing and laugh with village farmers and cowherds. Whether he acted predictably or perversely, he delighted in his own nature—and how could any but the wise truly recognize him?

In this opening we are presented with a figure whose popularity in Chinese Buddhism grew throughout the Tang dynasty: the antinomian monk, who manifests his superior wisdom through a deliberate violation of monastic moral codes. In the most shocking examples, this can mean heavy drinking, meat-eating, and sexual misconduct. In the case of Hanshan, it is mostly a scandalous disregard for monastic discipline and piety.[6]

The increasing popularity of the antinomian monk in the Tang dynasty, when the institutionalization of Buddhist sects reached its most developed stage, can be explained in a number of ways. John Kieschnick suggests that the comparative anthropological figure of the "trickster" is important here—the liminal or marginal person who derives cultural significance from the way he or she paradoxically confirms the norms of society by violating them. In this case, Hanshan's rejection of monkish norms supports the standards of monastic asceticism: "To a large extent it was asceticism that defined the monk, for it was asceticism even in its most formal aspects that set the monk apart, that pushed him into the outer boundaries of society—repositories of prestige, respect, and power. Ironically, the trickster derives *his* power from precisely the same source, though in his case it is not separation from secular society that distinguishes him, but rather, his separation from the monastic community, from the ascetic."[7] Bernard Faure, while agreeing with the "trickster" analysis, suggests that the rise of such figures in the Tang may also have been a means of replacing an explicitly supernatural and frightening figure (specifically, the magic-working monk, or thaumaturge) with another type of a less threatening marginality.[8]

These large-scale cultural and anthropological developments are relevant, but Ms. Chen would also final Hanshan's portrayal interesting in spiritual terms. First, his behavior indicates the boundaries established around the monastic community, and its strong set of moral interdictions and codes of behavior. As an eremitic layperson, the figure of Hanshan reminds us that clinging to institutionalized monasticism can lead to a smug complacency that makes enlightenment impossible. It is not so much that he reconfirms asceticism, but rather provides a constant irritant to monks by reminding them that if they have convinced themselves that they are nearing enlightenment, they very likely are not near it at all. In this, he plays a role quite similar to Vimalakīrti, the brilliant layman of the Vimalakīrti Sutra, who confounds the Buddha's disciples with his paradoxical arguments.[9] Ms. Chen would also see the similarities between Hanshan's behavior and stories told about the "Golden Age" of Chan, when masters and disciples would engage in agonistic and often violent exchanges in attempts to drive each other to Buddhist awakening.

Whatever the origins of the preface, it fits quite comfortably with Chan literature as it was evolving in the tenth and eleventh centuries. Just as Hanshan prods the monks of the Guoqing monastery by providing an example of the dangers of complacency, so Song dynasty practitioners (who were gradually institutionalizing Chan practice through set ritual procedures of meditation) would see the legendary Tang heroes as embodying a powerful and idealized questioning of duality.[10] And like these later Chan masters, Hanshan uses laughter and ridicule of the unenlightened as a major weapon. Third, Lüqiu Yin's own position as a secular Confucian official with Buddhist leanings allows him to claim solidarity with Hanshan and to incorporate him into a mainstream literary tradition already accustomed to non-Buddhist eccentrics. The "wise madman" had a long tradition in China before the arrival of Buddhism, particularly in Daoist texts like the *Zhuangzi* and the *Liezi*, in which eccentrics or fools are seen as embodying a higher wisdom, available only to those with more lofty attainments and insight: "How could any but the wise truly recognize him?" The preface situates the Hanshan poems as texts available for nonspecialist laypeople, as the Vimalakīrti Sutra is, and also suggests that they might provide a path to a higher enlightenment that even monks may not be able to attain, especially if they are unwilling to look below the surface.

At this point, the reputed author of the preface enters the scene:

> I was recently appointed to a lowly position in Danqiu. In the period leading up to my departure I was afflicted with a headache, and by the appointed day I was taking increasingly heavy doses of medicine. I then encountered a meditation master by the name of Fenggan, who said he had come from the Guoqing Temple at Tiantai, explicitly for the purpose of seeing me. I requested that he treat my illness. The master laughed in a friendly manner. "The body dwells among the four elements; illness arises from illusion. If you wish me to remove it, then I will need some clean water." I then offered him some, which he spit out at me. Immediately the headache left me.
>
> He then said to me, "Taizhou is a coastal area with unhealthy air—when you get there you must look after yourself." I then asked him, "I haven't had a chance to investigate whether the area has any sages—are there any worthy enough to take as a teacher?" He replied, "If you see such a one you will not recognize him—and if you could recognize him you won't see him. But if you do wish to see such a one, do not rely on externalities, and only then will he appear. Hanshan Mañjuśrī conceals his traces at Guoqing; and Shide Samantabhadra looks like a pauper. Both of them act like madmen and come and go as they wish. Shide is a servant at the storehouse of Guoqing monastery, and tends the fire in the kitchen." With that he took his leave.

Our magistrate is introduced to the existence of Hanshan through an intermediary: the mysterious marvel-working monk Fenggan. Later, we learn that Fenggan has a personal relationship with a tiger, a fact that likely made the other monks at Guoqing monastery uncomfortable (another irritant to monastic complacency!). Faure suggests that this connects Fenggan to other early Buddhist figures whose magical abilities are demonstrated through their taming of wild animals (obviously, the tiger also serves as a metaphor for taming the unruly mind of the practitioner).[11] This in turn hints to the reader that Hanshan too will possess aspects of the uncanny.

Lüqiu's headache and Fenggan's miraculous treatment would likely have resonated with a Buddhist reader. The monk cures Lüqiu's pain in part by reminding the magistrate that it does not exist: "The body dwells among the four elements; illness arises from illusion." This likely alludes to the Vimalakīrti Sutra,[12] and thus reminds the reader of the central conceit of that work: Vimalakīrti pretends to be ill in order to lure well-wishers to his dwelling, where he can engage them in discussions of the nature of nonduality for their own good. This is a classic example of the Mahayana doctrine of "skillful means" *(upāya)*, whereby teachers (especially bodhisattvas and buddhas) may employ seemingly deceitful methods in order to lead living beings to salvation. As a result, the reader will be led to think that Lüqiu's headache is itself a sort of "skillful means"—perhaps even one inflicted on him by Fenggan so that Fenggan will have an opportunity to meet him, to provide him with a lesson in the illusory nature of illness, and to mention the existence of Hanshan and Shide. Fenggan also hints at the supernatural origins of the two men, suggesting that one will fail to find them if one expects something impressive or has any preconceptions: "If you do wish to see such a one, do not rely on externalities, and only then will he appear." Here, he may be echoing the Diamond Sutra: "If you see the Marks [of Existence] as non-Marks, then you will see the Tathāgata."[13] In this particular case, Fenggan connects Hanshan with Mañjuśrī, a bodhisattva usually portrayed as a handsome young prince, who is a master of Buddhist wisdom *(prajñā*; in Chinese, *zhi)*. As such, he is an expert on instructing believers how to do away with conceptions of duality that keep them trapped within the samsaric realm. Fenggan connects Shide in turn with Samantabhadra, a bodhisattva skilled in meditation (*dhyāna*; in Chinese, *chan*). Mañjuśrī and Samantabhadra are often portrayed accompanying each other, symbolizing the mutual interdependence of wisdom and meditation. Fenggan's comment also suggests that being able to recognize the two men as higher incarnations is something that only one with an ability to see through duality can achieve.

> I then proceeded on my way; and upon reaching my post at Taizhou, I did not forget this business. Three days later, I personally visited various temples and meditation centers, and their accounts matched what the Master had said. I had inquiries made as to whether there were individuals named Hanshan or Shide in Tangxing county. The district staff of the time reported that seventy *li* west of the county seat there a was a cliff, and the elders there would see a pauper who would often go to the Guoqing monastery to spend the night. There was also a novice in the refectory by the name of Shide. I then went there personally to pay my respects. I arrived and made inquiries of the monks, asking them where a *dhyāna* [meditation] master by the name of Fenggan had lodged when he stayed with them; also, where Shide and Hanshan could be found. A monk by the name of Daoqiao told me, "Fenggan's lodging was behind the sutra library. No one is living there now, because a tiger comes by

there all the time and roars. You can meet Hanshan and Shide in the kitchen." A monk then led me to Fenggan's lodging, and when the door was open we saw only tiger tracks. I then asked the monks Baode and Daoqiao what task the *dhyāna* master had had when he lived there. The monks replied, "While he was here he did nothing but hull rice for the monastery's stores. At night he would sing to entertain himself."

Then we came to the kitchen and found two men laughing by the stove fire. I paid them my respects, but they shouted at me the whole time; then they took each other by the hand and broke into loud laughter. They cried out, "Fenggan—what a blabbermouth! But if you didn't recognize that he was Amitābha, why do you bother to bow to us?" At this point, the other monks started to gather, and were surprised in turn to see a high official paying his respects to two paupers. The two men then ran out of the temple, hand in hand. I ordered that they be followed; but after they rushed out they returned to Cold Cliff. I asked the monks repeatedly whether the two men might be willing to come back and stay, and I ordered that they be sought out and invited to return and take up residence.

I then returned to the county seat. I prepared two robes, some incense, medicine, and other things, to be given them as gifts. By then they still had not returned to the monastery, so my messenger went to Cold Cliff to present them. When he caught sight of Hanshan, Hanshan shouted out, "Bandits! Bandits!" and withdrew into a cave in the cliff. As he went in he said, "I urge all of you to strive to your utmost." The cave closed up on its own, and no one could go in after him. All traces of Shide also disappeared. I then had the monk Daoqiao and others prepare a record of their past deeds; but they only found three hundred or so poems that Hanshan had written on bamboo, trees, stones cliffs, as well as on the walls of local farmers' houses; also some *gāthas* that Shide had written on the walls of a shrine to the local earth god.[14] These they collected together and copied out to form a volume. I, who have found peace in the principles of the Buddha, have had the good fortune to have encountered these Men of the Way.

As Lüqiu goes off to his post, he finds himself in a typical position for a representative of the imperial government who happens also to be a lay believer. He desires to establish a teacher-student relationship with a local master, and he engages in the socially sanctioned behavior typical of wealthy laypeople in search of such teachers. A formal visit is followed by a second attempt to make contact through the bestowal of alms, in this case two of the four approved types of almsgiving to monks listed in the scriptures (clothing and medicine). There is also a secular trope underlying this narrative: the attempts of rulers to lure talented recluses into their service and the degree to which the truly virtuous ruler will abase his own pride in order to gain their assistance. Most famously, a third-century ruler of Sichuan, Liu Bei, visited the recluse Zhuge Liang three times before Liang would deign to grant him a hearing. Part of this is of course a testing; the recluse is more than willing to serve, but only someone who proves himself capable of honor and humility.

From this perspective, Lüqiu is seen as inferior, an ordinary person beset by ignorance who has failed some test he did not realize he was undergoing (in this case he has failed to recognize Fenggan as an incarnation of Amitābha).[15] He is never granted a third attempt: Hanshan and Shide disappear magically into a cave and are never heard from again. In this, the anecdote switches from secular motifs to a Daoist one: the two have very likely fled into a "grotto heaven" *(dongtian)* and have taken on identities as Transcendents.[16] As they flee, Hanshan cries out "Bandits!"—perhaps a hint at Lüqiu's failure to understand and an accusation that he is still beset by the bandits of sensory perception; or, more simply, he wishes to condemn Lüqiu's attempt to "bribe" him with conventional layman's presents.[17] Regardless, Hanshan and Shide have withdrawn into a deeper layer of reclusion inaccessible not only to ordinary ignorant individuals but to institutionalized religion as well: the monastery is no longer a refuge for them or a foil against which they can display their antinomian possession of a wisdom that surpasses that of ordinary monks. The importunate lay-believer has corrupted their purity.

But is that really what has happened? We must remember that our narrator has put himself in the position of detailing Hanshan's higher wisdom, and as such he must be able to recognize what that wisdom is; a truly ignorant man would not know how to represent an enlightened individual and would not recognize Hanshan's actions as embodying the antinomian critique of duality. In this respect, Lüqiu Yin the magistrate has become a fictional character taking on the allegorical role of the unenlightened person, while Lüqiu Yin the supposed author of the preface is well aware of this construction. We are thus presented with a piece of theater played by actors taking on roles for the sake of imparting a lesson, though they are no less real for that, from the perspective of our own illusory position in samsara.

In the words of the Chan master Huangbo Xiyun, the preface operates "like a magician preaching the Dharma to an illusory person."[18] Lüqiu Yin's stance bears an interesting similarity to the narrative role played by the Tang minister Pei Xiu, the reputed scribe of Huangbo's sermons, who often portrays himself negatively within the text, asking the Master questions in the role of a befuddled outsider. At one point, driven to distraction by Huangbo's contentious answers to his questions, Pei Xiu says, "Why are you always telling me that everything I say to you is mistaken?" To which the master replies, "It's you who don't understand what people say to you. What mistakes have you made?"[19] Of course, if Pei Xiu were as indeed as entirely ignorant as his dialogues suggest, he would likely not know how to transcribe Huangbo's elegant use of the question-answer dialectic to critique duality and his own supposed ignorance.

If this is the case, Hanshan's retreat becomes not so much a refusal to engage with the magistrate as it is an actual positive response meant to be taken as an acknowledgement of Lüqiu's worthiness as a student. As a reward, Lüqiu receives the poetry collection. It is not coincidental that Lüqiu has said nothing of these poems before this point; though they were supposedly composed over a period of years during Hanshan's residence on Cold Cliff, they only now appear, as if magically summoned by a bodhisattva's skill. Their transcription on natural surfaces is also meant to indicate their status as both texts and nontexts: Hanshan has refused to preserve them in conventional forms, thus going as far as he can to emphasize the contingent and impermanent nature of preaching: they are relicts, mere traces, no more substantial than the tracks of Fenggan's tiger. This does not mean that they are useless, or of importance only to the poet: rather, one of the lessons they convey is awareness of their ultimate disposability. In the end, understanding must still occur through an effort on the part of the practitioners. The poems Lüqiu has had copied may be Hanshan's wisdom embodied in textual form, but that does not guard against their ephemerality if they fall on deaf ears.

The preface ends with a thirty-eight-line eulogy *(zan)*, a typical element in many medieval Chinese biographies and prefaces. Eulogies are meant to give a ritual solemnity to the piece (they are written usually in four-syllable lines, a mark of deliberate high-toned archaism). They tend to restate the main points of the piece, thus serving as a summary. The ending of this is particularly important:

稽首文殊，	I make obeisance to Mañjuśrī,
寒山之士。	This gentleman Cold Mountain.
南無普賢，	All hail to Samantabhadra,
拾得定是。	For that is certainly Shide.
聊申贊嘆，	I shall lay out this song of praise,
願超生死。	And vow to transcend life and death.

There is an open emphasis here on Hanshan's role as an instructor of the monks and his semidivine status as an incarnation of Mañjuśrī; moreover, he will serve as an object of veneration for the monks of Guoqing for generations to come. The preface thus ends on a quite pronounced note of hagiography—it is the last thing our Ms. Chen reads before she begins the poems proper.

In Search of Hanshan's Dates

Let us assume for the time being that the poems really do represent a body of work written all or mostly by one particular figure, who might be largely characterized by what the content of the poems seem to suggest—a Chinese recluse with largely Buddhist (but also Daoist) interests. Is there anything in the preface on which we can rely? What can we conclude about it and its relative trustworthiness? And what external and internal data can we use to figure out who this author was? Much of this will bring us into the complex world of modern Chinese academic speculation—speculation that is often highly tenuous and problematic.

Scholars have exerted considerable energy to determine the birth and death dates of our reputed poet. One would assume that such data is not a matter of public record in part because of the poet's reclusive, antisocial nature. However, such difficulties afflict not just cases like that of Hanshan (or of prominent figures in the Chan movement, for that matter), but nearly all public figures in medieval Chinese history. We are often not sure what the birth dates are of prime ministers and other statesmen, because such information was not thought important by those who kept the public records. We will know, for example, when a certain figure took up a political office, when he submitted a petition to the emperor, or when he was dismissed or executed. But everything else, often including the milestones of private life, is left to speculation.

Chinese researchers of the past few centuries have become quite adept at calculating significant dates based on meager data. For example, casual comments in poems or letters may be seized upon as important clues: a prominent man may send a poem to a friend in which he remarks, offhandedly, that he is ten years older than the recipient. The recipient in turn may say in a letter to another friend that he was in his thirties when such-and-such a rebellion took place. A record may show that a third acquaintance of the first two was a client of a noted statesman whose death date is known for certain. The researcher will carefully piece these together, add suggestive passages from other texts, try to make them all fit a consistent pattern, and then arrive at reasonable birth and death dates; this type of close analytical work is characteristic of what is called *kaozheng*, "evidential scholarship." But very few students of early Chinese history and literature will admit how fragile this edifice is. In our hypothetical example, "ten years older" may be a poetic exaggeration or an approximation; the rebellion may have taken place when the friend was in his forties, and he has some personal reason to misrepresent his age; and the third acquaintance might be lying about his patrons in order to impress. And of course, all this data comes to us originally through handcopied manuscripts. Who knows what changes may have occurred in any given medieval text as it was written and rewritten by numerous hands?[20] We confidently copy out the dates of a historical figure that we garner from our modern dictionaries, unaware of the amount of sheer speculation that underlies such assumptions.

The search for Hanshan's dates is a particularly illuminating saga, since (as we shall see) there is no way to reconcile the available information, no matter how sophisticated our *kaozheng* work may be. Multiple narratives are more or less plausible, but no one of them makes complete sense, and the leftover puzzle pieces will not fit into the available spaces. This is exacerbated somewhat by the assumptions often underlying much of *kaozheng* work, which may be summarized somewhat unkindly in the following way: (1) a document that can be proved to have any evident factual errors becomes immediately suspect, and should probably be ignored in constructing analytical models; (2) a document that cannot be proved to have any factual errors can be accepted completely without reservation; (3) our current textual record is complete enough to arrive at a reasonable conclusion (we thus disregard the possibility that countless documents that could clarify our speculations have probably been lost over the centuries); and (4) consequently there *must be* an irrefutable conclusion based on the currently surviving materials (*kaozheng* scholars abhor a vacuum). These rules are understandable—it is painful to admit just how fragile our ability to recover the past truly is. Yet it gives *kaozheng* scholarship at times a certain claustrophobic feeling; every detail fits into the well-oiled mechanism with nothing left over. Rarely does anyone say "if" or "maybe" or "possibly"; the evidence is presented as obvious and leading to only one conclusion. In this, it can come to resemble densely argued treatises meant to prove that the Earl of Oxford wrote Shakespeare's plays.

We have already looked at the preface, attributed to a certain official named Lüqiu Yin, that gives us the only biographical account of Hanshan's life. Understandably, *kaozheng* scholars begin their search for Hanshan by trying to trace what we know (if anything) about Lüqiu Yin. The most distinguished voice in analyzing the data is that of the midcentury scholar Yu Jiaxi (1884–1955), whose monumental *Evidential Analysis of the Catalogue of the Four Treasuries* (Si ku tiyao bianzheng) was first published in 1937 and was substantially revised in a posthumous edition of 1958. In it, Yu examines the bibliographic notes assembled by the compilers of the massive imperial library, the so-called "Four Treasuries," between 1773 and 1782. Yu's article on Hanshan's poetry collection runs to a dozen pages of tiny print, composed in meticulous classical Chinese; his argument has been accepted whole or in part by almost everyone in China writing about Hanshan.[21]

Yu begins by noting that local records in the Tiantai area provide a list of magistrates for the Taizhou district throughout the Tang; he also notes that these lists derive ultimately from a record compiled around the year 1000. He thus assumes—not unreasonably—that the list is close enough to the Tang era to be reliable. This record indeed tells us that a certain Lüqiu Yin was a magistrate in Taizhou, and that he served there from 633 to 637. One bit of additional information supports Lüqiu Yin's time-frame: in the biography of a general-turned-monk by the name of Zhiyan (found in Daoxuan's *Biographies of Eminent Monks Continued* [Xu gao seng zhuan]), Lüqiu Yin is mentioned as a former colleague of Zhiyan's who came to visit him at some point between the years 621 and 643. We can now safely assume that "our" Lüqiu Yin was indeed a Tang official, and that he was active in the first half of the seventh century.

However, Yu points out (and here he makes a move much beloved of *kaozheng* specialists) that the preface mentions twice that Yin was specifically assigned to Tangxing county in Taizhou. Counties were frequently subject to renaming and reorganization, and in fact Tang administrative records tell us that this county never received the name Tangxing until 761; in Lüqiu Yin's time it was known as Shifeng. For Yu, this is an insurmountable obstacle: we have our proof that the entire preface is inauthentic, a later forgery. One might object that the mention of Tangxing might be the result of changes in the course of textual transmission: perhaps some later scribe saw the name "Shifeng" in the text and silently corrected it to the "proper," more recent name. Of course, such an objection would not in turn imply that the preface *is* authentic; rather it is interesting to note the *reasons* for Yu's rejection of it. Other features of the preface do not arouse his suspicion, ones that might stand out for a different sort of scholar: the archetypal and supernatural nature of the events described, for instance.

So where do we look now? Yu turns for the next part of his argument to the monk Zanning's work, the *Biographies of Eminent Monks Compiled in the Song Dynasty* (Song gao seng zhuan), composed from 982 to 988. Zanning gives a collective biography for Fenggan, Hanshan, and Shide; he also explicitly mentions the Lüqiu Yin preface (which also seems to serve as source for most of his biography of Hanshan). Some of his information on Fenggan is not found in the preface, however, and instead seems to come from an eighth-century work (no longer surviving) by a certain Wei Shu. At one point, Zanning writes, citing this work: "After Fenggan passed away in the Xiantian reign period [712–713], he practiced a manifestation [i.e., magically appeared] in the capital."[22] He also cites an incident related to Hanshan in his biography of the great early Chan master Guishan Lingyou (771–853), one that seems to have been popular in Chan circles by the tenth century:

> When Lingyou traveled to Tiantai he encountered Hanshan by the side of the road. Hanshan said to him, "After you travel over a multitude of rivers and hills you will arrive at a pool *[tan]*. Stop there. You will obtain a priceless treasure that will give aid to your many disciples." Lingyou thought about this as he traveled, and pondered on it in meditation. Thereafter he reached the Guoqing Monastery, where he met the extraordinary Shide, who gave him precisely the same message. Later he arrived at a place called Letan, where he visited Master Dazhi; there he suddenly understood the Meaning of the Patriarchs. Towards the end of the Yuanhe era, as he passed by Changsha, he came upon Dagui Mountain, where he decided to halt.[23]

At the very end of the Hanshan-Shide-Fenggan biography, Zanning adds the following editorial comment:

> Since Fenggan was wandering about the capital during the Xiantian era, we can assume that Lüqiu, Hanshan, and Shide were all men from the reign of Emperor Ruizong (r. 710–712). What do we then make of the fact that Daoxuan's biography [of Zhiyan] tells us that Lüqiu was a military official from the beginning of the Tang? The fact that the Lüqiu preface does not mention the time period of the three men is quite annoying. Moreover, the preface mentions that Lüqiu was a "recipient of the crimson [fish sack]," which indicates a civil office.[24] If this is true, perhaps there are two Lüqius? Moreover, Master Dagui Lingyou encountered Hanshan during the reign of Xianzong [805–820], when Hanshan indicated the way to Letan; and Lingyou then went on to meet Shide at Guoqing Monastery. From this we know that the three of them were still alive during the middle years of the Tang. So Fenggan died at Tiantai and then appeared again in the capital—and Hanshan and Shide were alive during the Xiantian era [712–713] but then were encountered again in the Yuanhe era [806–820]. Is this because their lifespans were extraordinarily long? Or because the periods in which they hid themselves and then manifested themselves were inconstant? The Judgment [on the *Yijing* hexagram *weiji*] reads: "But if the little fox, after nearly completing the crossing, / Gets his tail in the water, [there is nothing that would further]." That expresses the situation.[25]

Confronted with these different stories—Lüqiu's account, Wei Shu's account of Fenggan's death, and the Lingyou biography—Zanning's confusion is understandable. Rather than commit himself to a reality that would extend Hanshan's lifespan over two centuries, he eventually throws up his hands in exasperation and quotes a passage from *The Book of Changes* (Yijing) that suggests the folly of jumping to premature conclusions.

What does Yu Jiaxi make of Zanning's account? He stitches several conclusions together: First, Yu notes that Zanning is a serious and respected historian of Buddhism, and so is, by and large, reliable. Moreover, the fact that Zanning bothers to mention the chronological paradox inherent in the sources suggests that he views them critically. Second, Yu concludes that Fenggan's manifestation in the capital right after his death (c. 712)—though clearly a "fantastic" incident—does prove that Fenggan was present at Guoqing monastery up until the 710s. Hanshan thus must have known him there before his death. Yu's dismissal of the Lüqiu Yin preface thus does not result in a dismissal of the idea that Hanshan, Fenggan, and Shide were three actual, living men who did indeed know each other.

Further, Yu finds no explicit evidence to disprove Zanning's account of Lingyou's encounter with Hanshan, which could have occurred at some time before the Yuanhe era. In a further discussion of data surrounding Lingyou's career, he makes an argument that the encounter would likely have happened in the 790s, rather than in the 810s. Again, note that Yu does not entertain the possibility that the Lingyou anecdote is a legend that exploited Hanshan's increasing fame in order to legitimize Lingyou's enlightenment experience under his master Dazhi.

Finally, Yu concludes that Zanning would have thrown out the Lüqiu Yin preface if he had only dared, but felt he had to accept it along with the other data. But in fact, he argues, if we reject the preface we can just possibly imagine a Hanshan who was born roughly in 680, and died around his one hundred and twentieth year, shortly after meeting Lingyou (Yu remarks that Daoist and Buddhist monastics are often famed for their longevity, but that a life longer than 120 years stretches credulity). He quotes various poems in the Hanshan collection as well, arguing for a period of mountain-dwelling that lasted over seventy years.

Yu's tentative dates for Hanshan, stretching across the eighth century, have been accepted by many Chinese scholars of the past fifty years; in particular, his evidence for the dismissal of the preface (on the grounds of that disastrous mention of Tangxing county) has been adopted by many with little disagreement.

Yet a scholar with the same available data might arrive at a completely different conclusion. Wu Chi-yu, who published one of the few scholarly studies in English on Hanshan (in the journal *T'oung Pao* in 1957) also believes that the Lüqiu Yin preface is a forgery (though he seems to have been unaware of Professor Yu's work). Mentioning many of the same issues that Yu discusses, he concludes, "the preface does not conform to the ordinary formula of prefaces, to say nothing of its contradictions to the poems."[26] To prove this last point, he adds, as a footnote: "For example, in the preface Hanshan, Shide, and Fenggan are considered respectively as the incarnation of Mañjuśrī, Samantabhadra, and Maitreya [*sic*], while in the poems Han-shan never admits that he is no human being." But Professor Wu draws different conclusions from this dismissal than Yu, breaking the rules of *kaozheng* somewhat to claim that "the condemnation of the authenticity of the preface does not necessarily imply a denial of all the biographical elements contained in it. It may contain some factual elements, of course not the supernatural ones, nor those which are in contradiction with other authentic documents or with itself."[27] While he accepts that Fenggan died in the 710s (based on the Wei Shu anecdote cited by Zanning), he dismisses the Lingyou story as "a later legend not worthy of attention." He then returns to the account of the monk Zhiyan found in Daoxuan's *Biographies of Eminent Monks Continued*—the text that mentioned Lüqiu Yin as a former military colleague of that general-turned-monk. Combining that fact with a selective reading of some of the poems, he arrives at the "natural" conclusion: Zhiyan was in fact Hanshan!

Interestingly enough, another scholar—not of the *kaozheng* variety—also agrees with Wu that Hanshan was a seventh-century figure (or perhaps lived even earlier). The historical linguist E. G. Pulleyblank published an article in 1978 in which he analyzed Hanshan's rhyme-words (as in most Chinese poetry, the Hanshan poems rhyme the end characters of even-numbered lines).[28] Pulleyblank notes that as the Tang dynasty continued, the language changed gradually and many vowel distinctions tended to disappear in spoken dialect. The result is that the number of distinct rhymes became fewer over the centuries, and the number of possible rhyme words for each rhyme category increased. However, Pulleyblank notes, a large number of the Hanshan poems show a poet very picky about his rhymes—in fact, these poems show an awareness of rhyme categories that had already started to disappear at the very beginning of the Tang.[29] Professor Pulleyblank's conclusion runs as follows: the majority of the poems—about two-thirds—are probably the product of the early seventh century, or perhaps even earlier. The rest are by completely different poet(s), and are likely to be ninth-century creations. He labels the first group of poems "Han-Shan I" and the second "Han-Shan II."

Professor Pulleyblank's work is particularly illustrative as a contrast to Chinese *kaozheng* work. Both methods involve the careful and exhaustive enumeration of tiny details to produce a larger conclusion that attempts to be as objective as possible (and Pulleyblank's work is indeed unassailable in terms of its thoroughness and rigor). But while *kaozheng* scholarship puts a premium on the examination of the consistency of content within a small collection of pertinent texts, the linguistic method in this case relies upon analysis of usage based on reconstructed pronunciations, extrapolated from rhyme categories as attested by surviving dictionaries and by contemporary poetic usage, and is not concerned with "content" at all. In some ways, however, the two methods are not that different. Both assume a closed system of data that can be analyzed with a resultant series of conclusions. In order to arrive at any sort of stable conclusion, both methods assume that unknown historical factors cannot interfere with the process. For example, early in his argument, Pulleyblank notes:

> The basis for the conclusion that the original and larger portion of the Han-Shan poems comes from early T'ang [Tang] or Sui is that they rhyme even more strictly . . . than the court poetry of the early Tang. Since Han-Shan is clearly a rustic poet, this can only be because the distinctions he followed were part of his actual speech, not learned from a dictionary. It further emerges that he was probably a northerner. Though he is traditionally associated with Mt. T'ien-t'ai [Tiantai] in Chekiang, where the "Cold Mountain" at which he made his retreat is supposed to have been located, there are several references in the poems to northern places such as Ch'ang an [Chang'an] and especially Lo-yang [Luoyang].[30]

There are a number of assertions here that deserve further explanation. First, what does it mean to say that Hanshan was a "rustic" poet? What sort of level of literacy is Pulleyblank suggesting? (For example, if he was a rustic who learned poetry-writing from outdated examples, that might make him sound old-fashioned.) Do we know enough about regional dialects to assume that they would not skew the data to some extent? Is there a possibility that the author might be attempting an "archaizing effect," trying to make the poems sound older (or could such an effort have been attempted by one of the scribes who transmitted the Hanshan collection, who may have altered words)? Part of the problem here is the uniqueness of the collection: taken as a whole, the Hanshan poems are exceptional in their seeming closeness to Tang vernacular, yet we have no recourse except to compare their rhymes to a body of elite poetry. And the elite poems—written by known historical figures—are the only ones that we can conclusively date.[31] Professor Pulleyblank also suggests that Hanshan was a "northerner" because he mentions Chang'an and Luoyang. In fact, the extant poems never mention Chang'an, and they mention Luoyang exactly twice, both times when deliberately imitating popular poetry motifs inherited from Han dynasty verse composed five centuries earlier, when Luoyang was the capital. This suggests a poet who is quite familiar with the style of older, pre-Tang poetry, and is capable of imitating it. This might apply to rhymes as well. Finally, there is also the fact that the Pulleyblank model describes a movement from stricter rhymes to broader rhymes. From this, he concludes that *only* the "Han-Shan II" poems may be conclusively held to be later. However, this certainly does not prevent the "Han-Shan I" poems from being also written later: they might just as easily be categorized as *possibly* being written as early as the sixth or seventh centuries.

Professor Pulleyblank's account also opens up interpretive questions that are beyond the scope of his concerns: does situating Hanshan (or one of the Hanshans at least) in the seventh century rather than the eighth tell us anything about him as a poet? Does it make certain elements of his received biography more likely to be rooted in reality, or less? Is there a coherence to Han-Shan I's use of imagery, and is there one to Han-Shan II's? Are there perhaps multiple Hanshans in both eras? Pulleyblank does suggest that Han-Shan II represents a more doctrinaire Buddhist attitude ("many of these are didactic sermons"),[32] but that is about his only comment on content.

My own impressionistic perspective is that there is, generally speaking, a consistency in the poems that Pulleyblank attributes to "Han-Shan II." Most of the poems that quote sutras directly or refer to specific doctrinal points are in this group. However, there are many poems in the Han-Shan I group that also signify a rather later conception of Buddhism than was common in the sixth and seventh centuries and also belie the "folk poet" persona Pulleyblank imagines as characterizing the earlier author. HS 287, for example, seems to employ a fairly sophisticated "classical Chan" trope. Other poems in this group seem to be comfortable with rhetoric that had characterized Chan texts from the eighth century on, though admittedly it is difficult to pin down when certain forms of Chan language become widespread, especially when they can already be found to some extent in pre-Tang sutra translations.[33]

Generally speaking, I tend to side with the majority of Chinese scholars and imagine that most if not all of the Hanshan corpus was composed in the eighth and ninth centuries. However, I ultimately do not believe that this is an answerable question in any firm or permanent way. I merely mean to emphasize the degree to which our assumptions about the historical "reality" of Hanshan are rooted in very little. None of what we have—the fanciful preface, Zanning's exasperated collation of materials, Yu's and Wu's careful consideration of the data, Pulleyblank's rhyming categorization—give us an irrefutable answer to the question of when the poet lived.

But perhaps the poems themselves can tell us something about their author(s)?

CHAPTER 2

WHO WAS HANSHAN, AGAIN?

BEFORE we turn to the content of the poems (and consider them in the light of the poet's supposed life), we should look at the compilation of the collection itself. For some scholars, speculation about how the Hanshan corpus has come down to us is an integral part of who they think the poet was. But if we look at our textual sources, we shall soon see that these are no more reliable than the material we considered in the last chapter.

There are essentially two forms of data concerning the early circulation of the poems: mention of it in other texts—for example, in book catalogues and other bibliographic listings, and from comments made about it in other sources—and actual surviving editions. Because the earliest surviving edition dates from the twelfth century, we are wholly dependent on the first category of evidence in speculating about how the collection was first formed.

As we have seen, the Lüqiu Yin preface mentions that the monk Daoqiao supposedly copied the poems after Hanshan's disappearance from the various places that he wrote them—on walls, on rocks, on trees, and so forth. Yu Jiaxi does not doubt that the collection was indeed collected in this manner (in spite of his disbelief in the preface), nor do most scholars (perhaps this romantic myth of spontaneous inscription is just too powerful for them to surrender).[1] The question for Yu is how the collection progressed from this initial act of compilation (whoever did it) and became an actual circulated manuscript.

He continues his detective work, turning yet again to data found in Zanning's monk biographies. In Zanning's life of the monk Benji, there is mention that Benji composed a commentary for a work titled *Reply to Master Hanshan's Poems* (Dui Hanshan zi shi).[2] It is unclear what this "reply" means, or if this work in fact incorporates Hanshan's poems; it sounds more like the title of a collection of poems by someone else either imitating or responding to Hanshan's verse. In Zanning's biography of Hanshan, he repeats the story that Daoqiao gathered the poems after his disappearance, saying that he found "over two hundred poems." It then says: "Afterwards, the Chan master Ji from Caoshan composed commentaries and explanations, and entitled it *Reply to Master Hanshan's poems*."[3] Here, it seems clear that Ji is the same as Benji, and that the work in question was an edition of the poems with Benji's commentary added (the commentary serving as the "reply").

This version of the collection likely survived into the Song dynasty. The imperially commissioned bibliography *General Catalogue of Distinguished Letters* (Chongwen zongmu), compiled in the 1030s, lists "Master Hanshan's Poems in Seven Chapters," while the bibliographic treatise of the *New Tang History* (Xin Tang shu), roughly contemporaneous, lists a work entitled "Answering Master Hanshan's Poems in Seven Chapters," then includes a note: "With a preface by the Magistrate of Taizhou Lüqiu Yin; edited by the monk Daoqiao." This seems to be our earliest mention of the preface; from this point on, however, the curious "reply" in the title drops out.[4]

Interestingly enough, Yu feels he cannot accept Zanning's data exactly as it stands, because part of it at least seems to derive from the tainted preface. However, he *does* place particular importance on another anecdote from a completely different source. The massive tenth-century compilation of fantastic narrative, *Comprehensive Records of the Taiping Era* (Taiping guang ji, completed 978), has a short passage describing Hanshan, which it attributes to a work now lost, titled *Addenda to Biographies of Transcendents* (Xian zhuan shiyi) and supposedly written by the prominent Daoist philosopher and propagator Du Guangting (850–933). The text runs as follows:

> Master Hanshan—name and family unknown. In the Dali era [766–779] he lived as a recluse on Emerald Screen Mountain at Tiantai. This mountain was deep and remote, with snow at the height of summer (it is also known as Cold Cliff), so he took as his name Master Cold Mountain. He liked to write poems, and every time he composed a piece or a line he would write it on a tree or a stone. The curious would come afterwards and copy them, until over three hundred poems were collected. Most recorded the pleasures of living as a recluse in the mountain forests, while some satirized the fashions of the day and were able to serve as a warning on the decline of social mores. The Retired

> Gentleman of Tongbo Tabernacle[5] Xu Lingfu wrote a preface to the poems and assembled them into a collection, separating them into three chapters, and circulated them.
>
> A dozen years or so later Hanshan disappeared. In the twelfth year of Xiantong [872], there was a Daoist adept of Piling by the name of Li He, by nature narrow-minded and hot-tempered, who took pleasure in the humiliation of others. One day a poor scholar visited Li He and begged for food. He not only refused him any but abused him. The poor man bowed to him and departed. Several days later a man on a white horse accompanied by a group of six or seven attendants, all dressed in white, visited Li. He greeted them politely. Thereupon the man asked Li, "Do I seem familiar to you?" Li examined his features—and it turned out to be the poor scholar of before. He wished to apologize right away, but could say nothing in his shame. The man then addressed Li, "You cultivate the Way and yet you do not yet know how to begin—instead you delight in humiliating others. How could you hope for the Way? No doubt you know of Master Hanshan?" Li replied, "I do." "I am he. At first I thought you might be taught, but now I see it is impossible."[6]

Master Hanshan then preaches a sermon on charity and compassion before departing.

As with the Lüqiu Yin preface, we have a fanciful account in the form of a moral fable. It is related (not surprisingly) within a Daoist frame: Master Hanshan becomes a Daoist Transcendent *(xian)* rather than a bodhisattva. Many scholars would see this anecdote as a fine example of how Daoist and Buddhist circles tended to share stories, beliefs, and philosophical ideas during the Tang—sometimes harmoniously, sometimes as a form of competition. It is hardly surprising that Daoists would lay claim to their own version of Hanshan. Moreover, this narrative and the preface share a theme: the testing of the unenlightened. Li He here, like the monks of Guoqing monastery, does not recognize the saintliness of the ragged outsider and so demonstrates his own benighted nature.

However, Yu Jiaxi is much more interested in the opening paragraph that describes the compilation of the collection by the Daoist Xu Lingfu. Since he believes the Lüqiu Yin preface is a forgery, he accepts this anecdote as the earliest authentic description of Hanshan. His reasons run as follows: First, Xu Lingfu, the reputed editor of the Hanshan collection according to this account, wrote a description of the Tiantai district in which he tells of moving to the area in 815 (though he does not mention Hanshan). Yu therefore speculates that Xu must have learned about Hanshan some time after he wrote this account (i.e., after 815), and that he then compiled the collection from poems that survived in the region. Further, the Du Guangting anecdote lists Hanshan as a person of the Dali era (766–779), which fits with Yu's assumed dates for the poet. What's more, Yu notes, we know that Du Guangting spent some time in Taizhou in his youth, and may have discovered Xu Lingfu's writings then. At this point, Yu makes a speculative leap: some time around 900, the Chan master Benji took over the Xu edition of Hanshan, forged the Lüqiu Yin preface, and attributed the editorial work to a fictional "Daoqiao." He then composed a commentary on the edition, turning a "Daoist" work into a "Buddhist" work.

As with much of Yu's speculation, this is not impossible, but it is not really provable either. His argument seems not to evolve out of a reasonable consideration of the data, but rather out of a need to justify the *Taiping guang ji* anecdote for no other reason than it seems to be the earliest account of Hanshan (once the Lüqiu Yin preface is discounted). Needless to say, modern pro-Daoism adherents could use his arguments to claim that Hanshan was in fact a Daoist poet all along, instead of questioning the categories of "Buddhism" and "Daoism" as they existed in Tang popular religion. In the end, we are still confronted with unprovable and contradictory accounts concerning the compilation of the poems—and we still have no reliable conclusion about the author.

Two further notes might be worth bringing up here: though attention has primarily been paid to discovering who Hanshan was, scholars have largely ignored Shide and Fenggan. Due to the influence of the preface in later centuries, the two are constantly mentioned whenever Hanshan is introduced; but it is clear that their identities are even more shadowy than his. A handful of independent anecdotes concerning them do turn up in monk biographies, but all of them seem to be legendary. That being said, it should be emphasized that in premodern East Asia the Hanshan poems were almost always circulated together with the two poems attributed to Fenggan and the fifty-some poems attributed to Shide, and the work of all three poets was received as important and legitimate. This illustrates further the degree to which the preface (forged or not) became an accepted part of the Hanshan narrative. The associations of all three with the bodhisattvas Mañjuśrī, Samantabhadra, and Amitābha probably encouraged this.

Inventing a Poet

When we actually look at what the poems say about Hanshan himself, we run into a new series of problems. It cannot escape anyone reviewing the Chinese-language scholarship on Hanshan in the past few decades that a substantial portion of it attempts to reconstruct a biography for the poet based on the contents of the poems. This represents a curious combination of traditional reading methods with modern inclinations. There is little surviving evidence that premodern readers of Hanshan were interested in reconstructing a chronology of the poet's life in any detail. For example, Hakuin occasionally makes comments that suggest that he did take at least some of the poems as vaguely autobiographical, but he did not seem to consider that their most important aspect. This was partially due to the fact that the poems were most often read as Buddhist texts rather than as secular verse. As such, they were outside the mainstream of Chinese literary production, which was very much rooted in a poetics of self-expression and autobiography, especially beginning in the Qing dynasty (1644–1911), when commentaries on major Tang dynasty poets like Du Fu, Li Shangyin, and Wang Wei spent great intellectual effort in identifying the precise circumstances that produced each poem and in arranging them in a chronological sequence.[7] Biographical reconstruction continues to this day in much of Chinese scholarly writing on mainstream secular Chinese poetry. This in many ways represents the most extreme example of the "intimate friend" ideal of literature (*zhiyin*, "one who knows the tone"): if we can reconstruct the events behind every poem, we will have a guide to the poet's emotions and will thus understand him better as a human being.[8]

This biographical method would probably not have shifted to Hanshan interpretation were it not for two factors. First, as a corpus of poems that frequently employs Tang vernacular speech (as opposed to the usually "purer" diction of elite poetry), Chinese scholars have tended to see it as representative of a self-conscious "vernacular literature movement" *(baihua wenxue yundong)*, and as a symptom of a seemingly inevitable and progressive tendency to move from a hidebound classical literature toward one that more perfectly reflects the language of the "people." The poems are thus connected with other Tang dynasty texts that show similar propensities—in particular, much of the literature from the Buddhist caves at Dunhuang, especially the popular "transformation texts" *(bianwen)* and the poems attributed to the folk-poetry figure Wang Fanzhi.[9] This same trend would later encourage, so the argument goes, oral storytelling traditions in the Song dynasty and the evolution of vernacular drama and fiction in the Yuan and Ming dynasties.[10] With this elevation, there has likewise been a tendency for some critics to see the Hanshan poems as the product of a forward-thinking literary hero, someone who recognized the superiority of popular literature and chose to espouse it. As such, his life would deserve our curiosity and attention.

The other factor comes from more recent tendencies: increasing attention to religious texts, now much more available for study than during the Maoist era, as well as interest in the reception of Chinese literature in other countries. Chinese scholars soon noticed the fascination that Japanese and Korean readers had with the Hanshan corpus, and, even more intriguingly, the poems' impact on Gary Snyder and the circle of Beat writers in the 1950s. In the latter case, the Beat romanticization of the Hanshan figure as a courageous outsider telling unpleasant truths to a conventional society dovetailed to a certain extent with the Chinese predilection for a self-expressive and autobiographical reading of poetic texts.[11]

This is not to say that many Chinese scholars are not skeptical of this kind of interpretation, most notably Sun Changwu, perhaps the preeminent scholar on Chinese Buddhist literature, and the comparative literature scholar Hu Anjiang.[12] However, even those who express skepticism often seem to believe that there must be a core of "genuine" poems that arose from a distinctive personality and that these were diluted by later additions to the collection by non-Hanshan poets.

Biographical reconstructions of this sort track Hanshan's career as a sort of evolving spiritual journey. Usually they first take note of those poems that speak of life in ordinary secular society. Here, the evidence is conflicting and complicated. Was Hanshan a poor, suffering peasant? Was he the well-educated scion of a wealthy family? Was he a bravo who lived in the capital, indulging in hunting and other wild sports? Some readers might note that all of these life-roles are also conventional fictional personae in early Chinese popular poetry, but this has not prevented many from seeing such poems as autobiographical. Particularly important in this reconstruction is HS 101:

尋思少年日,	I recall the days of my youth—
遊獵向平陵。	I would go hunting at Ping Slope.
國使職非願,	No wish to serve as a state envoy,
神仙未足稱。	No interest in the Transcendents.
聯翩騎白馬,	Cantering along, astride my white steed,

喝兔放蒼鷹。	I'd release my hawk to flush out hares.
不覺大流落,	I didn't notice when I hit the skids,
皤皤誰見矜。	I'm gray-haired now, and no one cares.

The warning theme here is strong and universal: the young are oblivious to the vicissitudes of life and to physical and social decline. Compelled by habits of reading, some go further and take this as an autobiographical poem, and they wonder why he describes himself as a wealthy youth here while other poems describe early years spent in poverty. Perhaps the poems in which the narrator describes a life of poverty were written after the onset of hard times referenced in the seventh line?

Important as well for such readings is the second couplet, which holds out two supposedly more constructive careers for a youth: government service and Daoist self-cultivation. For biographical readers, the poet is here hinting at his future concerns; they then turn their attention to a number of poems narrated in the voice of someone seeking government office (e.g., HS 113, spoken by someone disappointed in failing the exams), and to those that express frustration over inability to achieve fame both as a civil and as a military officer—for example, HS 7:

一為書劍客,	I once studied civil and martial skills,
三遇聖明君。	And thrice met an enlightened lord.
東守文不賞,	But civil rank in the east did not win me reward,
西征武不勳。	And western campaigns earned me no distinction.
學文兼學武,	Study civil skills, then martial ones—
學武兼學文。	Study martial skills, then civil ones—
今日既老矣,	And now I've already grown so old,
餘生不足云。	Remaining years not worth a thought.

One may sense already just from HS 101 and HS 7 that the autobiographical assumption requires us to reconstruct a life particularly rich in incident: not only was the poet both poor and rich, but also he served as both a civil and a military official. And yet the drama is just beginning. Next he turns to Daoist self-cultivation and studies alchemical procedures in order to search for the elixir of immortality; HS 194, for example, describes his abode, where "in stone chambers and earthen furnace the smelting cauldron seethed." He is soon disappointed by his failure to discover eternal life, however, and becomes sharply critical of the search for transcendence, turning instead to the more elevated truth of Buddhism. In one of the longest poems of the corpus (HS 248), he castigates a would-be Transcendent for the tawdriness of his practice and claims that realizing the inner Buddha Nature is the only true path.

Having now brought the poet within the Buddhist fold, the biographers become undecided as to whether he was ever ordained as a monk. There are a number of poems that suggest criticism of monastic conventions, which may indicate that he at least spent some time in such a community.[13] However, the final stage and the fullest realization of his talent come when he embraces his existence as an antinomian recluse, resistant to all social and conventional forms of thinking.

Obviously, this romanticized biography is suspect. And yet it curiously resembles a medieval Buddhist way of thinking: that of *panjiao* or "division of the doctrines," an idea seen as having reached its fullest development in Tiantai thought. The doctrine first evolved due to the unease Chinese Buddhist monastics felt concerning the vast number of translated scriptures and the degree to which they seem to contradict each other. The concept of *panjiao* holds that the Buddha tailored his teachings to the capacities of different believers, reserving less lofty versions of the Dharma for those who could not comprehend the more advanced. For Tiantai, ultimate knowledge was contained in the Lotus Sutra. However, *panjiao* is adaptable to many different conditions. At its simplest, it may be seen in the original distinction Mahayana made between itself and other forms of Buddhism (the so-called Hinayana or "lesser vehicles"). It could be adopted as well within cultures that had religious traditions outside of Buddhism—rather than rejecting non-Buddhist doctrines outright, believers could judge native religious systems as valid but inferior to Buddhist truths. One of the most developed schemata that employ this method is found in Zongmi's *Inquiry into the Origin of Humanity* (Yuan ren lun), an essay written for lay believers. Zongmi (780–841), a prominent figure in both the Huayan and Chan traditions, brings the reader step-by-step from inferior forms of wisdom to the most profound, that is, from Confucianism, Daoism, Hinayana, Yogācāra Mahayana, and Madhyamaka Mahayana to Huayan and Chan. In this progression, the best elements of each doctrine are subsumed within the one that follows it.[14]

It is easy to see that the reconstructed biographies of Hanshan are essentially a progression through a *panjiao* schema, starting with his wild and unthinking days as a bravo, leading to his Confucian studies and attempts at holding a public office, his disillusion and subsequent conversion to Daoism, his conversion to Buddhism and monastic life, and his final existence as an antinomian hermit, the state in which the preface describes him. The endpoint of this story is particularly attractive, since it grants him romantic independence and freedom from the ritual and routinization of both monastic and lay Buddhism. It both allows him to fit in with later idealizations of Chan masters from the "classic period" and also makes him attractive to those who are interested in Buddhism for countercultural reasons.

There are however obvious problems with this construction, other than its tenuousness. First of all, most biographical scholars accept that Hanshan did indeed write his poems on various surfaces around and on Cold Mountain. So what do we make of the supposedly autobiographical poems that seem to place the poet in earlier periods of his life? To imagine that Hanshan made a sort of fictional persona of himself, pretending to be himself several decades earlier, would violate the very laws of traditional poetics that tend to govern biographical interpretations—laws that privilege poems as immediate emotional responses to external events. Such readings also tend to make self-identity reflect ideological and religious traditions in an overly simple manner. It has long been accepted that many Tang intellectuals felt comfortable combining elements of Confucianism with Daoism and Buddhism, and did not find them mutually exclusive. More important, we now have a much clearer sense of the way that competition and interaction between the Buddhist and Daoist traditions in the Tang resulted in a shared philosophical and religious language. It is not merely that the two traditions put their own doctrinal spin on the same Chinese words; rather, their very interpretations of those words tended to be shared, and a sort of dialogue (if often an antagonistic one) occurred between them.[15] This often makes the question of a specific poem of Hanshan's is "Daoist" or "Buddhist" pointless. Though some verses use jargon in ways so specific as to clarify their doctrinal pedigrees, the deeper meanings of many others will probably be constituted in the mind of the reader. If we try to reconstruct a life of Hanshan based on his ideological allegiances, we have to make specific choices about the orientations of specific poems and make them fit the narrative we want.

The immediate alternate to a biographical reading, of course, is to see the Hanshan corpus as a body of folk poems or semipopular poems, as Thomas Barrett and others have suggested:

> There is actually no evidence against the more radical conclusion that the poems were written by various hands over a span of time, and

> that what appear to be autobiographical references may be explained alternatively as falling well within the bounds of poetic convention—for example, the sort of false rustic persona that we also find in European literature. Is it only our own romantic individualism that prevents us from seeing behind the masks of convention a coterie of monks of the Tiantai mountains, detectable only by their penchant for including references to their distinctive philosophy in their verses?[16]

Taking this approach to the poems encourages a sort of sociological and linguistic analysis of recurring tropes and formulaic composition patterns. It has been suggested that many poems from the post-Han era that were interpreted by later readers as intense moments of self-expression from self-conscious poets were in fact composed out of a storehouse of shared conventions.[17] This trope-oriented poetry often stands behind some of Hanshan's recurring themes: the heroic bravo on horseback, the beautiful courtesan, the drinking party, the carpe diem injunction (with its representation of graveyards), the peacefulness of the hermit's life. Its presence tells us that the Hanshan poet or poets were rather familiar with the pre-Tang poetic corpus and were often attracted to conventional themes. A serious study along these lines would attempt to reach some conclusions about popular poetry composition in the Tang, asking what level of language was suitable for such poetry, what such poetry might suggest about ordinary literacy at the time, and how the poems shed light on other texts, such as Chan-related Dunhuang texts and the poetry attributed to Wang Fanzhi. Repeated lines and images would be mapped out and juxtaposed against the body of surviving Tang and pre-Tang verse. The result would reveal a more intimate sense of the social circumstances of their composition.

A worthy task—but not what this study intends. The fact remains that for one thousand years the poems have been read enthusiastically, most typically by Buddhists (both lay and cleric), and their attitudes toward the poems have neither embraced a detailed biographical analysis nor a sociological one. Those attitudes warrant discussion. While it is impossible for us to recapture to any thorough extent what our Ms. Chen thought when she turned the pages of her early printed edition, we can make some suggestions as to how one might read "as a Buddhist"—and how the poems might develop a greater richness and complexity as a result.

Creating Meaning in Hanshan

We have already briefly considered the biographical assumptions associated with HS 101 ("I recall the days of my youth"). From a nonbiographical perspective, this poem sounds not that different from earlier anonymous poems in the Chinese tradition, many of which possess just such a generalized moral: our early extravagances will disappear as we grow old, and our lives are far too short. It comes close to being a universal poem, the sort of verse that any premodern culture might produce. Yet a Buddhist reader might note that the text provides a striking example of one of the Three Marks of Existence, a central tenet of the faith—in this case, Impermanence (*anitya*).[18] To see this as a factor in interpretation is to recognize the ways in which Chinese cultural habits interact with Buddhist beliefs: readers predisposed to Buddhism would reorient texts from a non-Buddhist tradition to signify in Buddhist ways. But would such readers have a justification for imagining that the Hanshan poems are encouraging a Buddhist reading?

In fact, there are a number of poems in the collection that address the reader directly or attempt to explain to her what "Hanshan" is trying to do. These "meta-poems" provide certain rules of reading that a Buddhist might find particularly attractive. Most obviously, the very first poem (HS 1), employing a didactic voice, asks that the reader take on a certain Buddhist frame of mind:

凡讀我詩者,	All you who read my poems!
心中須護淨。	You must preserve purity in your minds.
慳貪繼日廉,	Work daily to clean out your stinginess;
諂曲登時正。	At once correct your deviousness.
驅遣除惡業,	Evil karma you'll drive away,
歸依受真性。	Take refuge, receive your True Nature.
今日得佛身,	Today you'll acquire your Buddha-body—
急急如律令。	Be quick to follow this command!

This poem is a combination of explicitly Buddhist terminology ("evil karma," "take refuge [in the faith]," "Buddha-body"); terms that often occur in a specialized sense in Buddhist texts ("preserve purity in your mind," "True Nature"); and words with moral implications that also became part of Buddhist rhetoric ("stinginess," "deviousness"). As Xiang Chu's detailed commentary on this poem indicates, all of these terms have a rich history of usage in the sutra literature.[19] *Stinginess* would be seen by Buddhist readers as the opposite of generosity, *dāna*; *deviousness* would be taken as a misdeed of speech (as opposed to misdeeds of the body and of the mind). Both can generate the "evil karma" of the fifth line. The practice that preserves "purity of mind" in line 2 will lead to the revelation of one's "true nature" (that is, the Buddha Nature) and to becoming one with the ultimate reality of the "Buddha-body" (that is, the *dharmakāya*). The rough equivalence of "purity of mind," "true nature," and "Buddha-body" would be familiar to anyone reading Chan and proto-Chan texts of the eighth century. The last line, "Be quick to follow this command," is an interesting adaptation of a phrase probably best known to Tang readers as a formula used at the end of Daoist spells, meant as a command for spirits to do the bidding of the spell-caster. Its use here is probably not meant to appropriate a Daoist phrase for Buddhist use, but rather to suggest in a humorous manner that Hanshan feels free to order us about the way a magician controls spirits.[20] The poem is not an obscure one, and the Buddhist resonances (for someone familiar with Buddhist texts) would be easy to hear. The more complex point for a Buddhist reader is how to interpret the transition from *preparation before reading* (what the poet says the reader should do before engaging with the texts) to the *results of reading*. I have translated the poem with the assumption that this occurs between lines 4 and 5; lines 2–4 suggest the preparation the earnest believer must make, and lines 5–7 are the benefits to be gained from approaching the texts in such a devout manner. But this division may not be important, because the reader might take the poem to be suggesting a process of mutual reinforcement: sincerity in approaching the poems requires, in a sense, *already* cultivating within oneself the very qualities that the poems are meant to impart or teach. The pious reader discovers through reading the poem that she in a sense has *already* read the poem; the Buddha Nature is always already within us, we just need to realize it.

A more complex poem (HS 141) carries Buddhist hermeneutics further by commenting on the idea that different readers are differently prepared to hear the message of the texts:

下愚讀我詩,	When low types—fools—read my poems
不解却嗤誚。	They don't understand and make fun of them.
中庸讀我詩,	When middling types read my poems
思量云甚要。	They think a bit, then say "quite essential!"
上賢讀我詩,	When lofty types—the wise—read my poems

把著滿面笑。	They break into the broadest of grins.
楊脩見幼婦,	When Yang Xiu saw "Young Bride,"
一覽便知妙。	In one glance he knew how marvelous!

Here the narrator grades his readers based on their intelligence and perceptiveness. Though this doesn't explicitly propose a "skillful means" model for the poems, it does suggest (as the doctrine of skillful means does) that those who hear the Buddhist path will differ in their responses. He makes the point in a more sophisticated way as well, enacting it through a particularly clever use of allusion. Those who are unaware of literary tradition would likely read the last couplet as "When Yang Xiu saw the young bride, in one glance he knew she was marvelous," but the well-educated would recognize the reference to a story found in *Tales of the World: New Series* (Shi shuo xin yu), a collection of anecdotes about the aristocratic classes compiled in the early fifth century. The story involves the infamous warlord Cao Cao (155–220), one of his ministers, Yang Xiu, and a Chinese character rebus:

> Emperor Wu of the Wei [Cao Cao] once passed by a memorial stele dedicated to Lady Cao; Yang Xiu was in attendance. Behind the stele someone had written:
>
> | | |
> |---|---|
> | 黃絹幼婦 | brown pongee young bride |
> | 外孫虀臼 | maternal grandson pound mortar |
>
> Emperor Wu said to Yang, "Do you get it?" He replied, "Sure." The emperor said, "Don't tell me yet, let me think about it a while." After they had ridden ten miles, the emperor finally said, "I've got it!" He then had Yang write down what he had figured out. Yang wrote: "'Brown pongee' is a kind of 'colored silk' 色糸, and those two characters form the character for 'supremely' 絕. 'Young bride' is a 'youthful woman' 少女, and those two characters form the character for 'marvelous' 妙. 'Maternal grandson' is the 'daughter's son' 女子 and those two characters form the character for 'wonderful' 好. 'To be pounded in a mortar' means 'to receive hardship' 受辛, and those two characters form the character for 'words' 辭. And so the phrase means 'supremely marvelous and wonderful words'" 絕妙好辭. The emperor also wrote down what he had thought. When he compared it with Yang's note, they were the same. The emperor sighed. "I'm ten miles less clever than you!"[21]

Hanshan's poems thus become a sort of rebus of wisdom, which those "in the know" will intuitively understand immediately. The poet has used a literati game as a metaphor for the search for enlightenment, one that perhaps evokes the strategies of "classical" Chan, which emphasizes the competitive and slightly agonistic nature of such a search. Regardless, it is the one of quick perception—the wise—who is superior to the ignorant and the slow learners.

By comparing Hanshan's verses to a rebus, the poem also suggests that the higher wisdom they impart is an index to deeper meaning—an index that on the surface may suggest nonsensical and wildly different from the "real" truth. This may suggest the distinction between "provisional" *(quan)* truth and "actual" *(shi)* truth in Chinese Mahayana thought. At this point, the "skillful means" concept really does enter into possible interpretations. By addressing an audience that would know the allusion and thus would not confuse the last lines for a description of a vulgar young man named Yang Xiu who is ogling a pretty woman, the poet suggests that Buddhist wisdom is also a form of knowledge that enables one to see through surface appearances (the superficial lesson) and capture the deeper significance. It also reinforces the theme—seen in the preface—that the "true" readers obtain a certain satisfaction from this privileged position, one that allows them to feel amusement and pleasure at their spiritual breakthrough.

Another meta-poem, HS 305, explicitly compares the Hanshan collection to the most famous poetry anthology in the Chinese tradition, the *Classic of Poetry* (Shijing). Victor Mair has noted that the Hanshan collection may have been kept at a little over three hundred poems in order to mimic its sacred predecessor;[22] HS 305 helps to confirm this speculation:

有人笑我詩,	There are people who laugh at my poems;
我詩合典雅。	Though they're in keeping with classical standards!
不煩鄭氏箋,	But I won't bother people with Sir Zheng's notes,
豈用毛公解。	Have no need of glosses from the Masters Mao.[23]
不恨會人稀,	I don't hate the lack of comprehenders;
只為知音寡。	That's just because my intimates are few.
若遣趁宮商,	I dispense with forcing tones on my lines,
余病莫能罷。	Since I can't cure myself of my errors.[24]
忽遇明眼人,	But should they meet up with clear-sighted ones,
即自流天下。	Then they'll circulate throughout the world!

The poet explicitly compares his work to the *Classic of Poetry*, and even suggests his own collection is superior to it, in that it is canonical in content but also readily understandable, free of the commentarial burden that weighs down the earlier classic (written in particularly archaic language, the *Classic of Poetry* could not be read by educated readers without substantial explanatory notes). At the same time, he introduces an element of traditional poetics, the idea that his poems are addressed to a reader (often quite rare) who can truly understand the poet by intuiting his personality through the text. As noted in chapter 1, Ouyang Xiu suggested that such a relationship existed between the Buddhist poet Miyan and his friend Manqing; in this poem Hanshan explicitly uses the term *zhiyin* ("one who knows the tone"). Though this seems to place the Hanshan poems in line with mainstream poetic composition, a Buddhist reader would understand it as a synthesis of Confucian poetics with Buddhist hermeneutics: just as a poet is lucky to find the rare reader who will appreciate his talent as represented in his verse, so a Buddha or bodhisattva is aware that the believer who understands his deepest meaning will be rare—in fact, the rarity of complete understanding (as in HS 141 above) is a mark of profundity and wisdom.

This is worth considering a bit further, because it touches at the most important intersection between a Buddhist poetics and the expectations of traditional Chinese readers. One of the assumptions of traditional Confucian poetics was the belief in spontaneous authenticity: the poet seeks to express as sincerely as possible the emotions that he feels at a specific moment in time in reaction to events around him. It is belief in this system that has led so many scholars to want to read the Hanshan poems as written over the long course of the poet's life, and as an autobiographical record of his spiritual journey. A central tenet of this aesthetic view is that excessive poetic craft—manifested through revisionism, flashy rhetoric, and authorial distance—often marks poems as "insincere" and consequently bad (or even immoral in some sense). Such poems may prove difficult to read, and that in turn makes even the best reader's experience of them one of effort, cogitation and confusion, rather than an intuitive and immediate comprehension that acts in harmony with the poet's intentions and personality.

Hanshan's poem 305 attempts in part to co-opt the claim of authenticity by boasting of its own metrical incompetence; it is rather the verse of the secular poets with their metrical proprieties that is guilty of artificiality and insincerity, and consequently might prove difficult to understand. In fact, Hanshan's directness of communication allows his poetry, according to this poem, to supersede all other Chinese verse, even the *Classic of Poetry*, which cannot be understood without annotation (in this way, he blasphemously groups this sacred Confucian text, said to be an infallible guide to moral behavior, with the fancy poems of the Tang elite). However—as we shall see in a moment—Hanshan is not simply interested in conveying his biographically inscribed personality to a talented reader. The "clear-sighted ones" he has in mind will have access to a deeper wisdom.

Finally, there is the concluding quatrain of the collection (HS 313), which serves as a sort of comic advertisement:

家有寒山詩，	If your household has Hanshan's poems,
勝汝看經卷。	That's better than reading sutras!
書放屏風上，	Write them out on a folding screen,
時時看一遍。	And read them from time to time.

Rather than replacing the *Classic of Poetry*, here the poems replace sutras; the poet suggests that they can serve a function in everyday devotion and contemplation. Though not entirely serious, this quatrain does suggest that the poems contain the same religious and moral truths as sutras, but are easier to understand and certainly more entertaining to read, just as they are more entertaining than the often incomprehensible *Classic of Poetry*. Again, we have the suggestion that the texts are examples of "skillful means." The association with devotional texts makes a strong statement about the author as the source of the poems' teaching: the poems are not the self-expression of an ordinary human being, but have a more elevated origin. The poems are not only poems in the traditional Chinese sense but also sacred writ.

In summary, a Buddhist reader would likely take away several "rules of reading" from these four poems that she might apply to the collection as a whole: First, she might conclude that the reader must place herself in a properly purified state of mind in order to receive the message of the poems, and that such a state of purification is both preparatory to, and a result of, the act of reading. Second, these poems suggest that work as a whole may point to a deeper meaning that is not immediately apparent upon a superficial perusal—in fact they may seem trivial or nonsensical to someone of insufficiently superior attainments, just as Hanshan in his beggar's rags goes unrecognized by most people who see him—but that a truly gifted reader will intuitively understand the poems at once. Third, like good mainstream poetry, the poems may find their most important audience among a limited group of such gifted "intimate readers." Fourth, the collection can serve a canonical purpose in that it can act as a guide for Buddhists, just as the sutras can. Fifth and finally, the poems' favorable comparison to the *Classic of Poetry* and to the sutras indicates that they participate simultaneously in secular and sacred textual traditions, primarily as a skillful means that utilizes the conventions of secular literature to point to deeper religious meaning.

A group of motifs that grow out of the assumptions of these poems concerns the division between ignorance and knowledge, the wise and the foolish. Hanshan tends to see the world divided into two camps, those who "get it" and those who do not. Of course, this is directly analogous to the enlightened and the unenlightened in Buddhist terms; but in poetic terms the themes get played out in more complicated ways. It is this division that accounts for the omnipresent role of laughter in his work: as Red Pine suggested, Hanshan always finds a reason to laugh. But even though this usually manifests as a contemptuous laugh of scorn for those still trapped in ignorance, it can appear in other ways as well: laughter at himself, at times, as a warning against arrogance; awareness that others are in turn laughing at him; and a Chan-inflected laugh seemingly employed to drive the ignorant to a greater awareness. Laughter can unite as well as divide: one can laugh *with* a person as well as *at* him. Another series of images that grow out of this division are ones connected to competition, shared knowledge, and friendship. As in the developing Chan movement, Hanshan's prodding and seeking can be seen as a method to compel people to deeper understanding. Heightened wisdom then creates a bond between Hanshan and his reader; the reader becomes a Buddhist *zhiyin* and can dwell with Hanshan as a recluse on his metaphorical mountain, taking the role perhaps of a new Shide or Fenggan.

But what are the greater conclusions to be drawn from Hanshan's assertions? In fact, these interpretative moves belong to a broader discourse already in existence within Buddhism that allows for a distinctive religious perspective on figurative language. That perspective helps create a specifically Buddhist poetics, a way of defining "Buddhist poetry" from the perspective of the reader.

Metaphor and Fable

Stephen Bokenkamp, writing on Chinese ideas of figurative language, especially the term *biyu* (the word now used to mean "metaphor"), notes that translators of Sanskrit texts used the term *biyu* to render a number of types of figurative language in the South Asian tradition—both the short comparisons of simile and metaphor, as well as the "extended metaphor" of allegory and parable. An essential point of his argument is that Buddhist writers saw such figurative language as didactic in nature, in that its purpose was to point to deeper truth. In discussing the Tiantai founder Zhiyi's consideration of the term, he notes that

> Zhiyi goes on at some length to explain how *biyu* allows one to plumb the transcendental verities of the Buddhist dharma by reference to mundane things: "For example, to compare the father-son [relationship] of this world with the supramundane [relationship] of master-disciple or to compare this-worldly extinction to *nirvāṇa* (出世滅)." He elsewhere praises *biyu* as a means of dissolving delusion and advocates ten similes (十喻 in this case) as the best way of helping others to apprehend the meaning of *śūnyatā* 空: "It is like illusion, like flame, like the reflection of the moon in the water, like the empty void, like an echo, etc."
>
> In this way, *biyu* becomes an expedient means *[upāya]* for apprehending the true nature of existence underlying the flux of illusory appearances normally taken for reality. While Buddhist metaphor and simile are held to point to "reality," it is finally a reality which is "fundamentally other from the concrete world."[25]

Even more interesting is the fact that an extended sense of *biyu* was applied to translate the term *avadāna*:

> To be scrupulously accurate, *biyu* is not a translation of *avadāna* at all, but a description of one of the primary attributes of the *avadāna* tale. The word *avadāna* originally referred to didactic passages in the scriptures which relate events in the previous lives of a Buddhist adept leading to enlightenment. The tales designated "*biyu*" in the scriptures are not confined to such stories but are what we would designate "allegory" [extended metaphor], or, in view of their religious intent, "parables." Since there was never a distinction drawn between *biyu* and "extended *biyu*," it was in this sense that the Chinese term must have occurred to early translators as a suitable designation for *avadāna* tales.[26]

This suggests a Chinese Buddhist conception of figurative language in general—from the simplest of metaphors to fairly elaborate narratives—as playing the role of pointing to deeper truths for the purpose of enlightening believers. Though the technical meaning of *avadāna* is somewhat limited (usually to the Buddha telling a story of a believer's past life to the believer), there is often little difference between *avadāna* and other forms of Buddhist narrative in terms of content: a past life is being related for the purpose of illustrating the workings of karma and the consequences of moral or immoral behavior. This is true of *jātakas*, for example, the tales of the Buddha's past lives, though they differ from *avadānas* in that we know beforehand that they tell of the Buddha, while *avadānas* leave the discovery of past-life identities for the end as a sort of revelation. In both cases, however, the Buddhist tradition often adapted traditional folk-tales (many of non-Buddhist origin) and gave them a Buddhist frame.

This also brings up a curious point at which figurative language runs up against the assumptions of Chinese poetics. The concept of "skillful means" *(upāya)* emerges in the Lotus Sutra specifically in the context of evaluating what is truth and what nontruth. In those passages, the Buddha explains that he may use language while preaching what is only "conventionally" true for certain specific situations or with some believers, but is not "ultimately" true from a perspective outside samsara. In this context, figurative language may be said to be "not true" in an absolute sense, though it is true contextually. If we think of the poems in the Hanshan collection as examples of *biyu* in a Buddhist context, we can imagine a location for them within Buddhist rhetoric that would free them from a conventional autobiographical reading, from the assumption that their narratives are supposed to reflect the actual experiences of a human being known as Hanshan; rather, as *biyu* texts, they open the back door to fictionality. We can then imagine a reading environment in which the recurring narrative tropes of the collection are interpreted as a representation of a complex range of human experiences, transcending any one life-experience but still expressed through a consciousness experiencing samsara. Buddhist narrative literature often incorporates a wide body of folk material and subordinates it to the context of karma and rebirth: though the ethical force of such tales is not necessarily Buddhist in origin, the understood frame converts these tales into specifically Buddhist stories that become part of a shared Buddhist cultural heritage. In the same way, the Hanshan corpus potentially takes a wide range of poems—some of them rooted in the imagery and tropes of a non-Buddhist tradition—and recontextualizes them as Buddhist lessons.

I am not suggesting here that we are meant to take the different narrative voices of the poems as the product of Hanshan's recollection of past lives. Rather, as a body of diverse texts written from many different perspectives, the poems are analogous to Buddhist tales in that they are meant to embody all of human experience. Just as the early narratives (*jātaka*s, *avadāna*s, and others) provide us with a cross-section of early Indian society, the Hanshan corpus taken as a whole reflects a large range of Chinese society; for a Buddhist-minded reader, these different identities reflect not just many different individuals, but also the countless states of being that we ourselves have experienced in the past and may very well experience again. In this sense, these poems are our own personal *avadāna*s, and Hanshan is presenting them to us for our own edification, just as the Buddha did. This is the reason why modern biographical readings of the poems often see Hanshan engaged in a sort of spiritual journey that ends in antinomian Buddhism: such readings detect that one of the principal qualities of the collection is its discontent and restlessness. But rather than serving as an indication of a self-expressive poet in search of inner peace, the poems can be read instead as catalogs of all the various forms of human dissatisfaction *(duḥkha)*. They are not fiction as such but skillfully evoked illusions that express our own impermanent lives.

This brings us back to the fact that the preface is quite emphatic in claiming that Hanshan was an incarnation of Mañjuśrī. This is not simply a figure of speech that is meant to point to Hanshan's wisdom. It is claimed twice in the preface itself, and the concluding poem of the collection hints at it as well. The preface to the Hakuin commentaries also goes out of its way to stress this—and to articulate the distinctive role this manifestation of Mañjuśrī plays as a skillful means for the benefit of sentient beings:

> Of old at Tiantai there was Master Cold Mountain—he was a responsive manifestation [i.e., incarnation] of the Dharma Prince Mañjuśrī, who is a master of controlling the passions, one who through the fruition of his merit has had a marvelous awakening. And yet it so happens that when he manifested himself in the world, there were no auspicious omens such as the release of light-beams or an earthquake; there was no splendid adornment on him, such as a body of purest gold—there was only a tousle-headed, dirty-faced, green-complexioned, frozen and starving old beggar. That's what we mean when we say, "Wealth and status will gnaw like vermin at your benevolent mind, while what is withered and pale will form a jade-like perfection in your dharma nature." His crazy

> songs are now The Poems of Cold Mountain [. . . .] Now when people like us select a teacher, it's no good to pick a Buddha or a Zen patriarch—only Master Cold Mountain can serve as a teacher.[27]

The poems are a skillful means from the mind of one of the most important bodhisattvas—a collection of Buddhist *biyu*. To the question "Who was Hanshan?" we can answer that Buddhist readers have known the answer all along: he was Mañjuśrī.

A Buddhist Poetics

If this seems to be basing a poetics on an essentially supernatural presupposition, I would suggest that understanding and appreciating a text may depend upon a sympathetic connection with the spiritual assumptions of the readers. We take this for granted when reading George Herbert or Rumi, and Hanshan deserves the same courtesy. In this case, of course, we have a body of poems that likely originated with a group of popular poets writing in the Tang. But once the collection was put together, a founding legend was attached to it, and it became part of a Buddhist reading tradition, such that this origin is much less important than the fusion of myth and history that grew up around it. In this we can follow John McRae's cardinal rule for examining the early Chan tradition: "It's not true, and therefore it's more important."[28]

The result of these speculations provides us with a larger theoretical basis for a distinctive Buddhist poetics, one tied to the idea of nonhuman revelation. This does not result in the sort of revelatory literature that has become part of the monotheistic faiths: not the Koran or the Torah or even mystic literature inspired by religious vision. Rather, it is a way of reading texts, a type of reader-response criticism focused on the idea of skillful means and the idea that the texts manifest their importance not at their source as unalterable truth—since in Buddhist terms an articulated truth is not Truth—but rather in how they are received and understood, and the benefits that may result from such a reception.

Perhaps the most famous source for the idea of a Buddhist creative literature can be found in the Lotus Sutra, immediately before the Buddha relates the famous parable of the burning house:

> At that time the Buddha spoke to Śariputra: "Did I not say before: 'The various Buddhas, the World-Honored ones, preach the Dharma

> through various causes and conditions and through skillful means by use of figurative *[biyu]* language, all for the sake of ultimate enlightenment'? All of this preaching is for the sake of converting bodhisattvas. And therefore, Śariputra! I shall now clarify this meaning further through the use of a figure *[biyu]*, so that all those who possess wisdom may be able to understand through use of a figure *[biyu]*."[29]

Here the Buddha speaks of two kinds of preaching. The first is the use of "causes and conditions," which implies a careful philosophical analysis of the process that creates the false sense of a Self and thus leads to suffering. The second form of teaching is through figurative language *(biyu)*, which will be understood by those who "possess wisdom *[zhi; prajñā]*." This resonates in a slightly skewed way with the Chinese *zhiyin*—though here the ideal reader is not the understanding friend as such, but one who is wise.[30] Imaginative literature then may serve a specific Buddhist purpose if it functions as a skillful means to enlightenment.

Two other passages, both from the Vimalakīrti Sutra, may prove illuminating. The first is a defense of language as a way of conveying truth: it is meant as a refutation of dualistic thinking that could potentially elevate silence as being somehow closer to the truth than speech. The wise goddess of the seventh chapter is conversing with the benighted Śāriputra:

> The goddess said, "Elder, how long have you been Liberated?" Śāriputra was silent and did not reply. The goddess said, "Why do you remain silent, in spite of your great wisdom?" He answered, "Liberation possesses nothing that can be said to express it. Therefore I do not know what to say." The goddess replied, "Spoken words and written text all are Marks of Liberation. Why is that? Liberation is neither internal, external, nor in between. Written text is also neither internal, external, nor in between. And so, Śāriputra, you may speak of Liberation without transcending written text. Why is that? All dharmas are Marks of Liberation."[31]

It is easy enough to deny the worth of explanations when dealing with the ineffable ("The Way that can be spoken of is not the Constant Way");[32] but this passage asserts that the decision to be silent establishes a false and misleading duality between speech and silence. Silence is in fact no better than speech—perhaps worse, because it creates a deceptive sense of wisdom, the sort that Mahayanists saw as typical of other Buddhists like Śāriputra, who is usually portrayed in this sutra as a confused "Hinayanist." Because both silence and speech can operate only as provisional means for conveying the ineffable, a bodhisattva may feel comfortable utilizing both.

The second passage comes from the first chapter of the Vimalakīrti, in the eulogy to the Buddha:

> Each sees the World-Honored One appear;
> This through his supernatural power, his distinctive characteristics.
> The Buddha with a single sound preaches the Dharma,
> While each sentient being understands in accordance with its kind.
> Each believes the World-Honored One is speaking to it,
> This through his supernatural power, his distinctive characteristics.
> The Buddha with a single sound preaches the Dharma,
> And each sentient being follows in accordance with its understanding.[33]

That the Buddha has the power to convey sermons with different content to different hearers at the same time is a quintessential example of skillful means. Of interest here, however, is the "reader-response" aspect of this assertion—the idea that through the wisdom of a Buddha or a bodhisattva, a listener is empowered to obtain whatever significance will mean most to her or him at that specific moment. The passage is *not* saying merely that different believers will understand the teaching differently—it is saying that the teaching really *is* different for each person. This too creates a radical revision of the idea of the *zhiyin*: the Buddha's words do not enable us to understand *him* as a personality; rather, we recognize that what we call and perceive as the "Buddha" is a fluctuating phenomenon without a definitive identity. If we are wise, we all become *zhiyin* of the Buddha, but that Buddha will be different for each one of us.

To read Hanshan as a collection of Buddhist poems, then, is to radically refigure the role of the reader as *zhiyin*. If Mañjuśrī stands at the poems' source in the way that the Buddha stands at the source of the sutras, he will be presenting us with a series of temporarily valid but ultimately illusory visions, each of which we may take for the moment as a true producing Self. But to be a true *zhiyin* is to possess *zhi (prajña)*; it is to realize that there is no object to receive our effort at understanding. It is to realize that the poet in fact does not exist, at least not as the emotionally expressive voice that secular poetics has posited.

All of these texts suggest a perspective on creative literature that celebrates its freedom to explore and to discover a range of ways of expressing the Dharma, as well as of embracing the interpretative strategies of the reader. Obviously, there are "bad readings," readings that would potentially result in the generation of bad karma both for oneself and for others, the Buddhist equivalent of heterodox readings. In spite of that, such a poetics does seem to offer considerably broader space for interpretation than do other religious hermeneutic traditions.

However, this should not blind us to the interpretative difficulties involved in taking the disparate body of Hanshan poems (probably written by different hands) and smoothing them out in this manner, creating one consistent reading. "Skillful means" does indeed resolve this issue; but it does so in order to compensate for the poetic voice(s) of the Hanshan poems—poems that often embrace irony, contradiction, satire, and other figures that point to reversals of surface meaning. In a Buddhist reading, such heterogeneity remains underpinned by a continuing and fundamental emphasis on faith; in this sense perhaps this freedom does resemble the hermeneutics of other religious traditions, in which ingenuity of interpretation is needed to reconcile incompatibilities.

There is a final point worth making concerning the implications of Buddhist ontology for the reading process, and what this ontology might suggest about the relationship between speaker/writer and hearer/reader. In East Asian Mahayana, we are constantly being told that we are in fact, already Buddhas—merely unrealized ones. Ultimately, part of the full realization of enlightenment, as it is ordinarily understood, is internalizing completely the idea that there is no Self, and that we all are entirely the same, rooted in the same Buddha-nature. One of the consequences of any form of preaching is the potential it creates for us to become the same with the one who preaches, to eliminate the false boundaries that separates subject from object. In literary terms, this establishes an intimate relationship between author and reader, in which the enlightened reader *becomes* the author, or rather, the boundaries that are said to constitute their identities are dissolved.

Stephen Owen observed some time ago that traditional Chinese reading practices chose to make the inscription of self and personality in the text the central goal in writing and reading poetry, and that any reading that does not take that goal into consideration will not understand much of what Chinese poetry is attempting to do.[34] But this is *not* what we should do with Hanshan; if we attempt to turn these poems into the product of a mainstream poet, then we end up with the forced biographical readings typical in much of the scholarship. Rather, the seemingly insuperable division between consciousnesses, the very Selves posited by poetics, is what Buddhist enlightenment is supposed to overcome. The Buddhist reading process, brief though its effects might be, can be seen as a technique, a skillful means that trains its readers in transcending the Self and recognizing their identity with the Other and with all sentient beings. In this sense, knowledge of the text becomes provisional *(quan)* truth, while knowledge of the mind that produces it becomes actual *(shi)* truth that arises with enlightenment. However, the sutra texts quoted above suggest that we can come to this consciousness only as specific individuals with specific levels of wisdom granted by our specific karmic inheritances: though we each will hear each text in a specific way that will make sense only for us, that very way is the path *(marga)* to liberation.

PART TWO

The Poems

CHAPTER 3

JUXTAPOSITIONS

IF we grant that the reader will recognize Buddhist content in Hanshan in the manner we have just explored, it remains for us to look at the poems themselves. Over the next four chapters, different aspects of the verse will be examined, together with the role that they play in creating a Buddhist reading. We will first consider matters of structure: how the poems are put together and how that may influence the way in which they convey meaning. This may be seen as a matter of juxtapositions: first, the internal juxtapositions of syntax and parallelism; and second, the external juxtapositions of poem contrasted with poem.

The internal structure of the Hanshan poems owes a good bit to mainstream Chinese verse, while at the same time moving away from it in the unexpected ways that they employ expected conventions and norms. Before investigating these deviations at greater length, it would be helpful to say something about the poems' forms and how they differ from the tradition out of which they grow.

The great majority of the Hanshan poems, 248 of them, are five-character octets: five syllables per line, eight lines each. As is common with almost all *shi* poetry, the basic structural unit is the couplet. The last words in even-numbered lines rhyme with each other, and, in a departure from most five-character octets in elite poetry, the opening couplet often rhymes as well. There are other forms in the collection, significant if not numerous, including sixteen poems of five-character and seven-character quatrains; thirteen poems of seven-character octets; twenty-nine poems with a larger number of five-character lines, the longest being thirty-six lines; and six poems of three-character lines.

The popularity of the five-syllable octet in the collection probably reflects the prevalence of regulated verse forms *(lüshi)* during the Tang. However, the Hanshan poems largely ignore the rules of regulated verse, with their proscribed tonal patterns; rather, the poems embrace the eight-line form's ability to create a brief vignette: each verse is long enough for some rhetorical elaboration, but short enough to contain an aphoristic punch.

The language of the poems is, for the most part, quite different from that of mainstream Tang elite poetry. This applies not merely to the use of vernacular expressions, but also to the widespread presence of function words, grammatical connectives, and pronouns. Taken together, they create a quality of "chattiness." Descriptive parallelism is employed, but it tends more toward the simple and repetitive rather than to the complex patterning found in the great Tang-era elite poets. The impression is of a poetry that would have been easy for semiliterate readers or listeners to understand. This does not mean that the poems do not contain any lines of sophisticated elegance; after all, even elite poetry can be quite easy to understand (this is true of much of Wang Wei's verse, for example). It is also likely that the poems at times deliberately shift between linguistic ranges for humorous or ironic effect. Perhaps the closest analogy to English-language poetry would be verse by poets who often exploit seemingly simple and popular poetic forms to express far deeper meaning: William Blake, Emily Dickinson, Stevie Smith. Rendering each poem in rhyming iambic tetrameter couplets would probably come nearest to the feel of the original. Here is HS 101 (discussed in the last chapter) translated in just such a way:

I now recall my younger days,
By Ping Hill we were on the chase.
A public post was never sought;
The Immortal's Way not worth a thought.
On shining steed without a care
I'd loose my hawk, flush out the hare.
How did I come to vagrancy?
All grizzled now—who frets for me?

This is little more than an exercise, and careful analysis of the poems really requires something nearer to the original in terms of vocabulary and word order. Nonetheless, throughout this study I have attempted translations that inhabit a more formal rhetorical register than free verse. As far as I can manage, I have tried to keep to iambic tetrameter lines (or iambic pentameter, when forced), but have left them unrhymed.

The doggerel nature of the verse also lets the poems "think" in a way fundamentally different from elite poetry. Here, for example, is a famous regulated-verse poem by Wang Wei (c. 699–c. 761), a poet with strong Buddhist sympathies who was also admired for his skill in regulated-verse couplet craft:

秋夜獨坐	AUTUMN NIGHT, SITTING ALONE
獨坐悲雙鬢，	Alone I sit, lamenting my graying temples.
空堂欲二更。	An empty hall, nearing the second watch.
雨中山果落，	In the rain the mountain fruit fall;
燈下草蟲鳴。	Under the lamp, the weed crickets cry.
白髮終難變，	White hair, impossible to change in the end;
黃金不可成。	And yellow gold cannot be created.
欲知除老病，	If you want to remove old age and sickness,
唯有學無生。	There is only the study of Non-Birth.[1]

Stephen Owen has identified the standard structure of a regulated octet as "tripartite": the opening couplet sets the scene, clarifying the location and/or time of composition; the closing couplet often gives an emotional response to the situation; and the two middle couplets, usually syntactically parallel and often descriptive, elaborate on the scene and the poet's reaction to it.[2] Here, Wang Wei exploits structure in a particularly elegant way: we have a statement of a problem (What shall I do about growing old? I'm thinking about that as I sit alone); followed by an observation the poet makes of nature that reinforces that consciousness (I notice the falling of autumn fruit, and the sound of insects that will die away with the first killing frost); followed by a rejection of certain forms of Daoism that would encourage alchemical practices for discovering elixirs of immortality or turning base metals into gold. In the end, the poet makes the essential breakthrough and decides that only Buddhism can cure the problem of aging (which is a form of Impermanence). Those unfamiliar with the term "nonbirth" may find it an odd phrase—it refers to the Buddhist belief that Impermanence can only be removed through attaining nirvana and thus ending not simply death but the rebirth that both follows and inevitably ends in death. Wang Wei has used the tripartite structure of regulated verse to work through an existential problem, and yet has also incorporated his own response to his environment as part of this work. Later traditional critics praised this attainment as "the fusion of emotion and scene": *qing jing jiaorong*.

And yet there is a certain restraint in Wang Wei, a genteel melancholy befitting this most aristocratic of poets. We have the impression that his lament over his graying hair, though real, is answered in a rather intellectual manner. Old age is a problem that can be solved through various possible methodologies, all of which can be weighed as he sits quietly in his room. Whether he actually succeeds in transcending his distress is left unanswered.

When we turn to the Hanshan poems, we find texts that are not committed to the obligations of traditional poetics, with its parallelism and tripartite structures. Instead, the eight-line form is employed for more explicit argument. Thus, HS 251:

何以長惆悵,	Why am I always so rueful?
人生似朝菌。	Man's life's as brief as a toadstool's.
那堪數十年,	Awful that in a few dozen years
親舊凋落盡。	Kin and friends will wither away!
以此思自哀,	For this my thoughts now turn to grief,
哀情不可忍。	A grieving mood I cannot bear.
奈何當奈何,	O what to do? O what to do?
託體歸山隱。	Pledge myself to a mountain refuge.

This poem possesses a breathlessness largely unprecedented in Chinese poetry. As with Wang Wei, the speaker is thinking through the problem of mortality; but there is no polite understatement in considering it. Rather, the speaker is made brutally aware of the increasingly frequent death of his friends and kin (described as fragile plant-life). He is also much more explicit in laying out the causal links of his thinking, taking advantage of colloquial poetry's tolerance of subordinating and connective phrases and repetition ("for this," "turn to grief," "a grieving mood"). This feeling he has is something he cannot stand—it is no longer a problem to solve, but an emotional crisis, ending in the cry of line 7, *nai he dang nai he*. *Nai he* (a phrase used to express emotional perplexity in the face of a dilemma) is often used in funeral texts, so here it does double-duty: the poet's lament for his dead friends and kin, as well as his desperate failure to find a solution. It is also the third vernacular phrase in the poem that expresses futility and frustration (line 3, *na kan*, means literally "how can [I] stand?" and line 6, *bu ke ren*, "cannot bear"). The last line then becomes a passionate release from the speaker's anguish as he decides what to do. As is typical for a number of Hanshan poems, it is unclear what specifically reclusion is meant to accomplish: Daoist cultivation or Buddhist monasticism? It doesn't really matter: the important issue is the desperation of the solution, the brake that stops the downhill slide into despair that marks the first seven lines. This is not Wang Wei holding up his finger and wisely pronouncing: "There is only the study of Non-Birth."

The function of Hanshan's writing is thus quite different from that of Wang Wei's. Like most elite Chinese verse, Wang's poem makes a claim to represent the mental state of the poet at a point in time. The Hanshan poem, by contrast, is an illustration of a state of mind characteristic of all of us, constructed for didactic purposes. We are meant to see ourselves in the narrative voice, and its urgency compels us to take action. This perhaps relates it less to elite poetry as it came to be imagined than to other genres composed in a generalized, universally adoptable voice: late Han "old poetry," Tang dynasty popular song, and many Song dynasty *ci* ("song lyrics"). However, the Hanshan corpus introduces a religious aspect to such universalism, which defines it as a genre distinct from other popular verse. For example, a Buddhist reader would specifically read this poem not just as a description of the brevity of life (common in "old poetry"), but as pointing to the special status we have as a result of being born human; because we are granted self-awareness, we have an obligation to use our time in this present existence to cultivate good Buddhist practice. The injunction to act quickly and immediately is a common element in the Zen masters—and an important point to remember for those who tend to emphasize the more serene and meditative aspects of Buddhism. So with Linji Yixuan:

> Followers—don't acknowledge any illusory companions, for in the middle of the night they will return once more to Impermanence. While you are in this present world, what sort of thing do you look for to obtain liberation? With the time you spend looking for a mouth of food or patching your rope, you must seek out [a teacher who] understands you. Don't waste the time pursuing pleasure. Time is valuable, every moment is Impermanence. Your coarser parts will be overwhelmed by earth, water, fire, and air; your finer parts will be oppressed by birth, abiding, change, and destruction.[3]

HS 251, simple and largely artless as it is, illustrates the strength of Hanshan's poetics. On the one hand, it relies on a simplicity of diction characteristic of early popular poetry, combined with vernacular expressions and explicit causal constructions; on the other, by restricting itself to an eight-line form, it keeps to the point and does not lapse into a rambling semicoherence (something that does happen in a number of the longer Hanshan poems).

Nonduality and Poetic Form

This in turn brings us to Hanshan's first major use of juxtaposition, one that may be contrasted with the parallelism of elite verse. This is the contrastive example, in which two types of behavior or two types of people are juxtaposed with each other through the suggested parallelisms of the couplet structure. A particularly clever example is HS 152:

人生一百年,	A human life: a hundred years.
佛說十二部。	Buddha's words in twelve divisions.
慈悲如野鹿,	Compassion is a wild-land deer,
瞋忿似家狗。	And anger a household dog.
家狗趁不去,	Drive the dog out: he always returns;
野鹿常好走。	The wild deer always wants to flee.
欲伏獼猴心,	If you'd control the monkey-mind,
須聽獅子吼。	Then pay heed to the Lion's Roar.

Lines 1–6 are six sentences placed in bald juxtaposition; they rely upon simple parallel contrast to create meaning. Since a typical reader would know that the opening line is a classic statement of the brevity of human life, the twelve divisions of the Buddha's teachings are given as a solution to the fact of mortality.[4] The meat of the poem, however, is the two middle couplets, which elaborate on metaphors that relate the classic Buddhist virtue of compassion and the classic Buddhist "poison" of anger to animal behavior. The poem is given a greater sense of unity through a chiasmus pattern (deer—dog—dog—deer); the metaphors themselves contrast domestic and wild behaviors. Part of the pleasure in the metaphors is their slightly paradoxical nature: the poem assigns virtue to a wild, untamable animal and vice to a domesticated one. Line 5 is particularly striking: we generally think of canine loyalty as a positive quality, but for the poet it becomes an emblem for the difficulty of shaking off negative behavior that has become habitual. The image is not original with the poet (it comes from the Nirvana Sutra);[5] but its contrastive use in poetic form works perfectly. The poem then closes with

two further animal images, both rooted in Buddhist clichés: that the restless human mind is a monkey that must be tamed, and that the teaching of the Buddha is like the roar of a lion.

Unlike HS 251, 152 is a preaching poem: rather than using a chain of emotional cause and effect to bring home the truth of the human predicament, it relies upon a series of explicit metaphors conveyed to an audience of believers to help explain the teaching. It is a different type of skillful means. The type of rhetorical balance found in it occurs fairly frequently in other poems with a didactic edge that are meant to illustrate and critique false conceptions of duality. Because these are particularly interesting examples of how Hanshan often uses seemingly simple language to explicate a difficult concept, they are worth exploring in some detail.

HS 241 is the most obvious example, in that it tackles the issue of duality head on, using a specific example found in the Mahayana scriptures:

常聞釋迦佛,	Śākyamuni, we've head it said,
先受然燈記。	Took Dīpankara's Buddha-pledge.
然燈與釋迦,	Dīpankara, Śākyamuni:
只論前後智。	Just say that one found wisdom first.
前後體非殊,	"First" or "second": the form's the same:
異中無有異。	No difference in their difference.
一佛一切佛,	Buddha, and each and every Buddha:
心是如來地。	The Mind is Tathāgata's ground.

Dīpankara is one of the Buddhas who manifested himself in our own cosmos, and who announced to "our" Buddha in one of his earlier incarnations (here called Śākyamuni, "sage of the Śākya clan," a term common in Mahayana) that he would indeed achieve full enlightenment. This annunciation, which occurs for all Buddhas, is known in Chinese by the technical term *shou ji* (literally, "receive the designation") and is mentioned explicitly in the second line. It provides one of the most important doctrinal examples employed in the Diamond Sutra, perhaps the most important sutra for Zen practitioners: "Because [I, the Tathāgata] truly obtained *no* Ultimate Perfect Enlightenment, Dīpankara presented me with the Buddha-pledge, uttering these words: 'In a future age you shall become a Buddha and be called by the name Śākyamuni.'"[6] Here, the sentence (like most utterances in the Diamond Sutra) is meant to undermine the idea that enlightenment is a concrete essence that can actually be attained through a process of striving; anyone who can fully realize that truth will in fact attain that very (nonexistent) enlightenment. The poet combines the Dīpankara-Śākyamuni connection with other sutra observations about the essential unity of all of the Buddhas: no matter in what chronological sequence they may have manifested themselves, they are nonetheless the same. The poem thus deals specifically with the need to remove the duality of "first-second," which we almost always instill with value judgments of one kind or another. At the end, it brings that critique of duality to the general Mahayana concept of the Buddha Nature, the ground of original reality that we all share with all beings, enlightened and unenlightened.

A more provocative example of duality critique occurs in HS 70:

豬喫死人肉，	Pigs will eat of dead men's flesh;
人喫死豬腸。	Men will eat of dead pigs' guts.
豬不嫌人臭，	Pigs don't mind that man-flesh stinks;
人反道豬香。	And men will say that pigs smell fine.
豬死拋水內，	A pig dies: throw him in the creek;
人死掘土藏。	A man dies: dig a hole to hide him.
彼此莫相噉，	If one stops eating up the other,
蓮花生沸湯。	Lotus will bloom from boiling broth.

As in certain *Zhuangzi* anecdotes, the poet here deliberately flaunts social conventions and standards of good taste in order to provoke the reader into considering unpleasant aspects of life, particularly mortality. A world of perpetual consumption (where "dog eats dog" becomes "man eats pig eats man") goes hand in hand with a jaundiced view of burial customs. Pigs and humans are indistinguishable save for how they end up: pigs in human bellies or drifting downriver; men in pig bellies or dumped in a hole.

The initial shock value here is directed toward a very clear Buddhist aim, one found in early Daoist philosophy as well: to divest oneself of false distinctions that have the potential to interfere with the clarity of one's vision. The use of parallel structures in order to set up a dualism that can then be critiqued is particularly sharp because it puts human readers (with our superior rites and customs) on the same level as pigs: pigs can judge us merely from the perspective of their satiated appetites, in the same way we do them. This radical decentralization of humanity's supposedly superior position has the additional value (from the perspective of Hanshan) of critiquing meat-eating as well: this is perhaps the single most frequently recurring moral issue in the poems, and one in which conventional Buddhist injunctions emerge most clearly. Sixteen poems in the Hanshan and Shide collections contain explicit references to this particular sin.[7] In this verse, the mutual consumption of pigs and humans becomes an illustration of how desires in general fuel the suffering of living beings; we face the danger of an evil rebirth not because a cosmic law enjoins us not to harm animals, but because we contribute to our own continually fueled desires and to the suffering of others through lusting after flesh and killing it. Or, as two other poems phrase it: "[Living beings] vie in seeking satiety and warmth, / Making plans to consume one other" (HS 92, lines 5–6); "They will consume each other in turn, / Stupid, mere foolish lumps of flesh" (HS 228, lines 3–4). Desire in this instance introduces us to an economy of death. The consumption of meat in turn transforms *us* into meat.[8]

Hanshan concludes HS 70 on a semi-serious note. If this endless cycle of violence and desire can be disrupted (a highly unlikely occurrence), we'll see lotus flowers springing up from boiling water. We might read this as a hyperbole confirming impossibility (compare "when Hell freezes over"; a figure of speech known in classical Western rhetoric as an *adynaton*). However, that would be to miss the main point. Victor Mair suggests the last image suggests a transformation through the power of faith: "The lotus blossoms symbolize rebirth in the paradise of Amitābha which Cold Mountain clearly hopes will replace the scalding broth."[9] I would add that a few other elements in this image have a Buddhist resonance. One is its resemblance to the very common cliché that enlightenment is like a lotus flower growing out of the muck of a pond bed: it remains pure white in spite of its origins. Another is the similarity of this "impossibility" to the "sacred vows" common in Indian folklore and found frequently in *jātaka* tales, in which a believer calls for nature to testify to the sincerity of her or his vows by producing a miracle: true faith can cause anything to happen and can emerge even from an inauspicious circumstance.

The other poems contra meat-eating also use contrasting dualities to make their point, thought they tend to focus on the karmic consequences of the sin. This can lead to a striking dissimilarity between premodern rhetoric and our modern reading instincts. For example, HS 56:

我見東家女，	I've seen that eastern house girl:
年可有十八。	Eighteen years old now, more or less.
西舍競來問，	Western neighbors all come with pleas,
願姻夫妻活。	Seek to wed her, live as man and wife.

烹羊煮眾命,	They stew a sheep, cook living things,
聚頭作婬殺。	All in their orgy of slaughter.
含笑樂呵呵,	Beaming, they laugh in their pleasure;
啼哭受殃抉。	Weeping, they'll receive their dues.

This little narrative arises out of the manipulation of folk-poetry tropes. Popular verse that contrasts "eastern and western neighbors" was quite common in the early tradition, and the most typical association with an "eastern house" in such poems is with a beautiful, unmarried girl.[10] Here we have just such a beginning, and the poem seems ready to celebrate her beauty in an epithalamium. The party turns ugly, however, and we move instead to the slaughter of animals, and a concluding contrast of joy and suffering.

Here the poem might invite modern readers to make an error in interpretation that evokes empathy for the dying animals. The phrase in the last line *shou yang jue* (literally, "receive calamity and gouging") could easily be interpreted to describe the suffering of the butchered beasts, whose "weeping" is ironically contrasted with the delight of the wedding guests. Henricks accepts this interpretation: "While bleating and wailing, the animals greet death."[11] However, this would go against similar passages in the collection in which present delight in animal slaughter is followed by punishment in a hell realm (HS 159, 233; SD 2, 4, 5, 12). Xiang Chu also notes cases where the word *jue* ("gouge") is used in the context of judicial punishment, and where the word *yang* ("calamity") refers specifically to rebirth in a hell realm.[12] It is most likely that this line refers to the future suffering of meat-eaters, and not to the present suffering of the butchered animals. This does not mean, however, that the parallel structure of the Chinese verse form is not establishing an important dualism that must be resolved in order to transcend suffering. Juxtaposing present and past in a karmic sense enforces the idea that suffering itself transcends our human identity—we will suffer as the animals have.

The fact that the vegetarian discourse in poems such as this one does not reflect a modern animal rights perspective that explicitly focuses on humane treatment does not make their ethical underpinning any less sophisticated, in spite of the practical (and seemingly "vulgar") threat of a burning hell. Rather, acknowledgment of the bad karma produced by eating meat as well as the decentering of human privilege in the mutual consumption of living beings that characterizes the world of samsara can lead us in turn to think of broader issues connected to the nonexistence of self and the importance of rejecting desire: this too is a potential avenue to nonduality, in that it obliterates the distinction between human and animal, eater and eaten. In comparison, a compassion that arises from seeing animal suffering would not be enough to lead readers to understand why the injunction against killing is intimately connected to larger ontological issues that involve justice and karmic redress.

HS 36 possesses childlike simplicity, rather like a nursery rhyme, and is perhaps the most striking example of the poet using Chinese verse structure to illustrate the problems of duality. It, like HS 56, may easily evoke a straightforward and unproblematic interpretation from a modern reader—in this case, a reader with a certain Beat sensibility. Behind its simple structure, however, is something more troubling and open-ended:

東家一老婆,	Old lady from the eastern house:
富來三五年。	She struck it rich some years ago.
昔日貧於我,	In days past she was poorer than me;
今笑我無錢。	Now she laughs that I have no money.
渠笑我在後,	She laughs that I've fallen behind,
我笑渠在前。	While *I* laugh that she's out in front.
相笑儻不止,	And if this laughter doesn't stop:
東邊復西邊。	An east side and a west side too.

The narrator is making fun of his neighbor lady for her arrogance and her snobbism, in spite of her humble origins. He in turn seems to embrace poverty as a noble quality, rejecting the greed that has corrupted her. This is not the end of it, however. To see how the poem is not content with such a reading, one must internalize the dialectic it constructs through simple juxtapositions.

In the opening couplet, the old woman enters the stage (note the possibly comic use of the "eastern neighbor" trope, here not the beauty that appears in HS 56, but a crone). A narrative is then constructed, line by line: first the woman is poor, then the woman is rich. In the third couplet, the woman laughs at the narrator for "lagging behind," with the implication that she now sees all people involved in a race to be rich, and that anyone who is not rich is "losing" and worthy of her contempt. In a Zen-like gesture, the narrator then turns this judgment nonsensically on its ear, claiming that anyone who *wins* such a race is actually the one worthy of contempt—and he in turn laughs at the woman for being in the lead. He has supposedly shown that wealth is a shallow thing indeed, and that he is superior to all that. He is very much the Beat nonconformist.

Most modern readers are likely to leave the poem here, accepting its seemingly antimaterialist moral; but this ignores the poem's need to confirm nonduality. The narrator in fact is trapped by asserting his own supposed spiritual superiority. Consequently, the poem must undermine this complacency by putting the two figures on the same level: "And if this laughter doesn't stop: / An east side and a west side too." This last couplet acts as an exchange of laughter that asserts that the narrator and the old woman are the same. If their mutual discrimination continues (this pointing and laughing at the other) then *it* is what ultimately creates discrimination, not their opposing attitudes toward wealth. "East" and "west" are mutually defined by their mutual contempt, and each becomes in the process "a side"—a flaw inherent in dualistic thinking. It is a particular strength of the Hanshan poems—and one not often acknowledged by modern readers—that the poetic voice has the ability to wryly undermine its own superiority, thus questioning its own seeming role as a model worthy of emulation. Hanshan's laughter is not merely directed at others; it is also directed at himself.

This sense of self-parody in the service of antidualism can be seen in HS 191, a poem striking for its ambiguity:

有身與無身，	"There is a self and not a self,
是我復非我。	There is a me and not a me."
如此審思量，	I pondered long and hard on this,
遷延倚巖坐。	For some time sitting against the cliff.
足間青草生，	Green grass grows up between my legs,
頂上紅塵墮。	Red dust settles atop my head.
已見俗中人，	And now those of the common world
靈牀施酒果。	Set wine and fruit on my "altar"!

The narrator has isolated himself from human society in order to engage in a lengthy contemplation of nonduality. The main subject of his meditation is the nonexistence of the Self—or, rather, as is fitting in Madhyamaka strategies, the way in which one may say that there both is and is not a Self. He "ponders" on this; the verb *siliang* used to express the act of pondering occurs eleven times in the Hanshan corpus, always in a favorable context, expressing a self-conscious use of the human intellect to arrive at a higher truth. This absorption in turn results in his utter indifference to the growth of grass or the fall of dust (dust, of course, being a common image for samsara).[13] The poem then concludes with a final hyperbolic image, one with humorous overtones. The local population, assuming that the narrator is either dead or a deity, comes to offer sacrifices to his spirit. *Lingchuang* (altar, literally, "spirit platform") could be used to describe altars both for doing honor to the dead as well as for worshipping divinities. In the latter case, the narrator has been mistaken for a statue.

As with HS 36, this poem might suggest at first glance an elitist interpretation in which the inferior knowledge of the local lay population mistakes deep spiritual practice for a manifestation of the divine or saintly. Such a reading bears an uncanny resemblance to the American Buddhist Red Pine's amusement at the folk shrines dedicated to Hanshan. In his commentary, Hakuin also reads the lay response to the meditator as a ritualistic ignorance:

> "There is a self and not a self, / There is a me and not a me." In this manner, completely alone, you embody the Ultimate in your investigations, sitting against a cliff; you always forget the differentiation between Thing and Self, and you cast aside both mind and form. "Green grass grows up between my legs, / Red dust settles atop my head"—but you are aware of neither. At this time you give rise to the Buddha's One Suchness, wherein purity and pollution are not two. The Diamond Undecaying Perfect Body suddenly rises up—a shining, Nirvanic, truly real and Perfect Body—and this is to become a son of the Buddha who can distinguish properly the Way. If you do not act thusly, then even if you practice a myriad acts of virtue or collect a multitude of good deeds, you would merely be some idle demon of the wilds clinging to the grass and the trees; when could you ever avoid drifting with change and sinking into suffering and misfortune? How sad that those of the ordinary world do not know of this sort of lofty inclination. Instead, they set out the wine and fruit of ignorance on an empty altar, imagining such an offering to be sufficient; they prepare their foul and stinking sacrifices in an empty shrine, thinking their sobs of mourning to be enough. No one knows that these are mere illusions of a dream, a darkness added to darkness, and suffering piled on suffering.[14]

Granted Hakuin's impatience with "lazy" practice and formalism in Zen, it is not surprising that he uses his reading as a way of contrasting the effort of the solitary practitioner with the ritualism of ordinary people. However, as in HS 36, juxtapositions keep the complete resolution of duality in suspension. Hakuin's comment itself emphasizes one of the classic tensions of

Zen thought, between effort and concentration on the one hand, and sudden breakthrough on the other. Because he sees the pondering *(siliang)* of the hermit in the first six lines as a movement along the path toward enlightenment, he sees its conclusion as an appearance of a new body, incorruptible, which "suddenly rises up" to replace the mortal, impermanent body. From the outside, one sees a motionless ascetic, not the earth-shattering transformations; one only sees the results. Hakuin thus revises the fairy-tale motif of a man turned to stone and instead sees a man turned to transcendent diamond, whose perfect form now appears to commoners as a sort of religious relic. That they mistake this superior man for the image of a god is understandable; it is not merely because the meditator has remained motionless.

That Hakuin sees a dynamic movement of transformation here is because he wishes to prevent any reading that would overemphasize the act of *thinking*. But the poem itself displays no such transformation; rather, the act of cogitation is left unresolved. If anything, the movement from couplet to couplet suggests that the poet is still struggling with the fundamental problem of nonduality: the poem moves from initial paradox to pondering the paradox to sustained obliviousness. The commoners then become not so much an example of inferior understanding, but instead a sort of theatrical punchline meant to underline the speaker's failure to achieve a breakthrough. If he has turned into a motionless idol, it is because he is caught up in a vertiginous Madhyamaka dialectic and has yet to surface again into our physical world. This is not a poem boasting of superior attainment, but a poem acknowledging continual striving for attainment.

Sequences and External Juxtapositions

It is unlikely that our knowledge regarding the compilation of the collection will ever improve. This also means that we have no data at all on the ordering of the poems—whether they were randomly assembled, perhaps as a result of collating various manuscripts, or whether the editor(s) did indeed order them according to threads of association running through the texts.[15] Any hope of tracing patterns is undermined further by the existence of two lines of textual transmission that assemble the poems in a slightly different order. However, this does not mean that a reader would not see resonances between poems and groups of poems; in fact, granted the collection's commonly recurring themes, a reader's experience would likely be a symphonic one, in which images become leitmotifs, deployed and redeployed in various ways, attaining greater depth and significance the more one reads. Such resonances create an external series of juxtapositions, in which the reader is invited to create meta-poems that possess grander narratives.

The following examples demonstrate this sort of resonance. The first example consists simply of two poems, adjacent in both textual transmissions. HS 142 is based on the popular *carpe diem* theme already present in popular Chinese poetry from the first century CE onward:

自有慳惜人,	Naturally there are stingy folk,
我非慳惜輩。	But I am not the stingy type.
衣單為舞穿,	Robe thin and worn through from the dance;
酒盡緣歌啐。	Wine gone—in song I urged us drink.
當取一腹飽,	You make sure that your belly's full!
莫令兩腳傈。	It keeps your legs from running down!
蓬蒿鑽髑髏,	When thorns and brambles thread your skull,
此日君應悔。	You'll likely lament this day.

There are a number of ambiguities here that complicate interpretation—in some cases, we can rely on previous poetic conventions to steer us in the right direction, but that is not a guarantee of clarification. For instance, is this poem in the voice of the recluse we think of as "Hanshan," or of some other, obviously fictional persona? The drinking and dancing might suggest the latter: unless, of course, one wants to see the poem as expressing a celebration of life that would be inappropriate for a devout monk but might be expected of Hanshan as an antinomian "crazy" believer. This might be supported by the use of the term "stingy," which could refer here to the lack of generosity shown by conventional Buddhist clergy. Or (if one is wedded to the autobiographical significance of the poem) it might date from the poet's "prereligious" days. As with other poems in the collection, the biographical projections typical of modern reading habits are often possible but unprovable.

If, on the other hand, the poem is voiced by a persona not identifiable as Hanshan, then we might further note that dancing and singing are often the prerogative of female entertainers in Chinese poetry, and that a number of the Hanshan poems emphasize this, notably HS 14 and HS 23—the latter written in a female voice. This allows us to read the poem as a sort of sexual invitation. The third couplet becomes a little unclear in this reading: it could be the speaker describing her own behavior at greater length ("I make sure to eat a bit, so that I can keep on dancing!"), or it could be an injunction to the partygoers ("eat a bit, and you'll continue to feel like dancing with me!"). This reveling is brutally interrupted by the image of thorns growing through the skull as the manifestation of the *carpe diem* theme. Chinese poetic convention guides us here: in such poems, the idea of "regret" (*hui*, which I translate here as "lament") does not mean, as it might in a more explicitly religious text, that one will regret having wasted one's life on follies like drinking and dancing. Rather, it means either that when one is dead, one will long for these days of celebration, and will think of them sadly; or that when one is dead, one will regret that one didn't celebrate *more* when alive. The image is most definitely meant to validate the celebration of the opening lines, rather than undermine them.

One word in this poem has been prone to misinterpretation, but will prove particularly important for careful readers: the last character in the third line, *chuan*. Because of its proximity to the word for "robe" or "clothes," translators have tended to interpret its meaning as "to wear," as is typical in modern Chinese.[16] However, the standard verb in the Hanshan collection used for "to put on [clothes]" is *zhuo*, which occurs five times with this meaning. *Chuan*, on the other hand, occurs four other times in the collection, and none of these uses refers to the wearing of clothes. It is much more likely that the word here bears the meaning found in those other occasions: "to bore through" or "to wear through." With that in mind, the literal, word-for-word meaning of this line is not "Robe is-single-layered, for-the-sake-of dance is-donned" but rather "Robe is-single-layered, because-of dance wears-through/shows-holes." In support of this reading is the parallel fourth line, which refers to the singer's wine at a banquet running out because of everyone's general high-spiritedness. In both lines, the passionate and unremitting song-and-dance results in items wearing out/running out.[17] It also conveys a touch of eroticism to line 3, if the poem is indeed voiced by a female entertainer, granted the conventions of Chinese poetry and its representations of the female form. Her robe is thin ("single-layered") not so much because of her poverty, but rather because of her desire to be seductive. And if that is the case, the fact that the robe is gradually "worn through" as a result of the dance makes it even more erotically charged. Because she is not "stingy," as she says in the opening couplet, she is indifferent to how many robes she ruins, or how much wine she drinks; presumably, she will not be stingy with her sexual attentions either. Of course, if this reading is correct, it makes the skull in the seventh line particularly poignant. The celebration of excess is still implied (with sex added to the drinking, singing, and dancing), but now with a certain gothic edge. The image is not so much a cold shower in this context, but rather a desperate call to seize the pleasure available to us.

The reader of the Hanshan collection might now turn to the next poem, HS 143:

我行經古墳，	As I passed by the old tomb mounds,
淚盡嗟存沒。	I wept all my tears for our life and death.
塚破壓黃腸，	Barrows fell in on cypress wood;
棺穿露白骨。	Coffins wore through, exposing white bones.
敧斜有甕缾，	This way and that the urns were leaning;
振撥無簪笏。	I poked about—no ornaments.
風至攪其中，	Then the wind came, churning all within;
灰塵亂悖悖。	Dust and ashes blew round about.

A visit to a graveyard occurs also in HS 11, and the use of graveyard images to emphasize human mortality occurs in a number of other places in the collection.[18] HS 143 is a straightforward poem of description, and holds few ambiguities. Yet the poem's power intensifies as it progresses from the poet's emotional response to passing the graveyard; to his vision of the collapsed tombs; to his search for relics (which have all presumably been taken by grave-robbers); and to the final image of a howling wind blowing the dirt of the tombs and ashes of the dead into an undifferentiated cyclone. The phrase "churning all within" does a nice job of uniting external scene with internal frame of mind, since it refers explicitly to the graveyard and implicitly to the poet's anguish.

And yet this poem benefits immensely from coming after HS 142, and it in turn deepens our reading of the earlier poem. We move from the unburied skull of 142, line 7 to the exposed dead of 143, line 4, so that what was merely a rhetorical device suggesting that we enjoy our present life becomes a pivot that moves us from *carpe diem* to *ubi sunt*; from "we shall all die tomorrow" to "the past is filled with graves." What really cements the two poems, however, is the reappearance of that problematic verb *chuan*, "to bore/wear though" in 143, line 4. As I commented above, this word only occurs five times in over three hundred poems; the appearance of this contextually rare word in two adjacent verses may make the linkage in the mind of the reader more likely. The meaning of this couplet is difficult to translate elegantly, because it describes a fairly complicated phenomenon. Literally, it reads: "Burial-mounds break/collapse, press-upon yellow innards; / Coffins penetrated/worn through, expose white bones." "Yellow innards" is not as appalling as it sounds in direct translation; it refers to the yellow inner wood of the cypress used for the construction of coffins.

The images here portray a cause-and-effect process with gruesome results: the barrows have fallen in, and the burial chambers have collapsed, dumping a weight of earth onto the coffins within. As a result, the wood of both outer and inner coffins has splintered, displaying the white bones of the dead. This pathetic exposure of things that should through propriety be perpetually covered has been prefigured by the bare skull of HS 142, line 7. But the use of *chuan* here also horrifyingly echoes the worn-through garment of that earlier poem. There, *chuan* indicated an eroticized exposure of white flesh through the holes of a dancing robe; here, it indicates exposure *(lou)* of white bones through the cracks of a violated coffin. And if that were not disturbing enough, the skull in HS 142 line 7 is "bored through" *(zuan)* by thorns and brambles, thus accentuating the association of *chuan* with penetration. I doubt that we would have associated the possibly sexual connotations of *chuan* and *zuan* merely by reading 142; 143 and its similar act of exposure and penetration draws our attention to them. Any sensitive reader at this point would be repelled by the sustained juxtaposition of pleasure and death.

Neither of these poems are explicitly Buddhist, and both draw upon tropes long present in Chinese secular poetry; however, needless to say, awareness of death and of the speed of passing time is an important part of the discourse of Impermanence in Buddhist writing. A Buddhist reader would be particularly sensitive the way these two poems interact: united by images and vocabulary that create intellectual and emotional associations that transcend the poems' borders, they resuscitate their cliché content and convey in a brutal fashion the true consequences of living in samsara. In particular, a reader might relate the poems to a form of Buddhist meditative practice, "charnel ground contemplation," in which the practitioner is invited to go to a burial ground, find an unburied or partially buried body, and meditate upon the process of decay as a guide to impermanence. One Hanshan poem even refers to this practice: "I gaze at the burial mound corpses: / The Six Paths do not hinder me" (HS 72, lines 7–8).[19] In this way, a typical trope of the Chinese poetic tradition—the view of a cemetery as a reminder of mortality—merges with actual Buddhist practice.[20]

A more complex form of external juxtaposition may be seen in HS 12–15. They form a sequential pattern not so much through shared images but through an intellectual process that creates a sort of meta-narrative illustrating a central problem of human existence (Impermanence) and a possible solution. Again, sequences like these were likely not created by author or editor, but evoke a natural response of the reader sensitive both to Buddhist concepts and to traditional Chinese literary themes. The text I follow here is somewhat different in the Guoqing transmission; in the latter, HS 14 is displaced to elsewhere in the collection.

鸚鵡宅西國,	In the western lands a parrot lived;
虞羅捕得歸。	He could return here in a hunter's net.
美人朝夕弄,	Ladies play with him night and day,
出入在庭幃。	He goes in and out of bedroom screens.
賜以金籠貯,	They granted him a golden cage—
扃哉損羽衣。	A prison! His feathered robe is spoiled.
不如鴻與鶴,	Much better to be a swan or crane
颻颺入雲飛。	That goes soaring amid the clouds.

The first poem in this sequence plays on the trope of the caged parrot, which probably originates with Mi Heng's (fl. 190s CE) canonical "Rhapsody on a Parrot" ("Yingwu fu").[21] A number of images here echo this rhapsody, which tells of a bird living happily in the western wilds. He is consequently hunted and captured by the emperor's foresters, who have heard of his beauty and talent. The parrot's position in Mi Heng is highly ambiguous: while well treated by connoisseurs rather than left to dwell among "barbarians," he nonetheless longs for his freedom. As William Graham discusses at length, this is usually read as a transparent metaphor for the position of the poet himself, who was a "free spirit" desirous of patronage from those in power but also wary of those same forces. Its appearance in the sixth-century *Selections of Refined Literature* (Wen xuan), a basic text for literary education throughout East Asia, would have made this allegorical connotation of the parrot immediately apparent to readers of Hanshan.

Even more than Mi Heng's poem, Hanshan's exploits within its small space the ambiguity of the parrot's position. This begins as early as the second line, "He could return here in the hunter's net." The "hunter" is the imperial forester; the parrot is described as being "able to return," as though his proper position in the world was as an exotic gift to the emperor (the verb *gui*, literally "to return," can also be used in any situation where someone or something, including tribute, goes to where it belongs). This connects the poem quite explicitly to the Confucian ideal of the imperial search for men of talent to serve the state, a search sometimes envisioned as a net. Yet Hanshan's parrot is not a privileged possession of powerful men, but rather the plaything of women, who bring him into their private spaces; he is converted to a sort of boudoir decoration, as parrots frequently were in the Tang. An explicit turn towards the negative finally comes in the sixth line, when his golden cage is no longer a luxurious house but a prison that causes the atrophy of his wings. The last couplet then introduces the expected comparison to the greater contentment of birds that are free from constraint. The overdetermined significance of the captive parrot in Chinese culture makes this poem adaptable to different situations. While Mi Heng's original poem stressed the connection between parrot and frustrated scholar, HS 12 also suggests a transvaluation reading à la Zhuangzi, where swans and cranes exist outside the world of human restrictions.

Those familiar with the Hanshan corpus might compare this parrot poem to a deer poem, HS 293:

鹿生深林中，	A deer is born within deep woods,
飲水而食草。	Sipping water, feeding on grass.
伸腳樹下眠，	With legs stretched it sleeps under the trees,
可憐無煩惱。	How charming! With nothing to vex it.
繫之在華堂，	But tie it to a splendid hall,
餚膳極肥好。	Feed it with morsels rich and fine,
終日不肯嘗，	And nothing will it even taste;
形容轉枯槁。	And its body will wither away.

The message here is largely identical with the parrot narrative: imprisonment, no matter how luxurious, brings suffering and etiolation. It is worth noting, however, that line 4 employs the explicitly Buddhist term *fannao*, the standard rendering for Sanskrit *kleśa*, the annoyances and disturbances that prevent the mind from attaining enlightenment. Though the word has now become a vague, nonreligious term for annoyance, the Hanshan corpus was composed at a time when it still possessed its doctrinal meaning.[22] Its use here suggests that we read the deer's predicament not simply as a violation of the creature's natural life, but also as a Buddhist parable for our own situation in a world of suffering. Both poems could see the animals as trapped within the tempting but ultimately restrictive bonds of karma, which prevents the free movement toward liberation; no form of sensuous delight, no matter how well meant, can contribute to a living being's ultimate happiness.

The slightly erotic connotations of the parrot poem, with its suggestions of a male creature introduced into the women's quarters and the seductions of luxury, also allows the reading to shift to another series of poetic tropes that appear in the following verse, HS 13:

玉堂挂珠簾,	Pearl drapes hanging in halls of jade:
中有嬋娟子。	Within, the loveliest of maids.
其貌勝神仙,	A visage surpassing goddesses,
容華若桃李。	Features like bloom of pear and peach.
東家春霧合,	In eastern house a spring mist forms;
西舍秋風起。	In western hall an autumn wind.
更過三十年,	Another thirty years go by:
還成甘蔗滓。	She's a wrinkled piece of sugar cane.

The parrot who was the plaything of women is now transformed into a woman, and the cage is transformed into a mansion: a cage for upper-class women, whose appearance outside the home was strongly discouraged. As in many Chinese erotic poems, the focus of desire lies concealed within curtains, gradually exposed to a male gaze. In the second half of the poem, however, we see time quickly passing. The poet quite skillfully uses simple parallelisms to introduce this idea: the fertile, erotic mists of spring turn into the chill and killing winds of autumn in the course of just a few words. The culmination is striking, with its use of a very unpoetic and atypical image in the last line: When sugar cane is pounded to yield its sweet juice, the result is a wrinkled, discarded husk. The source of the image is Buddhist, from the Nirvana Sutra: "Also, Kaśyapa—it [human life] is like sugar cane: after it has been pressed, its juice no longer has any flavor. Goodly man: the hale appearance of your flourishing years is like this as well. After old age presses on you, you will no longer possess the three tastes: the taste for becoming a monk, the taste for chanting the sutras, and the taste for sitting in meditation."[23] This metaphor does not occur in any mainstream Tang-era poems. Its use is a quite deliberate violation of poetic decorum, an insertion of a mundane image where a more delicate and restrained language to describe the sorrow of female aging would be called for. The shift of the image from its Nirvana Sutra context (where the loss of "taste" of the sugar cane is connected to the loss of "taste" in older humans for cultivating the Buddhist path) is also quite brutal: in this case, it is the withered body of the once-beautiful woman that has lost its savor for others, in the sense of beauty and sexual desirability. This (reinforced by HS 12 before it) emphasizes the ephemerality of beauty in the ordinary world. The woman of these lines may seem to possess a certain power through her glamour, but in the end she will never escape her own cage—the cage of Impermanence.

In HS 14, the theme of the previous two poems is repeated, with a synthesis of the images of both:

城中蛾眉女,	A moth-browed beauty of the town:[24]
珠珮何珊珊。	With jewel-pendants set a-jingling.
鸚鵡花前弄,	She plays with her parrot amid the blooms,
琵琶月下彈。	And strums her lute beneath the moon.
長歌三月響,	For three months her prolonged song still rings;
短舞萬人看。	Her brief dance draws a teeming crowd.
未必長如此,	But it can't stay this way for good:
芙蓉不耐寒。	A lotus cannot bear the cold.

As in HS 13, the poem opens with a cliché description of a beautiful woman. But while the woman in 13 was hidden behind pearl drapes, this woman is out in the open, swaying as her jeweled girdle-pendants tinkle seductively. This description suggests that we are dealing with a very different sort of person, one who is a public performer and possibly a refined prostitute. The two poems thus provide a sharp juxtaposition of the two most common representations of female attractiveness seen in male-authored Chinese poetry in the medieval period. By focusing on women in two consecutive verses, the corpus also shifts perspective from a generalized lament for human aging to a sort of mental exercise focusing on the decay of beauty as a discouragement to straight male lust. The poem takes a good bit of pleasure in invoking the woman's charm in the first six lines, creating a series of vignettes. In line 3, our parrot returns, in a reverse-angle echo of HS 12, line 3, "Ladies play with him night and day" (both use the same verb). Most important is the linkage of the woman to musical performance, the erotic art *par excellence* in early China. Each action in these lines puts increasing emphasis on her behavior as a form of sexual incitement: from her toying with the parrot (as the male spectators think to themselves how much *they* would like to be that parrot—not imagining what life must seem like from the parrot's point of view, as HS 12 has suggested); to her slender fingers running over the strings of the lute (here placed in parallel juxtaposition with the parrot); to her memorable singing and her compelling dance.

The fifth line complicates the poem somewhat. The most frequently cited source concerning the "prolonged song" is that it derives from the "Tang Asked" ("Tang wen") chapter of the early Daoist *Liezi*: "Once the woman Han E went east to Qi. She was low on provisions, so she went to Yong Gate and sold her songs there for food. When she left, the lingering sounds of her voice hovered about the rafters for three days before they dissipated, and those who passed by thought she hadn't left."[25] If this is indeed the source of the line, then either "month" is an error for "day," or the poet is deliberately exaggerating the singer's talents (suggesting that she is a greater singer than the woman of Han in the *Liezi* story). However, the line may also have its basis in the passage from the *Analects* in which Confucius is so struck by the music of Shao that "for three months he did not know the taste of flesh."[26] If this is the case, the poem contains a hint of blasphemy, as it compares the sexually aroused audience of the courtesan to the irreproachable Sage himself. It hints that all human activities, even supposedly high-minded ones, are ultimately motivated by desire. Just as in HS 13, though, the poet brings the poem to a blunt (if less coarse) conclusion: cold weather will kill off the flower, just as years will ruin the performer. She is described here by one of the standard terms for lotus *(furong)*; it should not to be confused with the more Buddhist-inflected word for the same flower *(lian)*.

If HS 12–14 gives a series of vignettes emphasizing the inevitability of change and the futility of pleasures, then what might one do to escape? HS 15 provides a solution, one that delicately plays off the previous three poems:

父母績經多，	My parents left me enough to live,[27]
田園不羨他。	So I don't envy others' land.
婦搖機軋軋，	Clacking away, my wife works her loom,
兒弄口嘔嘔。	My boy babbles as he tries to talk.
拍手摧花舞，	I clap my hands: urge blossoms to dance;
搘頤聽鳥歌。	Chin propped on arm: I hear birds sing.
誰當來歎賀，	Who might come to admire my life?
樵客屢經過。	Sometimes a woodsman passes by.

After three poems of observation, we have a poem with an explicit first-person narrator, who gives a classic version of rural contentment, playing on the sort of tropes common in Chinese poetry since Tao Qian. In this type of verse, sometimes referred to as "field and garden poetry" *(tianyuan shi)*, the joys of family life and simple domestic tasks are played out against a background of harmonious nature. There is nothing particularly striking here: even the woodsman who shows up at the end exemplifies the voice of idealized rural wisdom common to this type of verse. And yet there are subtle ways in which this poem serves as an answer to the earlier ones. If HS 13 and (especially) HS 14 suggested a male audience appreciative of female beauty and then horrified by its destruction, here we have a man serving as an audience to new performers. Rather than the songs of a courtesan, he hears the clacking of his wife's loom and the gurgling of his child. Then, as he leaves the house, he is entertained with another kind of song-and-dance, this from the flowers and the birds (these birds, like the swan and crane in HS 12 and like the narrator himself, are free of all conventional restraints). The woodsman's beneficent seal of approval then displaces the audience to yet someone else, a voice of authority who can praise and congratulate the narrator on his own successful performance as hermit.

The note of rural contentment is played out on numerous occasions in the Hanshan corpus. Most of these poems project the rural homestead as a dwelling free of striving and ambition and hence as a sort of modest secular representation of a post-samsaric existence; not surprisingly, they also bring in Daoist themes of harmony. In this particular sequence, they suggest a solution to the sorrows of Impermanence, suggested by the aging of desired women in HS 13 and HS 14. And yet—as we shall see in the next chapter—this eremitic solution is illusory. True liberation requires a more radical form of retreat.

CHAPTER 4

AT HOME AND ABROAD

In the last chapter, we saw a scene of domestic bliss that suggested that contentment lay in a simple, unadorned life of ordinary pleasures. It suggested that our habitation and the sense of stability and calm that it can provide play a major role in providing these pleasures. And in fact, the Hanshan poems do frequently mention dwellings, both figurative and real. Yet a survey of them gives us a much less sanguine view of the comforts of real estate. HS 184:

可惜百年屋,	Alas, the hundred-year-old house!
左倒右復傾。	Left side falls and right side topples.
牆壁分散盡,	And the walls are melting away
木植亂差橫。	And the beams are scattered about.
磚瓦片片落,	The tiles are falling one by one—
朽爛不堪停。	The rot's made it quite unlivable.
狂風吹驀榻,	One gust would bring it crashing down,
再豎卒難成。	With no way to put it right again.

The first line here gives a vital clue to the poet's deeper meaning: since "hundred years" is standard shorthand for "the human lifespan," the house is our own physical form.[1] As Hakuin explicates:

> "The hundred-year-old house" refers to the ephemeral, illusory substances of the Four Elements [earth, water, fire, and wind], and the corporeal self, a mere bubble or shadow resulting from the five *skandhas*, which will in the process of time wear out, grow weary, and fade.[2] "The

> walls are melting away" refers to blood and flesh gradually drying up and becoming exhausted, and the bones and joints becoming sore and painful. "The tiles are falling one by one" refers to the general shedding of one's hair and teeth. "One gust would bring it crashing down" refers to the season when the killing demon of Impermanence in a single instant carries everything away with it, so that one is confronted yet again with great difficulties.[3]

Hakuin's careful equation of each part of the house to a part of the human body is more than scholastic exegesis: it also means to emphasize the degree to which our selves are not coherent, but rather defined by an assemblage of discrete elements that convention refers to as a "Self." If we tend to view our Self as a psychological and organic whole, it should give us pause to see bits and pieces of us falling away with age, just like pieces of an abandoned house. This assemblage of parts is so tenuous, and ultimately so rickety, that a strong gust of wind will cause its collapse, that is, our own eventual death and redispersal into elements that were brought together only through a series of karmic circumstances. I suspect that Hakuin is interpreting "great difficulties" as referring to our rebirth and the return of another cycle of suffering.

Of course, the Mahayana tradition contains a famous metaphor linking the house to the Self—the Burning House found in the third chapter of the Lotus Sutra. A wealthy man possesses a dilapidated mansion that catches fire one day, threatening his children, who continue to play within, unaware of the spreading flames. The wealthy man attempts to warn them from outside the house, to no avail. Finally, he lures them out through promising them a number of beautiful carts if they leave, basing his description of each cart on the tastes of each child. When they finally come to him, he presents them with one supremely perfect cart, thus revealing that he had had to represent his gift somewhat inaccurately in order to persuade them to exit. The burning house, as the Buddha goes on to explain, is samsara; the promised carts are the various teachings he has employed as "skillful means," tailoring them to the individual propensities of different living beings; and the final cart is the actual reality of the teachings as perceived by beings who have escaped samsara.

In HS 190, Hanshan gives us a version of the parable with a rather cranky and irritated father. In it, the Buddha's loving compassion is conspicuously absent (as are the seductive glories of the decaying mansion):

摧殘荒草廬,	A broken down-hut in the weeds
其中煙火蔚。	Where smoke and flames come welling out:
借問群小兒,	I asked this gang of little kids:
生來凡幾日。	"Just how old are you anyway?
門外有三車,	I have three carts outside your gate
迎之不肯出。	To greet you, but you won't come out!
飽食腹膨脝,	Just stuffing yourselves till you get fat—
箇是癡頑物。	Oh what a pack of nincompoops!"

It is telling here that the main vice of the children is gluttony. In Hanshan's and Shide's satires on the secular householder life, the desire for food and drink is the most common indulgence of ordinary people, rather than the desire for sex. One might even argue that for Hanshan, consumption (particularly consumption of meat) is a force that holds families and households together, thus exposing the degree to which the human community is predicated upon universally accepted violations of the Buddha's precepts. In the last chapter we saw his rhetorical attacks against meat-eating. In HS 186, eating meat seems to be the defining mark of family life:

買肉血濉濉,	Buy meat—the blood is still dripping,
買魚跳鱍鱍。	Buy fish—their tails are still thrashing.
君身招罪累,	You bring sin's bonds upon yourself
妻子成快活。	To make wife and children happy.
纔死渠便嫁,	But die and then she'll marry again
他人誰敢遏。	And no one else can prevent it.
一朝如破牀,	One day, just like a broken bed,
兩箇當頭脫。	Two of you split from head to base.

The main purpose of the casual misogyny here is not to denigrate the faithlessness of wives as such (though that may be implied, particularly in a culture where chaste widowhood was a recurring subject for ethical sermonizing); rather, it is to establish that a householder's life cannot help but generate bad karma, and that the sins one commits in the process have no long-lasting benefits. We think to buy contentment and stability at the cost of other living things, but there is no guarantee of our success. This is (as is typical for the poems in general) an attempt to relocate our closest and most dearly held emotional ties into a context in which they seem nothing more than elements of a rational choice theory; marital affections are simply a bed that falls apart over time. This rhetoric of disenchantment has been a common method in Buddhist writing since the earliest sutras.

The insubstantiality of a householder's life can also be represented with a combination of pathos and irony, appealing more strongly to our sense of compassion but still attempting to question the fundamental laws of community. Here is HS 140:

城北仲家翁,	Old Man Zhong to the north of town—
渠家多酒肉。	His household's full of meat and wine.
仲家婦死時,	After the Zhong clan's wife had died,
吊客满堂屋。	The mourners filled his rooms and halls.
仲翁自身亡,	When Old Man Zhong himself passed on,
能無一人哭。	Not a single man was seen to cry.
喫他杯臠者,	Consuming all his roasts and wine—
何太冷心腹。	How cruel they were in their hearts!

Again, the force that maintains society's bonds is gluttony—more specifically, the meat and alcohol that should be incidental to social occasions and rituals like funerals but in the end serve as the main motive of attendance. Condemnation of "fair weather friends" is not uncommon in Chinese literature, but the focus on food and drink here makes the poem peculiarly typical of the Hanshan corpus. They suggest that the layperson's homestead is not a place of practice, and only produces constant suffering and perpetual cycles of Impermanence. They seem skeptical of the sort of "householder bodhisattva" exemplified by Vimalakīrti, who manages to reconcile his enthusiasm for the faith with ordinary social obligations.

One of the more famous Hanshan poems, 236, employs a novel metaphor for the uselessness of ordinary human motion and activity in the samsaric realm. *Kleśa*—the obstructions in ordinary life that prevent cultivation of the Buddhist path—are mentioned in the sixth line:

人生在塵蒙,	Humans born in this world of dust
恰似盆中蟲。	Are just like bugs in a bowl.
終日行遶遶,	All day they travel round and round
不離其盆中。	But never get out of the bowl.
神仙不可得,	No way to become Transcendent,
煩惱計無窮。	No end to Obstruction's schemes.

歲月如流水， Years and months pass, a flowing stream,
須臾作老翁。 And suddenly you're an old man.

Compounds describing motion back and forth (*wanglai*, "going and coming"; *laiqu*, "coming and going") occur about a dozen times in the collection, most frequently with a reference to useless and repetitive activity. It seems that when we believe we have found stability—exemplified in a classic householder's residence, a happy family life, abundance of food, and good relations with the community—we are fooling ourselves. We are, in fact, in constant movement: driven by karma, driven by our uncontrolled desires, driven by unavoidable human catastrophe. To stay in the burning house as if it were a refuge is in fact to be in constant flight from ourselves—as if we had a Self from which to flee.

Mountain Pilgrimage

If the public householder's life is doomed to failure, what is the true solution? At first, it may seem to be participation in a more bucolic, private community, such as the one we saw in HS 15 in chapter 3. In several poems, the narrator embraces life as a small farmer who renounces wealth and instead harmonizes with nature and the seeming naturalness of agricultural cycles; Tao Qian is the model here. HS 27 follows this line of thinking:

茅棟野人居， Thatched beams on a rustic's house,
門前車馬疏。 Few carriages before the gate.
林幽偏聚鳥， A forest deep where birds can flock,
谿闊本藏魚。 A valley broad where fish can teem.
山果攜兒摘， I take my son, pluck mountain fruit,
皐田共婦鋤。 With wife I go to plough the fields.
家中何所有， What can be found inside my house?
唯有一牀書。 Only furniture piled with books.

These poems are some of the least "Buddhist" poems in the corpus—unlike those we have examined elsewhere, they do not make it easy to repurpose secular elements in order to create a potential Buddhist reading.

However, most of the speakers of the Hanshan poems pursue a more radical eremitic existence, cut off both from idealized farming communities and even from monasteries (monasticism has its own problems, as we shall see in chapter 6). It is at this stage that a type of mysticism arises in the poetry, a preoccupation with isolated self-cultivation as a gateway to higher consciousness. A dangerous pilgrimage is involved, one that provides perils for both the physical body and for the spirit. This path can easily lead to missteps; the woods and the mountains are dark and dangerous. And it is in this world that Cold Mountain (the place itself) emerges in the poems, both literally and allegorically.

The place of practice as a deadly wilderness has its origins in Indian mythic traditions. Texts like the Rāmāyana see the world as divided into two spheres: the city, with its secular attractions and its community of families, and the wilderness, where ascetics go to practice. The wilderness is also the home of *yakṣas*, *rākṣasas*, and other demons who torment ascetics: demons who were thought to be real, but who also provided metaphors for the temptations that interfere with the development of spiritual power. The tale of the demon Māra distracting Śākyamuni under the bodhi tree in order to prevent him from attaining enlightenment owes something to this tradition. Though demonization of the wilderness is not so evident in Chinese texts, it does emerge in a number of places, notably in the *Summons of the Soul* (Zhao hun), a rhapsodic poem found in the Han-era *Songs of Chu* (Chu ci), in which the speaker attempts to lure the recently departed soul back to its earthly form by detailing the ogre-haunted horrors of the outer worlds and the luxuries to be found back in domesticated space. Similarly, medieval Chinese religion often expressed a tension between large, state-recognized faiths on the one hand and heterodox regional groups in the countryside on the other, often assuming that members of the latter who acted in the service of their deity were in fact deluded by a demon disguised as a god. This judgment was particularly applied to shamans, both male and female. The classic scene of a shaman exorcised or conquered by a representative of orthodoxy occurs with frequency throughout the Six Dynasties period (fourth to sixth centuries), especially with the rise of the large state-supported Daoist sects. In the developing Chan movement several centuries later, patriarchs often established their monasteries only after defeating or reasoning with the local mountain spirits, who were initially opposed to the representative of a rival faith setting up shop on their turf. This suggests that in China as well as India, the regional, the nonurban, and the wild (especially mountains) were seen as potentially dangerous, if desirable, places of cultivation.

This expectation is mitigated in Hanshan's case by the fact that his chosen place of refuge, Cold Mountain, was near the religious center of Tiantai, which had become the headquarters of a mainstream sect of Buddhism by the Tang and likely no longer signified "wilderness" for most believers.[4] Nonetheless, Cold Mountain is still a wild place on the periphery of Tiantai, and thus is set up in deliberate opposition to the "civilized" monastic enclave, as the apocryphal preface to the collection makes quite clear.

In most of the Hanshan poems, the mountain as a place of practice (or potential place of practice) is seen not just in contradistinction with the world of the householder, but also as a numinous and potentially dangerous location. One enigmatic verse, HS 144, a vignette in which the isolated mountain landscape and the liminal twilight contribute to a sense of profound mystery, emphasizes this:

夕陽赫西山，	Sunset shines on the western hills,
草木光曄曄。	Where grass and trees still glow in the light.
復有朦朧處，	And further on, a murkier place,
松蘿相連接。	Where the vines on the pine trees tangle.
此中多伏虎，	So many crouching tigers here,
見我奮迅鬣。	Who bristle with rage when they see me.
手中無寸刃，	Not an inch of blade in my hand—
爭不懼懾懾。	Who wouldn't then tremble with fear?

The lack of context for this scene invites a certain allegorical reading, though there is no weighted vocabulary here that would make such an interpretation obvious. Perhaps the missing blade in line 7 refers to Mañjuśrī's sword of wisdom, which can cut through the errors of discriminatory and dualistic thinking—an image that is evoked in HS 156, another mysterious mountain poem:

寒山有躶蟲，	On Cold Mountain there's a naked beast
身白而頭黑。	With pale-white body and jet-black hair.
手把兩卷書，	His hand holds a two-chapter book,
一道將一德。	One called "Way," the other, "Power."
住不安釜竈，	He's not set up house with kettle or hearth;
行不齎衣裓。	When he goes out, no supply of clothes.
常持智慧劍，	But he holds fast to the sword of wisdom,
擬破煩惱賊。	Planning to smash the *kleśa* bandits.

Hanshan's self-portrait here gestures toward cliché descriptions of Daoist Transcendents, whose power renders them indifferent to the weather. He also holds a copy of the *Classic of the Way and Its Power* (Daode jing), another name for the *Laozi*, and his identity as a being outside society is suggested in the third couplet: he has no house as such (the laying of a floor-hearth was one of the most basic stages of home construction in early China), and as a Transcendent he has no need for apparel. However, he also holds the blade of Mañjuśrī, which enables him to defeat the bandits that interfere with his practice, bandits who are analogous to the tigers in HS 144.

Regardless, it seems that reaching the actual site of a mountain retreat can be difficult in and of itself. In the introduction, we looked at HS 9, in which Hanshan essentially told an inquirer in search of Cold Mountain that he could only reach it by changing his way of thinking. In other poems as well, he emphasizes the idea of Cold Mountain as a mental state, a place that is attained in a spiritual sense. One method he uses to indicate this is to add touches of the uncanny to his portrait of it, as if he is delegitimizing the mountain's claim to any physical existence. We are meant to read such poems against the mainstream secular Chinese tradition, in which it is typical for the reader to assume that a real poet is climbing a real mountain at an actual historical moment. HS 28:

登陟寒山道,	Up I climb the Cold Mountain Road,
寒山路不窮。	Cold Mountain road that never ends.
谿長石磊磊,	Stream-bed long and boulders in piles,
澗闊草濛濛。	A broad ravine where grass grows thick.
苔滑非關雨,	Moss is slippery—but not from the rain;
松鳴不假風。	Pines do not need the wind to moan.
誰能超世累,	Who can transcend the bonds of the world
共坐白雲中。	And sit with me mid the white clouds?

The closing is a challenge to the reader, much as in HS 9—you can only come here if you have a mind like mine. And to do that, you must also have the courage to pass through an eerie landscape, where moss is wet for no reason and pine trees are rustling on a windless day.

In HS 2, the poet's isolation and rejection of community is even more apparent:

重巖我卜居，	By layered cliffs I chose my house:
鳥道絕人迹。	A path for birds; human tracks cut off.
庭際何所有，	What is there at the edge of my yard?
白雲抱幽石。	White clouds embracing the hidden stones.
住茲凡幾年，	Here I've lived for many years;
屢見春冬易。	I've seen the springs and winters pass.
寄語鐘鼎家，	I send word to households with bells and tripods:
虛名定無益。	No benefit at all from your empty fame.

Hanshan begins the poem with an act of plot-divination *(bu ju)*, the use of geomantic principles to determine the best place to construct a house. One must be careful not to exaggerate the importance of this act—it often simply means "choosing a place to live," and does not necessarily evoke larger issues of cosmic harmony. Nonetheless, finding a place to locate a monastery was a significant act, as seen especially in the legends surrounding notable Chan patriarchs and the communities they found. Such an act—sometimes referred to as "opening a mountain"—describes a potential act of civilizing, of bringing a previously uncultivated area within the jurisdiction of Buddhist compassion.

However, Hanshan's position as a civilizer is ambivalent, if we view this poem in relation to the narrative of the preface (as a traditional East Asian reader certainly would). Though his act of divination at Cold Mountain would normally have the potential to make his refuge a sort of annex to the main Buddhist community at Tiantai, it certainly does not function as such. Rather, he remains closer in type to legendary Chan monks who choose to remain wandering challengers, who go from temple to temple testing abbots on their intuitive wisdom through the posing of enigmatic questions or the execution of irrational acts, or who mysteriously appear to give hints to spiritual aspirants. A reader familiar with Zen literature might remember the uncanny appearance of Hanshan to Guishan Lingyou on his visit to Tiantai, when he told him to seek out his future master Dazhi at Letan (an anecdote mentioned in chapter 1). He also resembles Chan abbots in the early stages of their independence, when the act of temple-founding is followed not by the immediate establishment of a community, but by an extended passage of ascetic practice. Lingyou himself, for example, after building a dwelling at Guishan, "dwelt with the mountain monkeys and took acorns and chestnuts as his food."[5] He also remains much like legendary representations of Japanese *yamabushi*, figures who fight troublesome heterodox local spirits, while remaining (from the perspective of civilization) marginal and slightly dangerous figures.

The rest of the poem also sets up series of oppositions to the idealized Tao Qian community paradise: there are no roads to his dwelling, save those of birds; it is so high that the clouds are able to settle in his garden among the rocks (the mild personification of the clouds gives the poem a slightly eerie, supernatural quality). He is isolated from secular time frames as well, as he comes to embrace the years that come and go. While the conventional position of a Chinese poet is to see passing time as a depressing reminder of one's own mortality, Hanshan often sees it as a mark of transcendence; he has an ability to stand outside time, acknowledge its swiftness, but remain unmoved by it. When he does express consciousness of time, it can often be interpreted as sorrow for the Impermanence of living beings who remain unenlightened.[6] For himself, however, time can be viewed dispassionately or positively:

其中半日坐,	In the midst of this I shall sit half a day
忘却百年愁。	Forgetting the grief of a hundred years.[7] (HS 22, lines 7–8)

朝朝不見日。	I see no sunlight dawn after dawn,
歲歲不知春。	And know of no springs year after year.[8] (HS 31, lines 7–8)

快活枕石頭,	Delightedly I pillow on a stone,
天地任變改。	Letting Heaven and Earth transform. (HS 164, lines 9–10)

我更何所親,	Nothing more to care about;
暢志自宜老。	Doing what I want—the best way to age.
形容寒暑遷,	Though my form may alter with the seasons,
心珠甚可保。	I can preserve the pearl in my mind. (HS 278, lines 5–8)

As a recluse, Hanshan can embrace what horrifies others.

Many of the poems that describe living in the mountains are easily adaptable to an allegorical reading: Cold Mountain is a state of mind, and not simply a place. Not surprisingly, Hakuin takes this perspective in his commentary on HS 2:

> This poem is composed on the subject of dwelling in the mountains: secluded and quiet, lodged secretly in the lofty and leisured. With this it instructs and admonishes those of the floating world who are concerned with profit and fame.

There are three ways of "choosing a dwelling" *(bu ju)*:

To be cut off by the vast ocean of life and death, and to adhere obstinately to an island in the sea; to bury yourself in a dark, unenlightened valley and sink into the moats and gullies of love and hate; to take your place with the poison tree of arrogance; to bathe in the deep mire of heterodox views; to be where flames all around rush upon you and the winds from all directions blow upon you, so that a multitude of bitterness afflicts you, so that in the end you are plunged into the Hell realms; that is the ordinary man "choosing a dwelling."

To resent that the three Forms of Existence are scattered;[9] to fear that the four Forms of Birth are a worry and a hardship;[10] to enter into the secluded valley of the doctrine of the "emptiness of the Self";[11] to stick to the foundation of a one-sided view of reality; to plow a burial ground in a high field; to plant scorched grass, beans, and wheat; to open up stony fields for cultivation; to sow the withered seeds of insignificant tares; to fertilize it with the manure of conceptual thought; to wash in the muddy puddle of quietism; to try to polish the broken tile of "storehouse-consciousness"; and to experience the life-spans, past, present, and future, of many kalpas; that is the practitioner of the lesser vehicle *(hinayana)* "choosing a dwelling."

To swim perpetually in the sea of the four universal Bodhisattva vows;[12] to have always acknowledged the Buddha's land of calm illumination;[13] to divine the splendid realm of absolute reality; to accrue the saintly wealth of sky-flowers; to climb upward in seeking lofty halls; to go deep in order to transform the gullies and ditches; to nurse well the trees in the garden of all good works; to sprinkle the rain of the undiscriminating Dharma; and to travel together with all living things the path of perfecting Buddhahood: that is the practitioner of the greater vehicle "choosing a dwelling." That is the dwelling place of a true priest: a nine-walled palace of red-hot iron.[14]

Hakuin has created metaphorically three different kinds of reclusion and has been careful to distinguish each one of them. The ordinary reclusion dismissed at the beginning is a sort of morose, lazy eremitism, indifferent to activity and feeding off its own ignorance. Perhaps Hakuin is attacking what he saw as a common vice of hermits, the tendency to embrace a misanthropic isolationism as true cultivation. Next, his Hinayana practitioner is a hard-working farmer—bringing his own private plot of land into productivity through labor-intensive means. Such an effort, though not evil in and of itself, only reaps minimal benefits over countless lives. Hakuin also breaks momentarily from elaborating on the farming metaphors to introduce the famous Zen image of polishing a broken tile (more frequently, polishing a brick). Its origins lie in a famous anecdote told about the early Chan master Nanyue Huairang:

> There was a novice, Daoyi [later, Huairang's famous disciple Mazu Daoyi] who would sit in meditation each day in the Dharma Transmission Court. The Master [Huairang] knew this was a man capable of being a vessel for the Dharma. He went and asked him, "What do you plan to accomplish by sitting in meditation?" Daoyi replied, "I plan to become a Buddha." Huairang then took up a brick and started to whet it against a stone in front of the building.
>
> Daoyi asked, "Master, what are you doing?"
>
> "I'm polishing this into a mirror."
>
> "How could a brick ever become a mirror?"
>
> "How can you turn into a Buddha by sitting in meditation?"[15]

Here, Hakuin seems to be alluding to practitioners who labor through meditation and other practices to access the layer of universal consciousness underlying all phenomena, the "storehouse consciousness" or *Ālaya-vijñāna*. Since the theory of the eight consciousnesses belonged initially to the highly scholastic Yogācāra school of Mahayana, he is likely criticizing overly cerebral approaches to attaining enlightenment.

Hakuin's ideal hermit is still dwelling in a rural landscape, but he has become a healthy countryman, engaged in the benefit of all—not in the brooding inertia of the first kind of recluse or the back-breaking and useless toil of the second one. There is a certain delight in the good practitioner's actions here—swimming, climbing, traveling—indicating a true freedom within the bounds of eremitism. This is an interesting move, because it suggests that Hakuin sees Hanshan ultimately returning to a concept of community, though not a community of Tao Qian farmers. Rather, he belongs to a community of bodhisattvas, who participate with ordinary people in the suffering of samsara yet manage to remain above it. Hakuin seems to be attempting a reconciliation of Hanshan's severe reclusion with the social obligations of the Mahayana practitioner. But how such a higher community might be constructed remains a question.

Finding the Source

In fact, this search for the next stage (and whether one accomplishes it alone or with others) emerges in a number of poems and is highlighted by Hakuin's comment on them. HS 280, for example, suggests a possible role for a community, even on the lonely heights of Cold Mountain:

本志慕道倫,　　I deeply honor men of the Way;
道倫常獲親。　　And they always permit me their company.
時逢杜源客,　　At times I'll meet one who's stopped up the source
每接話禪賓。　　Or see someone who'll talk of Chan.
談玄月明夜,　　Chatting of mysteries on a moonlit night,
探理日臨晨。　　Or probing principles in a sunlit dawn.
萬機俱泯迹,　　When myriad motives all vanish away,
方識本來人。　　You'll recognize the original man.

This poem has numerous semitechnical expressions that make straightforward translation difficult. The first line more literally reads, "Through my deep-rooted aspirations I admire people who associate in the Way," indicating the speaker's almost intuitive recognition of a group of practitioners who share his goals (and perhaps have something to teach him). "People who associate" *(lun)* implies members of a peer group who bond over a shared interest or social position; and the Way, though of course linked with Daoism, can also imply the Buddhist path as well. The next couplet describes two members of this fraternity. The interesting expression "stop up the source" likely has its origins in a passage from a Tang Buddhist encyclopedia in which the speaker is giving advice on how to avoid the evil karma that will result in rebirth in Hell:

> To try to hold down the current is not as good as stopping up the source. To fan boiling water is not as good as stamping out the fire. Why? The source produces the water; if the source is not blocked up, then the water will never run out. Fire boils water. If the fire is not stamped out, then the boiling will never cease. Therefore the man who blocks up the source will not have to hold down the current, and yet it will dry up on its own. One who stamps out the fire will not be fanning the boiling water and yet it will stop on its own.[16]

The text then goes on to make the obvious comparison to karma: it is a good bit easier not to generate evil karma to begin with, rather than to find a way to deal with its consequences later. For Hanshan here, the meaning extends to the more drastic action of removing oneself altogether from the generation of karma, as suggested in the seventh line, "When myriad motives all vanish away." A more literal translation would be "have their tracks eliminated," the word "track" *(ji)* also referring to mountain tracks or trails, the paths that humans or animals make—in HS 2, *niao ji* is the "path of birds" that provides the only access to Hanshan's abode. Thus, though the community of practitioners Hanshan meets will "chat" and "probe" deep issues with him, the end result will be to remove the traces of human activity from the vastness of the hills—except, of course, for his poems, left behind for similarly discerning practitioners. This is a community whose function as such is its own eventual abolition.

Hakuin seizes upon the expression "stopping up the source" as worthy of elaboration. As in his comments on HS 2, he creates a hierarchy of increasing competence, suggesting what constitutes a successful "stopping up the source." His use of water metaphors gives a particularly good example of his satiric wit as well as the sublimity of his descriptions:

> There are four ways to "stop up the source." It is essential for the practitioner to understand them thoroughly.
>
> One way is to plant your frame erect, teeth clenched with determination, staring straight ahead of you with your hands balled into fists, unaware of anything that comes and goes. In this way you wish to stop up the mind's source, hoping to immerse yourself in and draw strength from the tranquil waters of meditation. This is the way people currently "plug up the source." It is like people on a raft using all their efforts to try to halt the river's current, with no idea that they're being carried off by it the whole time.
>
> Another way: in some silent place under a shady cliff observe the four Dharma gates,[17] cutting off vision and cogitation, making empty the world of dust, and in this way wishing to plug up the mind's source. This is "plugging up the source" characteristic of the *śravaka*.[18] This is like spreading a screen, hoping to divert the flow of a river as you might with a net; and yet the water will keep rolling along.
>
> Another way: engage in a barren sort of meditation, keeping to a biased view of reality derived from focusing on the emptiness of the

Self. You pay no attention to the appearance of myriad conditions; you resemble an incense burner going out in an ancient shrine, or a withered tree turning to dead ashes. You hope in this way to achieve no outflowings.[19] This is how the *pratyekabuddha* stops up the source.[20] This is like standing in the middle of the river, hoping to block the current with your body. Though it may seem like your legs are standing securely in it, how can this deal with the sea of life and death?[21]

But if there is someone who has a great capacity for faith, yet also a nature capable of great doubt, and who yet has a will that allows for strong enthusiasms, then he will take up a single word-head[22] and through it he will seek his way back to the source of his own mind. Then in an instant all will open up at once into a vast expanse and he will kick over his own mind's source, tearing down the obstructing embankments that had been separating the main current from its tributaries. The earth of old will be enveloped in a rolling darkness; Heaven and Hell and the Buddha Lands and the Realm of Demons all will turn to a sea of perfume, true and pure with no outflows, with nothing within, without, or in between. And slowly great clouds of compassion will spread out from this, letting rain a great Dharma rain that will soak every kind of grass and tree, and will bring the withered things back to life from their great drought. The glittering flames of the Burning House will be blown out, and all evil [karmic] seeds will be washed clean. And this will pass through kalpas of dust and sand without the loss of a single drop.

This is when a bodhisattva "stops the source"—and how is that something some ordinary priest could do? "Ho ho ho!" laughs Hanshan. "The turning wheel of the Three Realms!"[23]

This magnificent bit of rhetoric may at first seem like overkill, or rather, like a classic sermon built upon the smallest of scriptural bases, since it is all rooted in the need to explain a two-character phrase. However, for Hakuin Hanshan is ultimately an exemplary practitioner, a bodhisattva, and so it is important to see his actions, as described in the poems, as harmonizing with Zen theory—especially because the poem sets up "stopping up the source" as parallel with "speaking of Chan," thus suggesting to Hakuin the link of the first action with exemplary Zen conduct. What might Hanshan and his companions be talking about? Precisely what constitutes bodhisattva Zen, rather than inferior or even fraudulent practice. Hakuin reserves his greatest satiric contempt for the first class of practitioners, casual meditators who think Zen just requires sitting in one place and not thinking (as in much of his writing, he is probably attacking followers of the seventeenth-century Rinzai master Bankei Yōtaku [1622–93], who espoused a type of quietistic meditation, especially for laypeople). He then moves on, in classic Mahayana style, to the errors of the lesser vehicles. As with his discussion of HS 2, he tends to be critical of a passive eremitic practice, one that separates itself from the trials of ordinary existence.

In his description of the heroic actions of the bodhisattva, Hakuin first introduces the idea of going upriver to the source (the other groups had merely attempted to block the river in ridiculously futile ways, much as the Tang encyclopedia text had warned against trying to "hold down the current"). But as Hakuin's spiritual hero tracks down the source (accomplished through finding the "source of the mind" in koan practice), he does *not* in fact "stop up the source" and make the river dry up, as the original text had suggested. He rather releases a flood upon the world by breaking down the embankments that had controlled the original current's flow. Paradoxically, the bodhisattva finds his victory not in making the current stop (an action that perhaps would only benefit himself), but by creating an ocean where current and forward movement (the driving force of karma) disappear completely, eliminating distinctions and dualities. Then, in an ecstatic rhetorical move, Hakuin shifts attention to a series of Buddhist tropes, beginning with the rain that brings life to all beings, an allusion to a parable in the Lotus Sutra in which the Buddha describes his teaching:

> Dense clouds grow thicker, covering the three-thousand-fold universe, saturating everything at once. Grass, trees, forest groves, and medicinal herbs, ones with small roots, stems, branches, and leaves, ones with middling roots, stems, branches and leaves, ones with large roots, stems, branches and leaves; trees of all sizes—in accordance with their degree, so they receive. Rain from a single cloud matches the nature of each plant so that each is able to grow, flower, and produce its fruit. And though they all grow from one soil and are nourished by one rainfall, each plant and tree has its distinguishing marks.[24]

The bodhisattva similarly draws up his moisture from the vast ocean he has created—an undifferentiated ocean of emptiness, no longer controlled by samsaric laws—and distributes its moisture upon all living beings, in accordance with their individual natures.

Hakuin then moves to the Burning House parable, and closes his ecstatic vision with an image of the bodhisattva's cleansing flood continuing cosmic age after cosmic age. Then coming violently back to earth, he evokes Hanshan's own contempt for the monks of Guoqing Monastery as described in the collection's preface. We should not confuse Hanshan's friends in HS 280 with some banal monastery, filled with mediocre priests. Hanshan, Hakuin argues, is not a simple recluse talking to coreligionists, but a cosmic warrior among other magical bodhisattvas. When he stops up a source, the result is apocalyptic.

For Hakuin, Hanshan's engagement with fellow practitioners suggests the generation of a transcendent, salvific power. It is still unclear, however, where Hanshan will find his companions to aid him in this task. We would first imagine that he could turn to his two supposedly magical companions, Shide and Fenggan—the two men most likely to help him form such a community. The Shide collection references Hanshan by name three times, usually focusing on the aspects of their friendship already suggested in the preface. Perhaps because they were written after the trinity of sages had become famous, these poems tend to portray Shide as a slightly insecure friend of Hanshan's, eager for the hermit's approval and quick to mention to others how close they are. SD 16, lines 3–4 alludes to the legend that Shide was a foundling raised in the monastery (hence, his name, which literally means "gathered up"). SD 15 is also typical of how Shide supposedly sees their relationship:

寒山住寒山，	Cold Mountain lives on Cold Mountain,
拾得自拾得。	Shide is himself—Shide.
凡愚豈見知，	How could common fools recognize us?
豐干卻相識。	But Fenggan knows who we are.
見時不可見，	When you look at us you can't see us;
覓時何處覓。	When you search for us—nowhere to search!
借問有何緣，	And if you ask us what we're doing here—
向道無為力。	In the Way there's an actionless Power.

This could almost be a poem addressed specifically to poor Lüqiu Yin, who tried so desperately to make contact with the two sages and learn from them; yet it also sets up a somewhat defensive "us versus them" dynamic, as Shide boasts of the duo's abilities in comparison with ordinary people. Their superior practice allows each to be the other's *zhiyin* (understanding friend); it lies beyond the ordinary, even rendering them invisible to mediocre practitioners. The final couplet provides a touch of supernaturalism combined with doctrine: the seventh line could be read more precisely as: "If you ask about what karmic conditions [have created the situation that accounts for our presence here]," while the eighth line uses the technical term no-action (Ch: *wuwei*; S: *asaṃskṛta*), referring to actions that occur independent of the causes and conditions that govern the workings of karma. Though developed in complex ways in the Indian schools, the term tends to have a simpler meaning in Chinese Buddhist texts, perhaps encouraged by its prevalence in Daoist writing. In Chinese Buddhism it often refers to a recognition of the need to act in a way that does not produce karmic results, as opposed to performing the good works (*youwei*, purposive action) that may generate a kind of merit but do not lead to an ultimate escape from samsara.[25] The final couplet might thus be interpreted to mean: "If you ask what karmic forces have brought about our activities here, I reply that in fact we are possessed of a power that can act independent of karma and can thus practice the Buddhist path freely." The suggestion, as in Hakuin's reading of HS 280, is that the two of them are functioning as bodhisattvas.

However, if we turn to the only poem in the Hanshan collection that specifically mentions Shide and Fenggan (HS 40), we see Hanshan returning to a previous stance and ultimately denying the value of friendship and community:

慣居幽隱處，	When I've gotten too used to a hermit life,
乍向國清中。	I'll often go off to Guoqing Temple.
時訪豐干道，	Sometimes I'll visit Fenggan,
仍來看拾公。	And often I'll come to see Shide.
獨迴上寒巖，	But I'll go home alone and climb Cold Cliff,
無人話合同。	Because there's no one I can really talk to.
尋究無源水，	I'm seeking water that has no source—
源窮水不窮。	For sources dry up while this water doesn't.

This is a little surprising, considering the legends that grow up around the trinity from the preface on, all of which imply a close friendship. Here, the poem hints that Hanshan can only get so much benefit from socializing with his fellow eccentrics. When the day is over and he is trudging back to his home, he has to acknowledge that no one understands him or his concerns (line 6 more literally might be read as "there is no one whose conversation falls in line with mine"). The reason for this, Hanshan suggests, is that Fenggan and Shide are not quite engaged in the same enterprise that he is—a pilgrimage that involves seeking out the water that has no source. And yet the verb that he uses here, *xunjiu*, is exactly the verb one would use in following a stream up into the mountains to find its actual origin point; the character for a water source, *yuan*, consists of a marker for "water" combined with the character that means "origin." So what can he actually be looking for, if not a source?

To explore what this means takes us back to the same series of images we encountered in the phrase "stopping the source"—in particular, the idea that a vital part of escaping samsara lies in tracing the flow of karma back to its origin and finding a way to stop it. This can be found through two meanings of the verb *qiong*, which occurs twice in the last line. One definition is "to run out" or "to become exhausted," and could thus describe a stream drying up or running out; the second definition is "to seek to its source," essentially a synonym for *xunjiu*, to go upstream in order to *find* the origin of a stream, river, or creek—in allegorical terms, to seek out the ultimate nature of reality, for which the Hanshan corpus often uses the term *zhenru* (Sanskrit *bhūtatathatā*, "true suchness").[26] Thus, the last line could mean: "Though a source may become exhausted, this water [for which I am seeking] will never be exhausted." Or, alternatively: "Though one can discover the ultimate source of a spring, this water cannot have its source discovered." But what lies at the heart of these two possible readings? Which one does Hanshan intend? And how does his intention play into Buddhist themes of karma and the source of its production?

Hakuin once again has something to say:

> These two lines are the central meaning of the entire piece. "Water without a source" means that above everyone's Mind there is another erroneous mind that continually arises and dissipates; it is like a floating mist or trailing smoke that continues both day and night. It is like a stream flowing through a ravine continuously, never drying up through the four seasons. If the two [inferior] vehicles attempt to draw from it until it is used up, so that they will arrive at a day when it is completely dry, so as to become enlightened, then they will pass through countless kalpas in a state of constant hardship; while the bodhisattva merely seeks out the Great Matter of enlightenment at its root.
>
> But what does it mean to "seek out"? Those who can distinguish the path will arouse their spirits and will personally go to seek for the

> water in the place where it arises. But where does this water arise? What place acts as its root? He will seek for it everywhere, until both the place he seeks and the mind that seeks for it disappear in one stroke. At this time, when falsity melts away and iron mountains crumble, he will split the steep cliffs with his hands; and only then will he again attain a state of peace. This is "seeking to its end a water without a source."
>
> And yet, though one seeks it to its end, the water as before will continue to flow without exhaustion. He previously could not make out the original source with his ignorant and wild mind—a mind that arises and then dissipates. But after he has succeeded in seeing how to be liberated, then the great Dharma rain that derives from the most marvelous and mysterious ocean of encompassing wisdom, every drop perfectly bright and every drop all-pervasive, will soak the stems of every kind of plant; each drop will appease the hunger and thirst of creatures dwelling on the Six Paths; they will not be exhausted in the course of three great kalpas, and all living beings will be saved without exception. Such is searching out the source where the water will never be exhausted.[27]

Hakuin is obviously working through this poem with much the same perspective that he brought to bear on HS 280, but here he proceeds a bit further with his argument. Here, it is important not to see the water as a *positive* image, as other translators have—Hanshan is not looking for some perfect well that will always provide him with fresh spiritual drinking water. Rather, he is trying to find its source in order to *block it*—because the water is, once again, the river of samsaric karma that is carrying us all along against our will. Once more Hakuin critiques the lesser vehicles, who hope to exhaust the river by drawing out the water, much as desperate men might try to bail out a sinking boat. The true bodhisattva will realize that one must go to the source. But in the process of seeking out the source, he will fail to find it—*because it does not exist*. The river in fact has no true beginning or ending—it simply flows. The bodhisattva at this stage has made an essential error by assuming that the causes and conditions that govern karma have an actual, real, locatable existence. This paradox will confuse him, and out of the resulting imbalance will come the flash of enlightenment that will enable him to transcend object and subject, the thing sought and the mind that seeks it. For Hakuin, of course, this is the agonistic struggle characteristic of the student engaged in koan study (or, one might add, someone reading Hanshan's poems). This breakthrough will release the compassionate power of the bodhisattva, who now realizes that the river continues to flow regardless of his actions. But here, as in his commentary on HS 280, the river becomes a sea that in turn generates the nourishing clouds of dharma rain that will save all living beings.

How to interpret the end of the poem, then? Hakuin seems to be reading it to mean: "I am seeking the source of a water that has no source that can be found, because ordinary sources can be found and stopped, but it is the characteristic of this water to have no source and to never run out." It becomes, in fact, a mature Zen paradox. Hakuin's interpretation of this ending can then be extended to the rest of the poem: the reason why, ultimately, Hanshan must return alone to Cold Mountain is because he is engaged in a difficult and seemingly absurd task in which only he can engage. Perhaps unlike both Fenggan and Shide, he possesses higher perceptions and ambitions: "Those who can distinguish the path will arouse their spirits and will personally go to seek for the water in the place where it arises." And so he climbs back up, looking for the source that doesn't exist. His search for a residence has thus passed through two rejections. His initial pilgrimage to Cold Mountain resulted in his rejection of an easier, society-based reclusion, modeled on either the bucolic comfort of Tao Qian's peaceful village or the mutually supportive practice of the monasteries. Yet once he attains Cold Mountain, he must confront the fact that he has further to go, and that even his fellow bodhisattvas cannot help him to achieve the final stage. He must leave them behind as well, and go to climb the Cold Mountain that lies beyond Cold Mountain.

Roaming at Rest

At the beginning of this chapter, we saw Hanshan's critique of householders' lives: that they go searching for stability and luxury, but that any sense of permanence is an illusion. Rather, living beings caught in the rounds of samsara are compelled to move restlessly, back and forth, constantly struggling with their ephemeral existences. Hanshan's answer to that, of course, is to become a true recluse—the only possibility for genuine practice.

But reclusion does not necessarily imply stasis, in spite of the poems that describe the hermit tranquilly watching the years pass by. Rather, it opens up the possibility of a new kind of movement, no longer restless and compulsory, but genuinely free, much like the ideal figures of the *Zhuangzi* with their "roaming at will" *(xiaoyao you)*. Hakuin stresses this in his commentary on HS 2, where he praises the activity of the true bodhisattva recluse, one who is able "to travel together with all living things the path of perfecting Buddha-hood." It is not surprising then to see Hanshan describing the actions of the true recluse in terms of freedom. HS 247:

我見出家人,	I see those who "leave the household"—
不入出家學。	They don't enter into its practice.
欲知真出家,	If you'd know true "leaving the household,"
心淨無繩索。	The mind is pure, with no ropes that bind;
澄澄孤玄妙,	Pellucid, alone, darkly mysterious,
如如無倚托。	Completely itself, no dependencies.
三界任縱橫,	Through the three realms it rambles free,
四生不可泊。	Unmoored to any form of birth.
無為無事人,	Free of actions, free of affairs,
逍遙實快樂。	How great the joy to roam at will!

The poem begins as an anti-clerical satire, directed at "those who leave the household" (*chu jia*, a standard term for monks). But it moves quickly to an evocation of spiritual liberation that transcends monastic regulations and ordinary practice. This poem operates firmly within a Daoist-Buddhist realm, evoking postenlightenment bliss in language that occurs in both traditions. However, such terminology can only suggest the incommunicability of such a state, only vaguely convey a sense of movement and freedom. HS 246, on the other hand, gives the free-rambling bodhisattva a mission, thus fulfilling Hakuin's vision for him:

一生慵懶作,	I've been lazy all my life,
憎重只便輕。	Hated the hard, just went for easy.
他家學事業,	Other folks might learn a career—
余持一卷經。	I just have my one-chapter sutra.
無心裝褾軸,	No plans to mount it on a scroll—
來去省人擎。	Then I'd have to carry it around.
應病則說藥,	Based on the illness I give prescriptions,
方便度眾生。	My Skillful Means save everyone.
但自心無事,	If your mind's free of all affairs,
何處不惺惺。	You'll be brilliant at everything!

We start with a self-effacing assertion of worthlessness—the speaker claims he's congenitally lazy and unwilling to learn a trade. What he has instead is nothing but a sutra in one chapter—that is, the enlightened mind.[28] If that is the case, what would be the purpose of manifesting it in concrete form, dragging it along with you wherever you went? Better simply to exert one's newly liberated mind in skillful means, prescribing whatever medicine each individual needs. This medical metaphor is a common one, perhaps most clearly stated in the Vimalakīrti: "They [bodhisattvas] are great physician kings, skilled in healing the illnesses of all; they give them medicine in accordance with their illness, making sure that they take the dose as prescribed."[29] The playfulness of the poem derives from the contrast of this medical competence with the speaker's avowed refusal to learn a useful trade. The ending emphasizes this irony: while the speaker has a mind in keeping with enlightenment ideals—it is "actionless" (*wuwei*; that is, independent of actions that generate karma) and "without affairs" (*wushi*; a term indicating the mind's ability to remain unmoved by samsaric interference)—both terms reinforce the self-accusation of laziness. *Wushi* in particular echoes line 3, in which the speaker says that others learn "a career" *(shiye*, a term that incorporates that same term for "affairs," *shi)*. It is as if the poet is saying that as long as one does nothing and has no skills, he will be skilled in all things. In this way, the contrast between the seeming inactivity of eremitic cultivation on the one hand and salvific labor on the other are reconciled.

At the beginning of this chapter, a cranky Hanshan condemned, in HS 190, the fat, stupid children who refuse to come out of the Burning House of samsara. Stay there and make a home of it and you will burn up; leave it and a new world of freedom is open to you. The collection's other Burning House poem (HS 255) is considerably more upbeat:

余勸諸稚子,	I am urging all you youngsters
急離火宅中。	Get out fast from the burning house!
三車在門外,	Three carts wait for you here outside,
載你免飄蓬。	To free you from endless wandering.
露地四衢坐,	In open air, sit at the crossroads,
當天萬事空。	Face the sky—all things are empty.
十方無上下,	In all directions, no up or down—
來去任西東。	You can come and go, now east, now west.
若得箇中意,	If you can get this essential thought,
縱橫處處通。	All paths will open up to you!

The fourth line literally reads, "to transport you [so that] you avoid [becoming a] tumbleweed." Tumbleweeds are a recurring poetic cliché in Chinese verse, describing a speaker who is condemned to endless and uncontrolled wandering. Taking the Buddha's vehicle, by contrast, we enter the space of the crossroads; we may wander any road we choose, out in the open air, with complete freedom.[30] Our actions are no longer driven along the samsaric Six Paths by the winds of karma, with their never-ending suffering; we can now go anywhere we like.

CHAPTER 5

TROPES

We have seen in chapter 3 that poems sometimes form sequences that suggest fruitful juxtapositions and larger narratives, even if those sequences are often created in the reader's mind. Another way that the collection creates a sense of unity for the reader is through the use of recurring tropes, whose potential Buddhist significance allows for the exploration of aspects of samsara and nirvana from various perspectives. In the following pages we will look at four of these. Once again, much of their power lies in a combination of secular Chinese conventions with more religious ones.

Blasted Trees

Four poems in the collection deal exclusively with the theme of a dying or ailing tree. One possible reason for this trope's mild popularity in the collection is the way that it compels allegorical readings. This in turn encourages a Buddhist-inclined reader to discover ways to fuse secular and religious motifs.

The secular tradition behind these poems can be traced relatively easily: they belong to a small but quite well-defined subgenre that Stephen Owen has referred to as "the barren tree." He sees the type deriving from Yu Xin's (513–81) *Barren Tree Rhapsody* (Ku shu fu), which largely defined the boundaries for the rhetoric and "plot" of future poems on the same topic.[1] A series of shared themes seems to be common to the subgenre. First and most typically is an allegorical identification between the tree and the poet (or some other human), who may be complaining about the failure of his own political career and his subsequent "withering away," often in obscure circumstances.

Such arguments usually allude explicitly or implicitly to a common Chinese character pun: *cai* 材, meaning timber, and *cai* 才, meaning talent. Second is a counter view, inspired by Zhuangzi's parables, in which trees that are ugly, withered, or barren actually survive because they are perceived as useless and therefore are not abused or cut down. Not surprisingly, the second scenario is often used as a form of consolation for the despairing situation of the first. Occasionally the poem (when it is not self-portrait) might suggest that a barren tree (i.e., a certain public figure) is in fact *not* fit for use (may in fact be rotting), and that the allegorical referent's failure to find a position in administration is actually a good thing. Another occasional theme is the intervention of the true craftsman, who sees the seemingly abandoned tree, recognizes it for its value (essentially acting as a *zhiyin*), and then gives its timber/talent a noble purpose. The reading tradition will almost always assume that the tree is a stand-in for an individual: it is rare to encounter a barren tree poem composed for the pleasures of pure description.

On the Buddhist side of things, there is no clear, universally recognized trope that makes use of a dying or barren tree. However, one passage in the Nirvana Sutra does suggest a plausible Buddhist context for the metaphor. In it, one of the Buddha's disciples is commenting on the Buddha's transcendence of samsaric suffering:

> World-honored one—Suppose that outside a large village there happens to be a forest of śāla trees, and in that forest there is a single tree, one that preceded that forest, a hundred years of age. At that time the forester waters it, and cultivates it in accordance with the seasons. But the tree starts to rot away, and its bark and branches and leaves all fall away, leaving only its inner core. The Tathāgata is also thus; all of his former parts have all been removed, leaving only the true Dharma behind.[2]

Here the dying tree is perceived as a positive image, because it stands for a being who is transitioning out of the cycles of desire and rebirth. What remains to the tree is only the true Dharma, its inner core, much as one who is enlightened no longer has any "outflows" and will achieve the state of parinirvana at death.[3]

Beyond this image, it is perhaps not surprising that a Buddhist-oriented writer might use images of a withered tree in a positive sense. Not only would such an interpretation suggest that continuing life, no matter how flourishing, is a perpetuation of suffering; it also embraces an ascetic ideal that would find the withered and bare representative for the refusal of the sensuous delights of the world. One can trace this view in the native Chinese tradition as well, as far back as the opening of the second chapter of the *Zhuangzi*, in which an observer praises a sage for the strength of his meditative absorption: "What state is this? Can one's body indeed be caused to become like a withered tree, and one's mind like dead ashes?"[4] It is also likely that this celebration of withering would appeal to Chan and proto-Chan tendencies that were generally hostile toward religious ritual and fond of paradox. However, these associations should not keep us from seeing that a dying tree could also be read as a symbol of Impermanence and Suffering, and an exemplar of our own inevitable decline and death. With that in mind, we note that the Hanshan tree poems cover all of these themes. They often seem to imitate the secular poems in form, but often put a distinctively Buddhist spin on the topic that removes them from the secular tradition.

The least potentially Buddhist of the poems (and the one closest to the tradition Owen has defined) is HS 10:

天生百尺樹，	Heaven gave rise to a lofty tree,
翦作長條木。	Men trimmed it to form long beams.
可惜棟梁材，	A pity—this wood for rafters
拋之在幽谷。	Got thrown into some hidden gulch.
年多心尚勁，	Core still strong after many years,
日久皮漸禿。	Though bark peeled away as the days passed.
識者取將來，	But if a knowing one will bear them off—
猶堪柱馬屋。	They can still prop up a stable!

Here the tree has already been converted to worthy timber (suggesting that someone at some point recognized its value), but that timber was unceremoniously dumped in the wilderness before it could be used for its ideal purpose, as the beams of a house. Nonetheless, it continues to long for usefulness, even as its bark begins to peel away. We have the contrast of "superficial exterior" and "valuable essence" implied in the Nirvana Sutra quote, but the poem also suggests that someone who can see the inner essence (past the decline of surface attraction) will recognize its value—a fairly clear-cut reference to the timber/talent theme of the secular poems. The slightly novel (and comic) moment comes at the end, however, when the man who has come to rescue the timber can find nothing to do with the boards except use them to prop up a horse stable. Is this a sarcastic undermining of the secular theme, suggesting that recognition is inevitably a disappointment? Or are we supposed to see it as the timber's statement about its own desperation, that it would be happy to serve, even as a stable prop? The applicability to a human situation is obvious, and points to a subtler psychology than many of the secular poems on which it is based.

As the tree poem that most clearly lies within a non-Buddhist tradition, HS 10 challenges a serious Buddhist reader to repurpose it. Hakuin doesn't disappoint, though his opening comments clearly suggest that he worries that people will mistake this for a mere poem about office-holders:

> Though this poem seems to narrate the lament of a worthy man consigned to the wilderness, its deeper meaning is to condemn the sterility of the lesser vehicles, with their biased view of reality. "Heaven gave rise to a lofty tree" means that the inborn and essential self-nature of every person is in each case a perfect Buddha Mind. If someone determines its existence, grasps it, and nourishes it through the practice of the four all-encompassing Bodhisattva Vows,[5] then the Seven Characteristics of Awakening,[6] the Eight Correct Paths,[7] the Four States of Fearlessness,[8] and the inexhaustible Entrances to the Dharma[9] will all be perfect and complete within his body, like a tall tree, complete in its flowers, fruits, and branches.
>
> The Buddha temporarily made use of techniques of a middling or lesser value, lecturing on the Four Truths or the twelve different kinds of doctrine, calling them two forms of "gradual teaching." Through these you awaken to the emptiness of the Self, a principle that gives a biased view of reality; you then obtain the minor benefits of nirvana with remainder,[10] and you then have no wish to study the awe-inspiring deportment of a bodhisattva, or have any desire to purify a Buddha-land.[11] This then is "being trimmed to form long beams."
>
> If you imitate the so-called "way" of Daoist Transcendents, of Brahmin heterodoxy, or of ordinary people, then you might seem to be some kind of splendid wood formed into long boards. But in comparison with practicing the bodhisattva vows, with their benefit both for the self and for others, you're just a withered and rotten piece of wood dumped in some hidden gulch. This is why the poet finds it lamentable.
>
> "Core [heart] still strong after many years" means that after you have endured lives past, present and future, and the suffering of sixty kalpas, you have no intention of retreating from hardship, and your

mind of faith is still firm—just like an old tree passing through months and years with its core still firm and solid.

"Bark peeled away as the days passed": Eventually you give up your diligent polishing, and your erroneous views and thoughts completely drain away—this is just like a rotting tree whose bark peels away, leaving what is true and solid to remain.

But even if on some future day you act as an assistant in the worlds of gods or men, aiding the Buddha in propagating the teaching, you will only keep to your own quietistic practice as some beggarly manager, reduced merely to suppressing the Horse of the Will and the Monkey of the Mind. This is why the poet says "still prop up a stable."

This poem is thus a narration that exclusively relies on profound Mahayana teachings to critique and eliminate [inferior doctrines].[12]

Hakuin's clever interpretation suggests that the poem describes the gradual decline of a true believer to a level of inconsequence; he thus reorients the message away from a secular reading. Starting out as a flourishing tree, the potential bodhisattva originally contains within himself the perfection of all wisdom. The first misstep is when he becomes enamored of lesser vehicles—this is the stage when he is cut into boards and loses his greater ambitions. But worse is to come; he starts heeding non-Buddhist teachings, and becomes useless, tossed aside in the wilderness. Only the continuing existence of a steadfast mind sees him through this period. Still, when he finally achieves some progress, he will find his position reduced to a servile one, concerned only with the most basic meditative practices to keep himself and others under control. Hakuin comically ties the stock phrase "the Horse of the Will and the Monkey of the Mind," a popular Buddhist expression used to describe the restlessness of the human intellect, to the poem's image of a stable. All of this is meant not as a lament for an official whose talent has gone unused, but a critique of a bodhisattva who refuses to use his talents or squanders them on inferior tasks.

The next tree poem, HS 155, shifts the area of argument:

有樹先林生，	There's a tree, older than the forest;
計年逾一倍。	Twice as old, by the count of it.
根遭陵谷變，	Roots shifted with the hills and valleys,
葉被風霜改。	Leaves have changed in the wind and frost.
咸笑外凋零，	All will laugh at the outside withering;

不憐內文綵。	No one admires the grain within.
皮膚脫落盡,	But when its bark will peel away,
唯有貞實在。	Only the Real and True remain.

Though the poems are structured similarly—an opening demonstrating the impressive age of the tree, middle couplets that describe failure or decay, and a conclusion that asserts continuing worth—it is clear that this tree is not a pathetic symbol of abandonment but of continuing value and importance, even if it is recognized by few. Here we have a quite definite allusion to the passage in the Nirvana Sutra quoted above, where the Buddha is likened to a tree that precedes the forest around it in life, and that has withered away, leaving behind a pure essence, the true teaching or Dharma. The poem's only difference from the Nirvana Sutra passage is the emphasis on "lack of recognition," an import from the secular tradition with its complaint that talent goes unrecognized—and further, the enlightening and critical laughter of Hanshan is replaced by the scornful laughter of ignorance. This Buddhist context suggests a teaching that may catch on only among the chosen few, those mentioned, for example, in lines 5–6 of HS 305 (discussed in chapter 2): "I don't hate the lack of comprehenders; / That's just because my intimates are few." That image of the unheeded speaker makes it not unreasonable to see the tree as a symbol for Hanshan himself, especially when one takes into account the idea that an unprepossessing exterior may discourage a superficial audience from paying attention. Again, the theme of *zhiyin* is recontextualized and given a Buddhist flavor. Such an attitude may be seen, for example, in the famous HS 221:

時人見寒山,	When people these days see Hanshan,
各謂是風顛。	All of them say he's a madman.
貌不起人目,	A face that draws no one's attention,
身唯布裘纏。	A body wrapped in a hempen coat.
我語他不會,	What *I* say they don't understand,
他語我不言。	And what *they* say I'd never speak.
為報往來者,	But I tell anyone who passes,
可來向寒山。	"Why not come to Cold Mountain?"

The play on the poet's name and the place name is obvious here, ending as it does the first and last lines of the poem. But it emphasizes that his failure to present a distinguished exterior keeps people from paying him any attention, and that they don't understand what he has to say anyway—though he has a symbolically appropriate teaching to impart, "Come to Cold Mountain." As with the tree, no one sees the Real and True inside the poet.

Hakuin elaborates on HS 155's symbolic significance:

> Hanshan is here speaking of himself—he is a shadowless tree on the mountain of his residence. . . .
>
> "Roots shifted with the hills and valleys": when Hanshan first perceived Principle and entered into the Way, all Emptiness in every conceivable direction was annihilated; and at that very moment, his own fundamental root was eliminated as well. Thus the tree's "roots shifted with the hills and valleys." "Leaves have changed in the wind and frost": After this, the tree passed through three thrice-extended kalpas purifying and refining its true nature, suffering through frost and snow; and both the branches and leaves of *kleśa* and the flowers and fruits of divine insight dried up and withered away. And now it has attained its original appearance, an abbot's staff in the form of a mountain, with absolutely no external adornment. Thus the poet says, "when the bark will peel away, / Only the true and real remain."[13]

Hakuin is eager to emphasize Hanshan's existence outside time (and outside karma). For Hakuin, Hanshan is the incarnation of a bodhisattva, already free of most human suffering. He has attained a sudden enlightenment, in which he and the world exterior to him were similarly transformed/annihilated (a favorite representation of Hakuin's for satori: seen also his comments on HS 280 and HS 40, discussed in chapter 4); the bodhisattva's "roots" (a Buddhist term for capacities) changed with the landscape around him. There followed a period of training and endurance, in which everything extraneous was stripped away, leaving the pure essence. Hakuin sees the tree in semimagical terms, and ends by comparing it to an abbot's staff *(zhuzhang)*, an object that often was used to express both the rhetorical and the supernatural powers of classical Chan monastics. As Steven Heine describes it, "the staff . . . , a seven-foot-long, untrimmed stick that every Zen master traditionally cut for himself in the mountains, represents the structure and charisma of the master's authority. It is an important symbol of the abbot as a mountain steward . . . as well as a spiritual leader capable of taming wild nature."[14] By equating Hanshan both with the tree and with a found object on his own mountain ("a shadowless tree on the mountain of his residence"),

Hakuin emphasizes the poet's symbolic power over Cold Mountain and over the spiritual realm in general. The abandoned timber of HS 10 has become a magical staff.

The other two tree poems leave themselves open to fairly straightforward Buddhist interpretations that focus on impermanence and suffering. HS 192, for instance, describes a blasted tree, and concludes: "The sphere of life is just like that; / Pointless to resist Heaven and Earth." HS 216 is quite similar: the poet observes a tree growing out of a cliffside and on the point of perishing, and he laments that it will be "reduced to a pile of ash" (suggesting it will be used for firewood). Though neither poem is explicitly Buddhist, they tend to reinforce for a Buddhist reader the concept of Impermanence.

Small in number though these blasted tree poems are, they give us insight into how a Buddhist readership would be likely to take images, tropes, and even vocabulary from Buddhist and non-Buddhist texts and use them to suggest Buddhist content. It is perhaps this method, more than anything else, that comes to define a potentially "Buddhist" quality in the collection, and which makes it a recognizable if unique literary work within traditional Chinese literature. We will continue to see this method occurring in poems with other themes, though none of them are linked to such a clearly defined "subgenre" within the secular tradition as the blasted tree.

Jewels and the Buddha Nature

Hanshan's jewel imagery comes from two main sources. The first derives simply from a Sanskrit term, *maṇi*, that may refer to any legendary gem that has magical properties: the power to remove difficulties, heal illness, purify water, et cetera. The term recurs often throughout the sutras, and *maṇi* are often differentiated by various descriptions, as, for example, Night-Shining *maṇi*, Great-Lamp *maṇi*. Generally speaking, they are portrayed as giving off magical light, and are usually functioning talismans of some kind. By extension, they can symbolize the religious or magical power held by buddhas, bodhisattvas, or believers.

The other major source of jewel imagery is one of the more famous parables from the Lotus Sutra:

> "World-Honored One! It is like a man who comes to the house of an intimate companion. He becomes drunk there and lies down. At that time his companion, having official business and needing to depart,

sews an invaluable gem into his clothes, giving it to him upon departure. But his friend, lying there drunk, knew nothing of this.

"He later arose and went traveling and he journeyed to other lands. He went seeking everywhere in order to provide food and clothing for himself, suffering greatly in the process. When he managed to obtain even the slightest amount, he would make do with it. Later, his close companion encountered him and said to him:

"'Bah, old friend! How did your food and clothes get in such a state? Some time ago on such-and-such a day, because I wanted to make things easy for you so that you could enjoy the pleasures of this life, I sewed an invaluable gem into your clothing. It's still there right now, and you don't know it! You've been suffering all sorts of hardships and annoyances to make a living, and you've been a complete fool. You can now trade the gem for what you need and get whatever pleases you, with nothing lacking.'

"The Buddha is like this. When he was a bodhisattva, he taught and converted all of us, causing us to give rise to a mind wise in all things. And yet we immediately abandoned and have forgotten all of it and became ignorant."[15]

The speaker here is one of five hundred *arhats* who now acknowledge the superior vehicle of the Buddha's new teaching—or rather, as this story suggest, an *old* teaching they had forgotten over the course of their rebirths.[16] It will enable them to give up their previous path, with all its pointless and unnecessary toil. Within the East Asian Buddhist tradition, the parable comes to represent the doctrine of the *Tathāgata-garbha* (literally, the "Tathāgata-womb"). This concept expresses the belief that in our unenlightened state we already possess the potentiality to become enlightened—or, to state the doctrine even more radically, we already exist in a state of enlightenment, but simply have not come to awareness of it yet. As the doctrine became increasingly popular, the simpler terms "Original Nature" *(ben xing)* or "Buddha Nature" *(fo xing)* came into ordinary discourse to represent this idea, pervasive in early Chan texts. The idea also contributes to Chinese arguments concerning "sudden enlightenment," since it suggests that a final spiritual breakthrough could arise from the abrupt recognition of one's inner potential. It also tends to encourage the belief that everything present in the world of suffering (humans, animals, demons, even plants) has the seed of enlightenment within it.

A number of poems develop the jewel image at great length, demonstrating the degree to which it permeates Buddhist rhetoric about Buddha Nature. One of the simplest is a quatrain, HS 196, which plays indirectly upon the Lotus Sutra parable:

千生萬死凡幾生，	Thousand lives, ten thousand deaths, how many lives at last?
生死來去轉迷盲。	Life and death, we come and go; we grow more lost and blind:
不識心中無價寶，	Not knowing the invaluable jewel within the mind:
猶似盲驢信脚行。	Just like a blinded ass allows his legs to choose the path.

"Invaluable jewel" is the exact phrase used in the Lotus Sutra; here, however, the ignorant are not compared to feckless youths who must struggle to earn a living, unaware of their wealth. Rather, they are blind asses, wandering the Six Paths of Rebirth again and again, heedless of where they are going (the ass occasionally occurs as an image for stupidity and ignorance in the poems).[17] As one might expect from "Buddha Nature" rhetoric, the ass's general blindness results from a blindness in one specific instance: failing to acknowledge the existence of the jewel that would result in liberation. The ass's resulting directionlessness evokes the futility seen in the bugs in the last chapter: we are always striving to go somewhere, but lack the ability to recognize that the proper direction is a pilgrimage directed towards one's own self and towards significant awakening and recognition.

A futile wandering also occurs in one of the most astonishing poems in this group. HS 199 introduces a fairy-tale narrative (in fact, one of the very few detailed narratives in the entire collection). It suggests a sort of quest, not unlike Hanshan's quest for the source in the last chapter—but in this case, the adventurer chooses the wrong way to go about it:

昔年曾到大海遊，	So many years ago I went and traveled to the sea;
為采摩尼誓懇求。	So I might pluck the *maṇi* gem, I swore to seek it out.
直到龍宮深密處，	Down I went to the Dragon Hall's most secret place below—

金關鎖斷主神愁。 I tore apart their golden gates—
the sentry spirits vexed!
龍王守護安耳裏， The dragon lord kept jewel close,
he hid it within his ear;
劍客星揮無處搜。 Guardians swung their flashing blades—
no place that I could search.
賈客却歸門內去， This merchant found his way back home,
withdrew within his gate,
明珠元在我心頭。 Not knowing that that brightest gem
resided in the mind.

There is some overlap of Chinese and Indian Buddhist lore here. Chinese dragons *(long)* are often associated in the translation of Buddhist texts with the snake-like *nāgas*, a nonhuman race often admired for its wisdom. Buddhist legends surrounding the prominent Mahayana philosopher Nāgārjuna portray him as a tantric magician who acquired significant scriptures from a *nāga* king when the latter pitied his ignorance and invited him to his underwater palace.[18] This legend provides the supposed reason for his name (rendered in Chinese as Longshu, "Dragon-Tree"). In general, dragon-*nāgas* were seen as wise, often helpful, but also dangerous nature spirits, capable of producing or controlling floods and gifted with supernatural powers and magical arts.

In our poem, the narrator does not come to an underwater palace by invitation (as Nāgārjuna did), but plans to wage war upon it. His vow to find the *maṇi* gem seems oriented toward personal gain; we learn in line 7 that he is a merchant playing the role of a pirate-adventurer. Obviously possessed of extraordinary courage and magical power, he attacks the dragon-king's palace directly, smashing through its doors in an effort to track down the gem. Unfortunately, the king falls back on a last line of defense, concealing the gem in his ear and unleashing his swordsman-guards on the intruder. The protagonist soon has no choice but to retreat in failure. The classic Buddhist paradox is enunciated at the end: the whole quest was useless, because the gem was not to be found anywhere else; it always existed within the seeker's mind.

Some of the individual details of the verse invite allegorical readings. Obviously, the fact that the merchant attempts to gain the gem by force is a cause for suspicion, especially when compared with the means employed by Nāgārjuna, who was personally invited by the *nāga* king to consult his secret scriptures. The other error on the merchant's part, of course, is to externalize the gem, seeing it as something that can be acquired, possessed, and possibly traded. Rather, the gem is something inalienable to the individual; it can be recognized, acknowledged, and possessed (in the same way that we possess certain qualities), but not separated from oneself. The withdrawal within the gate at the end might signify the merchant's withdrawal within the gates of his own senses, a self-examination that can result in awakening to the Buddha Nature.

Such a self-examination is described in great detail in HS 204, which relates the process that ends with realizing the gem within the self:

我家本住在寒山,	From the start, my home has been here on Cold Mountain,
石巖棲息離煩緣。	Where I roost atop the stony cliff, cut off from karmic pains.
泯時萬象無痕跡,	All phenomena, when submerged, leave no trace behind them;
舒處周流遍大千。	Unspooled, they'll then flow everywhere, through the endless universe.[19]
光影騰輝照心地,	A flashing image of shadow and light glows against the ground of Mind;
無有一法當現前。	Yet not a single dharma comes to face me in the Now.
方知摩尼一顆珠,	At last I know that solitary single *maṇi* gem
解用無方處處圓。	Is boundless in its usefulness, perfect in every way.

The doctrinal rhetoric of this poem is on a higher level than that of almost all the Hanshan poems, and it perhaps requires a more elevated style in translating. But as it stands (and without some explanation), it might sound like high-flown nonsense. A reasonable reading is possible, though certain lines are open to debate. As in so many of the poems, the narrator locates himself on Cold Mountain as a way of asserting a place of practice free from the interference of *kleśa*. The phrase "from the start" suggests that though Cold Mountain may be a place to which we seemingly move, it has always already been our residence, our original condition from the beginning (our "original nature," *ben xing*). Once we come to grips with this state as our home, we can separate ourselves from the karmic noise that distracts us and focus instead on transcendence. The first stage of this separation is acquiring the ability to move outside all phenomena, so that one may dismiss them from the mind or reveal them, as one requires. Hanshan might be describing the meditative process itself, though the idea that reality can be manipulated to this extent echoes HS 161, where the poet celebrated the malleability of the Buddha Nature in similar terms: "Contract it all within the mind, / Or stretch it out to everywhere." Perhaps there is no real difference: part of the recognition of the Buddha Nature is also the recognition that it is no different from phenomena. Yet the third couplet also expresses the separation of the Mind from phenomena, or at least the Mind's ability to mark phenomena without having them impact it to any extent: though they flash against the "ground of Mind" (*xin di*, a term sometimes used in Zen discourse to represent the mind in a state of enlightenment), not a single dharma actually manifests itself in the present (*dharma* here is used in its alternate meaning found in Buddhist philosophy, a phenomenal element of the samsaric world). This state of liberation comes about through the discovery of the *maṇi* gem, the metaphorical embodiment of the Buddha Nature, which is now fully understood and acknowledged. The last line consists of a particularly dense play on words: it might be rendered, literally and character by character, as "[I] understand the use of no-method/square, every place round." The gem is round, and consequently perfect ("round" to mean "perfect" is a common locution in Buddhist texts). To be round is, by definition, not to have square features *(wu fang)*; the word *fang* can also mean "method" or "direction" (as in the technical term for "skillful means," *fangbian*). To have "no method" or "no direction" can mean "to have no one specific method," that is, "to have boundless methods." There may also be yet another pun, as *wu fang* written with a slightly different second character can also mean "no obstructions." To paraphrase this couplet: "I now know that if you really understand how to use this one simple magical gem (that seems so modest and small), then you realize that it is truly perfect, just as a sphere as perfect; the perfection of its sphere is a manifestation of the fact that it is open to all movements, in all directions, without obstruction (it can roll everywhere, unlike something that is square). And this symbolizes that it masters all conceivable skillful means in bringing sentient beings to enlightenment."

The last poem, HS 245, is a vivid narrative vignette, and luckily a great deal less complex than HS 204:

昔日極貧苦,	In former days I was impoverished,
夜夜數他寶。	Night after night, counting others' jewels.
今日審思量,	Today I thought about it well:
自家須營造。	I must plan on my own behalf.
掘得一寶藏,	So I dug up a buried treasure,
純是水精珠。	All of it a crystal gem.
大有碧眼胡,	But many a blue-eyed merchant Hun
密擬買將去。	Would plot to buy and carry it off.
余即報渠言,	And I reply to all of them:
此珠無價數。	This gem is beyond all price.

A significant Mahayana text, the Avataṃsaka Sutra, may be the source here:

> Just like an impoverished man
> Who counts others' treasures, day and night,
> Yet even half a coin he lacks;
> Hearing much is just like this.[20]

Counting another's treasure is an image for someone who reads or studies the Buddha's teachings in an academic way without seeking to apply them to his own life (the phrase "hearing much" often means "studying the doctrine in detail"). In our poem, the narrator decides it is finally time to acquire the treasure on his own. And at this point, the allegory becomes a little confusing. Making plans for himself, he goes out and "finds" a treasure. But how does this come about? Usually the "discovery" of a treasure is serendipitous, not something one undertakes as a conscious action (when the merchant in HS 199 went out to storm the dragon king's palace, his adventure ended in failure). But here, the search is portrayed a little differently. The narrator does not have to rely on the Buddha to discover his treasure; he relies on his own instinct and (presumably) his newfound resolution to find it. Perhaps Hanshan here manifests an awareness of the characteristic Zen emphasis on self-reliance and personal responsibility in practice. In any event, this mode of searching fits well with the idea that he should be looking after his own state, and not "counting others' jewels." The result is a successful quest, the acquisition of the treasure that results in a permanent awareness of transcendence.

At this point, our barbarian enters the poem. In Tang China, blue-eyed foreigners can signify a number of things. For those hostile to Buddhism, the Buddha himself was a foreigner; for the Zen movement, their founder

Bodhidharma was an Indian foreigner (and Zen writers emphasize that fact as a part of their iconoclastic rhetoric). Of course (as this poem suggests), foreigners were often merchants, and were often noted for their skill in bargaining as well as their interest in obtaining exotic or unusual goods. In this case, the primary purpose of the foreigner's presence is to indicate the extraordinary value of the Buddha Nature, as something that even foreign merchants would try to acquire. It is not impossible, however, that Hanshan introduces this subtle reference to a non-Chinese merchant in order to refer back to one of the other themes of the poem, the futility of "counting others' treasures." If Buddhism is considered merely a doctrine that can be studied through reading translations of foreign texts, then it is somehow alien to native practitioners; what good could it possibly do someone in China? But finding one's own Buddha Nature *is* native, close to home; it is digging a hole in your own backyard. It has nothing to do with exchanges that might be carried out with mysterious aliens. When the narrator replies, "This gem is beyond all price," the term he uses for "price" *(jiashu)* contains within it the word "to count"—the exact word he used when he said he was "counting others' treasures." The Buddha Nature cannot enter into the economy of exchange; it cannot be "owned" and so cannot be given away.

The Moon

Anyone familiar with Chinese Buddhist literature (especially Zen literature) would hardly be surprised to learn that the moon features prominently in the Hanshan collection. There are various reasons, both doctrinal and psychological, for the popularity of moon imagery. While any source of light could be a metaphor for wisdom, ultimate truth, or enlightenment, the moon is more dramatic than others: it sheds light in the midst of darkness; it can actually be observed (as opposed to the sun, which is too bright to observe directly); and its constant cycle of waxing and waning can provide additional metaphors related to the changeable qualities of human nature. Moreover, the moon can be seen reflected in surfaces (especially water), allowing for metaphors suggesting illusion, secondary reality, and Impermanence.

While the Hanshan poems usually evoke the moon for atmospheric purposes, hanging it in the sky to create an atmosphere of loneliness and reclusion, there are a handful of poems where it most definitely has an allegorical significance. Perhaps the simplest of these poems, HS 51, is also the one that has garnered the most interest among later readers, especially Zen masters:

吾心似秋月,	My Mind is like the autumn moon,
碧潭清皎潔。	In a jade-green pool, clear and bright.
無物堪比倫,	There's nothing to which it can compare,
教我如何說。	So what would you have me say?

Simple though it is, this poem offers some problems in interpretation. The opening couplet (as rendered here) may describe the reflection of the moon in the pool, since the pool is unlikely to be bright by itself. Also, the flickering nature of the moon's reflection, though filled with light, can be seen as exemplifying the essentially "empty" nature of our minds, even if they are attuned to an ultimate reality behind illusion. However, the syntax does not demand this, and in fact the poet may simply be comparing his mind to two *separate* things—bright moonlight and clear pond water.

As Xiang Chu's commentary to this poem attests, it inspired a substantial number of responses from later Zen masters.[21] There are many reasons for this. First of all, it is short and epigrammatic: as a five-syllable quatrain, it has the shortest acceptable form for an independent verse in the Chinese poetic tradition. Such poems became increasingly popular among Zen monks in the following centuries, and they often used this precise form to express enigmatic truths, adopting the Sanskrit term *gātha* to describe them. They are particularly common as "deathbed" poems, in which the monk means to encapsulate his wisdom in pithy form before he passes into nirvana. Later readers would have seen this verse here as a very specific statement of Hanshan's view of reality, one that could be evaluated and discussed in comparison to verses by other Zen masters. Second—as we saw in chapter 2—Hanshan's own poems occasionally encourage the reader to "decipher" the deeper meaning of the verse. HS 141 suggests that to the wiser reader, the poems provide a sort of rebus that holds the key to superior knowledge, a knowledge that moves beyond surface meaning. Hanshan thus provides a challenge to his readers, and hints that they should not be content with an initial response. Third, Hanshan had the audacity to begin the verse with a bald assertion in the form of a simile; in the world of Zen discourse, where critiques of duality were common and simplistic views of reality discouraged, he seems to be inviting refutation and competition from later masters. I think it likely that many later masters responded to it in imitation of the most famous poetic exchange in the Zen tradition, the one between Shenxiu and Huineng in the Platform Sutra. The unenlightened Shenxiu composes a quatrain that, like Hanshan's poem, proposes a simple simile to describe the mind:

身是菩提樹,	The Self is a Bodhi Tree,
心如明鏡臺。	The mind is like a stand for a bright mirror;
時時勤拂拭,	Constantly strive to polish it,
勿使惹塵埃。	Don't let any dust alight!

Huineng replies with a reassertion of nonduality:

菩提本無樹,	Bodhi originally has no tree;
明鏡亦非臺。	And the bright mirror has not a stand.
本來無一物,	Originally there is nothing at all,
何處惹塵埃。	So where could the dust alight?[22]

The temptation for a Zen master to play Huineng to Hanshan's Shenxiu must have been irresistible. This would not necessarily mean that such a master would consider Hanshan as unenlightened, as Shenxiu is usually portrayed. Rather, Hanshan would be seen as providing an opening gambit, initiating a new episode in the never-ending competitive dialogue on nonduality and the striving for enlightenment that characterizes Zen literature in general.

Finally, the poem was likely to provoke responses because even at its simplest level it leaves itself open to misunderstanding. The Song dynasty intellectual Hong Mai (1123–1202) wrote of this problem in one of his collections of philological notes: "People have said, 'Since his mind is like an autumn moon and a jade-green pool, why does he then go on to say that there is nothing that compares with it?' Probably he meant that if there *weren't* those two things for comparison, what would he have been able to say? Readers ought to assume *that* in seeking the meaning of the poem."[23] If Zen responses to the poem are any indication, Hong Mai's comment was an unconvincing attempt to smooth over an obvious difficulty in interpretation. The fact that this difficulty concerns communicable speech (or lack of speech) made it even a more satisfying target. Hakuin, for his part, shows an awareness of the need to reconcile the poem's seeming paradox:

> He says that his Mind in meditation is lofty, at ease, perfect and bright, just like an autumn moon, which is completely radiant without a single spot or flaw to mar it. But even though the autumn moon has no flaw, it is merely a silver plate that rises and sets; and so he rejects that metaphor. He then compares his mind to a jade-green pool, gleaming, bright, and pure down to its very depths. But even though the jade-

green pool is gleaming, it has enclosing hills and limiting embankments all around it; and so he rejects *that* metaphor. Then he gazes all around him, and finds that there is nothing else he can use as a comparison. That is why he says, "So what would you have me say?"[24]

A sampling of Zen responses shows the way in which readers manipulated the problems inherent in this poem's mind-moon simile. Taken together, they offer a marvelous demonstration of the act of Buddhist reading, each individual practitioner hearing the words of the bodhisattva differently and attempting to solve their mysteries.

First, from the conversations of the prominent Song dynasty master Hongzhi Zhengjue (1091–1157):

> Master Hanshan says: "My Mind is like the autumn moon, / In a jade-green pool, clear and bright." This merely indicates that it is bright like an autumn moon—I'm afraid this is still not right. He also says: "There's nothing to which it can compare, / So what would you have me say?" That is, "Since there's nothing, then why should I speak?" And so he *says* this. This is no good, no good at all. This sentence is also unacceptable.
>
> Rather, call the mind far-reaching, unsurpassed, lodging in nothing, not finding lodging in any particular place—that is the pervasive Mind. How would it be in any particular place? It is pure, naked, dispersed everywhere, not pausing anywhere.[25]

Though Hongzhi doesn't compose a poem as a direct challenge, he does pick the individual images apart, just as Huineng did to Shenxiu's verse. First, he protests the limited nature of the simile—that the only basis for comparison is the brightness of both things. Second, he takes Hanshan to task for talking about the fact that something need not be talked about. Finally, he expresses what the Mind is *really* like, which, not surprisingly, is not really anything. Hongzhi plays with the verb "to lodge" *(ji)*, which is often employed to describe the process of making a simile or a metaphor: one "lodges" the object in the thing that resembles it. Hongzhi thus suggests that just as the Mind has no set abode, so it resists all form of comparison.

The late Song master Shouning Daowan chooses to express his critique of Hanshan in the form of an eight-line poem:

古人見此月,	The ancients saw this moon,
今人見此月。	The moderns see this moon.
此月鎮常存,	This moon always has existed,
古今人還別。	While ancients and moderns part.
若人心似月,	If a man's "mind is like the moon,
碧潭光皎潔。	In a jade-green pool, clear and bright,"
決定是心源,	The moon must be the *source* of the mind.
此說更無說。	Nothing more to say about it![26]

The mind of the individual, says Shouning, is nothing like the moon—people die and are born and are Impermanent, while the moon is always above us. If one wants to compare the moon to something, it is to the *source* of the mind, that is, the source of reality that is behind everything. Of course, Shouning is deliberately misunderstanding Hanshan here, since Hanshan's conception of Mind is not the Impermanent phenomenal mind, but the Buddha Nature itself; Shouning is probably using his critique as an excuse to remind his disciples of this fact, and not accept a facile reading of the original verse.

Finally, we have an excerpt from a sermon by the late Ming master Zhanran Yuancheng (1561–1626), who also critiques the moon simile, but from the opposite direction:

> On the Mid-Autumn Festival, the Master ascended the Hall [and spoke]:

吾心比秋月,	"'Say that the Mind is like the autumn moon—
秋月有圓缺。	The autumn moon will wax and wane.
世間無比倫,	Nothing to compare with it in the world,
教我如何說。	So what would you have me say?'

> "Well then! They say that Old Man Hanshan was an avatar of Mañjuśrī. Then how could he be so close-mouthed so that he couldn't say anything? He took a path off into the mountains, daring to measure himself against the Ancients. So I'll compete with him myself and give you a two-couplet *gātha*:

吾心非秋月，	“My Mind is not an autumn moon;
秋月有盈缺。	For an autumn moon will wax and wane.
萬物有無常，	All things in the world possess Impermanence;
這個不生滅。	But *this* neither arises nor perishes.”[27]

Here, Zhanran taunts Hanshan-Mañjuśrī for his inability to expound the teachings of wisdom—precisely the purpose of this particular bodhisattva. It is up to Zhanran to take over the position and “clarify” the message. Note that he misremembers the Hanshan original (he is probably recalling it from memory); conveniently so, because he invents an aspect of the simile that was never there to begin with, the idea that the Mind, like the moon, waxes and wanes. As a result, he makes a critique that is the precise opposite of Shouning’s: the mind is not like the moon because it is in fact permanent (that is, the Buddha Nature is), while the moon is changeable and unreliable. As this range of critiques suggest, whatever aspects of the moon are discussed, Zen masters exploited them in order to engage the short Hanshan poem in a dialogue that lasted for centuries.

Two other poems use the moon as a symbol for the elucidation of doctrine, and both of them suggest that the poems themselves need to be transcended by the practitioner. Of some importance here is a favorite Zen metaphor, derived from the Śūraṅgama Sutra:

> The Buddha told Ānanda: “All of you continue to listen to the Teaching with a mind attached to karmic conditions. As a result, the Teaching also is conditional, and you will not obtain its Nature. It is like a person showing the moon to someone by pointing at it with his hand. The person being shown on the basis of the finger ought to be able to see the moon; but if he looks at the finger, taking it for the moon, he will not only mistake the moon but will also mistake the finger—all because he mistakes the indicating finger for the bright moon. And not only will he mistake the finger—he will fail to distinguish darkness from light. That is because he takes the finger as the nature of the bright moon, and so will fail to understand the individual natures of light and darkness.”[28]

Of the two poems, HS 279 uses more philosophic language to discuss the moon:

巖前獨靜坐，　I sit in lone silence before the cliff,
圓月當天耀。　While the round moon glows in the sky.
萬象影現中，　All images flicker within its light,
一輪本無照。　Yet that single wheel never shines at all.
廓然神自清，　In vacancy a spirit, clear in itself,
含虛洞玄妙。　Filling the void, a hollow mystery.
因指見其月，　Follow your finger to see that moon:
月是心樞要。　The moon is the pivot of the Mind.

This poem shows a particular love of paradox, emphasizing the degree to which the moon illuminates everything through its nonexistence. Line 3 reads literally as "the reflection-shadows of ten thousand *xiang* manifest themselves in the midst [of the moonlight]." "Ten thousand *xiang*" (phenomena/images) is a phrase that emphasizes the illusory, projective nature of samsara (it is also used in HS 204, discussed above); the poem also associates them with "reflections/shadows" (*ying*), a general noun used to describe visual effects produced by light. All in all, we have a line meant to emphasize that the moonlight makes the world more illusory, rather than less, exposing its figments to our sight with the ultimate purpose of doing away with them. The reason for this, the next line suggests, is that the moonlight itself is illusory and possesses no absolute existence, and for that reason it can reveal the truth of the world in general. The last couplet evokes the tripartite move of the metaphor of the finger pointing to the moon: our mental process in understanding all of this shifts from finger to moon to Mind, and thence to the transcendence of the teaching itself.

The remaining moon poem, HS 287, uses plainer language to make its point. In many ways, it embodies typical Zen rhetoric as it came to be recognized in the modern era. If one had to pick one Hanshan poem that could be labeled "Zen" as it is now popularly understood, it would be this one:

高高峰頂上，　High up, on the top of the peak:
四顧極無邊。　Infinite in all directions.
獨坐無人知，　Alone I sit: no one knows I'm here;
孤月照寒泉。　A lonely moon shines on the cold stream.
泉中且無月，　But there is no moon in the stream;
月自在青天。　The moon's right there, in the night sky.
吟此一曲歌，　And as I chant this single song:
歌終不是禪。　At the song's end, there is no Zen.

Many readers familiar with Tang poetry will read this and think of a famous quatrain of Wang Wei's, "Lodge within the Bamboo" (Zhu li guan):

獨座幽篁裏，	Alone I sit in remote bamboo thicket
彈琴復長嘯。	Strumming my zither, whistling long notes.
深林人不知，	Deep in the forest—no one knows I'm here.
明月來相照。	The bright moon comes and shines on me.[29]

There are definitely some similarities between the two: the solitary sitting, the moon shining, the assertion in both cases that no one knows of the poet's presence. Wang Wei entertains himself with activities characteristic of a well-educated gentleman-recluse, playing the traditional *qin* (a zither-like instrument cultivated by the elite) and engaging in a form of hygienic breath control practiced among Daoists (here, inadequately translated as "whistling"). Hanshan, on the other hand, is sitting in meditation. When the moon arrives in the Wang Wei poem, it possesses a certain aesthetic grace that completes the genteel scene. The moon in Hanshan's poem is a manifestation of Mind, summoned by the effort of practice. Instead of aiming its light at the poet (thus accompanying him in his solitary plight and providing a revision to the proposition "no one knows I'm here") it instead shines on the stream, which allows the speaker to draw a typical Zen-like insight about the necessity of not mistaking a reflection of the moon for the moon itself. Not only that, but the poet ends with a neat self-referential gesture: just as the reflection of the moon is not the real moon (it is merely, metaphorically, a finger), the poem that Hanshan is chanting is not true Zen meditation, but only a reflection of it. This insight arrives in the last line, just in time for the mini-sermon to end in silence, which will become the true sermon.[30]

Ladies

There is one small body of poems in the collection that seems genuinely out of place, no matter how one interprets its origin or its purpose. It describes the activities of attractive women from a voyeuristic male perspective, without the slightest hint of deeper philosophical profundity. These verses can be distinguished from a number of other poems that do describe the sexual attractiveness of women, but then go on to emphasize that beauty fades with age, thus using female beauty as an ideal example of Impermanence (two of these, HS 13 and 14, were discussed in chapter 3; HS 170 is another example).

Rather, these poems suggest an attention to other aspects of the feminine, one that seems at odds with Buddhist practice, at least as seen from a certain Buddhist misogynist viewpoint in which female sexual attractiveness is to be avoided at all costs.

It is of course a very old theme in Buddhist religion, that women are a threat to (male) practice. The origins of the belief stretch back to significant elements in Indian myth: ascetics are frequently distracted from generating meditative power by beautiful women, who are sometimes employed as weapons for precisely that purpose. The most famous example in early Buddhism are legends surrounding the Buddha's breakthrough under the Bodhi tree: the god of samsaric suffering, Māra, sends his daughters to seduce him, in order to prevent him from saving the world through the insight he would win. Examples of women as manifestations of samsaric temptation are unfortunately far more common in Buddhist literature than examples of them as agents free to pursue their own enlightenment. It was also generally accepted that individuals incarnated as women were paying off karmic debts, and that women could not achieve nirvana in their own lifetimes. Mahayana, in its attacks on dualistic thinking, undermined this position to some extent, and there are some famous counterexamples in its literature: the goddess in the Vimalakīrti Sutra who turns the Buddha's disciple Śāriputra into a woman in order to illustrate the illusive nature of gender divisions, for example; and the "Devadatta" chapter of the Lotus Sutra, which describes the young daughter of a *nāga* king, who achieves enlightenment when she hears instruction from Mañjuśrī (though even in her case, she briefly has to incarnate as a man before she can attain Buddhahood). Generally speaking, traditional Buddhist attitudes lean towards the misogynist, and there is nothing in the Hanshan poems that show any explicit sympathy for women in general or for female practitioners.

Our interest here is in a number of poems that are mildly erotic in content and not Buddhist at all, and how a Buddhist reader might account for their presence, even though they suggest the disruptive element of female seduction.[31] Let us begin with HS 23, probably the most extraordinary of the group:

妾在邯鄲住，	I, your handmaid, live in Handan city,
歌聲亦抑揚。	And I soar through the notes of my song.[32]
賴我安居處，	Tarry here in this place of leisure!
此曲舊來長。	This tune has always lasted long.

既醉莫言歸，	And when you're drunk, don't speak of home—
留連日未央。	The day lingers—it's still not late.
兒家寢宿處，	My house is also a place of rest—
繡被滿銀牀。	With embroidered sheet on silver bed.

There is no mistaking it: this is an invitation verse from a prostitute. At first she lures the customer with her singing and invites him into the brothel for drinking and entertainment. Then, when he's drunk, she insists he stay the night and brings him to her bedroom.

Since this is the only poem in the Hanshan collection obviously written in the voice of a woman (the pronoun in the first line signifies this), we might pause to think about the possibility of allegorical readings. It is true that the *bhakti* devotional tradition in India did produce forms of poetry in which spiritual relations were eroticized and in which the voice of a courtesan-prostitute is prominent, but this was not common in Chinese Buddhist verse.[33] The Chinese tradition included an allegorical habit of eroticizing political poems, in which ignored statesmen or bureaucrats write themselves as spurned concubines or imperial consorts; but again, this seems odd in the Hanshan context, even if we accept the poems as autobiographical. Hakuin, plainly thinking the problem needed to be reconciled, ventures into largely unchartered waters:

> By "I, your handmaiden," Hanshan is referring to himself. "Handan" indicates that he himself originally possessed a home. "And I soar through the notes of my song" means that there is only One Vehicle of perfect sound, that should be sung to people of varying capacities, both those superior and inferior; its clever subtlety is like a song that follows one's thoughts, high and low. "This tune has always lasted long" means that there has never been any other tune from every sort of Tathāgata, from Bhiṣma-garjitasvara-rāja [The King of Awe-Inspiring Sounds] of the past right to the present day.[34] "And when you're drunk, don't speak of home, / the day lingers, it's still not late": All sentient beings are deeply intoxicated from drinking the evil wine of the Five Impure Ages.[35] The Buddhas with their numerous skillful means attempt to lure them out of their current mindset, which will not seek liberation. In the burning house they remain, thinking that their long night of suffering is merely half a day—and not realizing that the fire is coming at them from all directions. "A place of rest": Within the halls of enlightenment,

among its furnished dwellings, all tastes are accommodated, like a thousand layers of painted silk sheets. The "silver bed" is the carriage all of white in the open air, driven by a white ox.[36]

The song of the courtesan is the preaching of the Buddha—always the same, always perfect, though tailored in its melodies to the capacity of each individual. Hakuin inverts the invitation to stay, turning it into a description of the deluded instead: "Though already drunk, they don't speak of going home, but linger there, through half the day." Finally, he relocates the action of the poem to a new home outside the Burning House, one equipped with luxurious furnishings. The sheets become a symbol for the joys of existence in nirvana, and the bed is the One Vehicle, driven by a white ox.

If Hakuin bravely takes on the challenge of making HS 23 about the Dharma, he largely gives up on the other poems in this genre, occasionally making comments that Hanshan is being too profound or puzzling for easy comprehension.[37] Most of these are sensuous descriptions of women engaged in activities in the open, usually gathering flowers. In two of them, HS 50 and HS 61, ominous weather or the presence of flirtatious males threatens to disrupt the outing. One could argue that Impermanence is sneaking into these two poems through the distress caused by a threatening male presence, with its hint of sexual seduction or assault. However, I think that is stretching matters, and not even Hakuin, with his penchant for allegory, attempts to make such a reading here. The poems really do not seem to go beyond vignettes with mild erotic connotations.[38]

But then we come to HS 62, a poem quite similar to HS 61 in its opening, but with a bizarre ending:

群女戲夕陽,	A bevy of girls play in the sunset;
風來滿路香。	A wind comes, filling the road with their scent.
綴裙金蛺蝶,	Skirts embroidered with golden butterflies,
插髻玉鴛鴦。	In the coils of their hair, jade mandarin ducks.
角婢紅羅縝,	Pigtailed maidservants in red silk aprons;
閹奴紫錦裳。	Court eunuchs in purple brocade robes.
為觀失道者,	They've come to watch the man who's lost,
鬢白心惶惶。	Going gray, uneasy in his mind.

Unlike the women in HS 61, these are most definitely court ladies. They are gorgeously attired, and they have maids and eunuchs in attendance. But what are we to make of the last couplet, with its mysterious and anxious stranger? The women do not come simply to visit him, but rather to *watch* him, with a disconcertingly subversive female gaze; the verb *guan* usually implies a certain objective distance between the one who sees and what is seen.

It is impossible to provide any definitive solution for how these poems are to be read in a Buddhist manner. I suspect that most readers who read the collection in a Buddhist sense largely skipped over these or, like Hakuin, decided there was some mystery here too deep to fathom. But I would like to suggest one Buddhist theme that might have some resonance with these poems, and that might have affected such readers, at least on a semiconscious level.

In one of the most famous *jātaka* tales, the Buddha's past incarnation is a holy man by the name of Kṣāntivādin (Pali: Khantivādi; the name means "sage of forbearance"). One day he is meditating in the royal park of the local king precisely when the king decides to have an outing with some female entertainers. In the midst of the revelry, the king becomes drunk and falls asleep in the lap of one of the girls. The entertainers, seeing their chance for a bit of freedom, decide to roam the park. Soon they encounter the ascetic. "As the women were wandering around they saw him and said, 'Come here ladies. Let's sit down and listen to something from the recluse sitting at the roots of the tree until the king wakes up.' So they went and paid respects to him and sat in a circle around him. 'Please tell us something that is worth listening to,' they asked. The Bodhisatta taught *dhamma* [Sk: *dharma*] to them."[39] Shortly after, the king wakes up. Learning that his entertainers have all gone off to attend upon an ascetic, he storms off in a rage. He confronts Khantivādi and asks him what he is teaching. When the sage replies "forbearance," the king proceeds to sever his various limbs from his body in an attempt to force him to surrender his greatest virtue. Khantivādi remains steadfast, and later dies of his wounds. At that moment the earth swallows up the king in punishment for his horrific deed.

The women are an intriguing aspect of this narrative. Though the tale does not make it explicit, it is their interest in the sage that enrages the king. He feels sexual jealousy as they transfer their rather frivolous and sensual attention from himself and the flowers to an ascetic's sermon. A more poetic and elaborate version, found in a Sanskrit retelling, describes the singing girls at much greater length, suggesting that they themselves are an erotic force of nature:

> As they rambled about with typical restlessness, the confused jangle of their jewelry mixed with the sound of their chatter. Behind them came their maids, bearing the umbrella, fly whisk, throne, and other insignia of royalty, all brightly decorated with gilt. Deaf to their maids' protestations, the women rushed up and greedily picked from the trees any blossom that was within easy reach, and the tender shoots as well. Though they themselves were covered in flowers woven into wreaths and ornaments, if they encountered on their way a bush with pretty flowers or a tree with trembling buds, they could not pass it by without greedily stripping it.[40]

This mad female tornado of flower-stripping desire is tamed by Khantivādi's example, and this the king cannot stand. It is their conversion that triggers the significant events of the tale. Here women are viewed ambivalently, to say the least: they are capable of listening to the Dharma and subduing their passions; but in the end, since they are things that can be possessed (*either* by the king *or* by Khantivādi, who in his own way espouses them), they cannot avoid becoming the subject of a property dispute.

The bevy of ladies in Khantivādi also mimic the daughters of Māra, a potentially disruptive force to the spiritual practice of an ascetic. Those troublesome daughters appear in the fourth chapter of the Vimalakīrti Sutra. The bodhisattva named "Upholder of the Age" is describing an earlier encounter with the lay bodhisattva Vimalakīrti:

> Once I was residing in a quiet room when Pāpīyas[41] came to visit me in the guise of Indra, king of the gods, accompanied by twelve thousand heavenly maidens, strumming on instruments and singing. He and his retinue bowed low to my feet, clasped their hands together with respect and stood at one side. I mistook him for Indra and said to him: "Welcome, Kauśika![42] Although you are possessed of good karmic virtue, you ought not to act willfully, but should observe the Impermanence of the Five Desires[43] in order to seek out the roots of goodness, taking advantage of your body, life, and wealth to cultivate the unyielding Dharma." He then replied, "Upright one! Please accept these twelve thousand heavenly maidens, who may attend upon you." I said: "Kauśika! Do not press upon me these unlawful things, I who am a monk and a son of Śākyamuni Buddha. It is not suitable for me to accept." Before I had even finished speaking, Vimalakīrti entered

> and said: "That is not Indra. It is a demon who has come to vex you." He then said to the demon: "You can give *me* the women; it is suitable for one like me to take them." The demon, terrified, replied, "Are you trying to make trouble for me, Vimalakīrti?" He then tried to vanish but found that he could not, no matter how hard he exerted his supernatural powers. Suddenly a voice could be heard in the sky: "Pāpīyas! If you give him the women, you will be able to leave." The demon was frightened; looking all around him in perplexity, he finally surrendered them. Vimalakīrti then said to them: "Since the demon has given you to me, you should now all set your minds on obtaining the highest unsurpassed enlightenment."[44]

Vimalakīrti then preaches to the maidens. But Pāpīyas has not completely given up:

> "I now wish to return with you to my Heavenly Palace." The women replied, "We have experienced the joy of the Dharma with this layman; and so great is this joy that we no longer wish to delight in the Five Desires." The demon said to Vimalakīrti: "Will you surrender them? It is befitting of a bodhisattva to give all he owns to others." Vimalakīrti replied, "I have already surrendered them. All of you depart now! And may you cause all sentient beings to fulfill their Dharma vows." Thereupon the women said, "How can we reside in a palace of demons?"[45]

Vimalakīrti then reassures them that the teaching that they have received is an Inexhaustible Lamp, a lamp they can carry back with them to their demon palace, keep lit, and transfer to others. In that way they can maintain their virtue in the midst of evil. With that, the chastened devil and the ladies depart.

The anecdote is a good example of the sutra's humor. Like Khantivādi, Vimalakīrti seduces the women of a king, using the Dharma; but unlike the former case, which ended in jealousy and horrific violence, here it turns ridiculous. First, we have the bodhisattva Upholder of the Age, who is too clueless to see that the supernatural being visiting him is actually a demon, bent on destroying his virtue; as a consequence, he is reduced to moralizing bluster. Then Vimalakīrti calmly shows up and offers to take the maidens off his hands. The demon, rendered powerless by the layman's powers, can only get his ladies back and return home by reminding him of the obligations of a bodhisattva to practice the Perfection of charity *(dāna)*. Vimalakīrti graciously agrees to this proposition. Meanwhile, the maidens, who have "experienced the joy of the Dharma with this layman" find themselves totally uninterested in the joy of conventional vice, and fear that they will fall back into old ways if they return to their palace. They only agree to depart when given reassurance that they can keep their virtue there, and even spread what they have learned. In this narrative, women still largely lack agency, but the text subverts their traditional role as an incentive to lust and violence by satirizing it.

It is not impossible that Hanshan readers would be familiar with some of this material. The Khantivādi *jātaka* had been translated quite early,[46] and its popularity in general made it a likely candidate for oral circulation; there is a significant allusion to it in the Diamond Sutra. The Vimalakīrti Sutra was, of course, well known to the average literate Buddhist. My point here is not that Buddhist readers would have thought of these two stories as the direct source of the Hanshan erotic poems. Rather, they would have been conditioned to have certain expectations when confronted with large groups of potentially unruly women, especially if they were out picking flowers or generally presenting their seductive side. Such women are dangerous but also convertible to the Dharma; and in the case of the Heavenly Maidens of the Vimalakīrti, they may in fact be a positive force in disguise, yet another skillful means that might be opening an erotic path to enlightenment.[47] Such a reading might be the solution to the enigmatic ending of HS 62, in which the women confront "a man who's lost, / Growing gray, uneasy in his mind." Either he is a descendent of Upholder of the Age, helpless in dealing with a serious challenge to his virtue, or he is a genuine lost soul, and the women have come to save him.

In light of this, let us conclude with HS 35, which bears an uncanny resemblance to the Khantivādi *jātaka* in its depiction of girls rioting in the garden:

三月蠶猶小,	Third Month, when silkworms are still small:
女人來采花。	Women come out to pluck the flowers.
隈牆弄蝴蝶,	Leaning on walls, they toy with butterflies,
臨水擲蝦蟆。	At water's edge, tossing things at the frogs,
羅袖盛梅子,	Gathering up plums in the sleeves of their robes,
金鎞挑筍芽。	Digging up shoots with their golden hairpins.
鬪論多物色,	Playing games, they make much of beauty:
此地勝余家。	"This place is way better than home!"

CHAPTER 6

SATIRE

What emotion is represented most often in the Hanshan poems? In spite of their modern reputation for eremitic Buddhist transcendence, we might very well choose "anger." On the surface, this seems quite surprising. Anger is (along with ignorance and desire) one of the "three poisons" that are responsible for suffering in the world. However, we must be careful not to equate Buddhism only with the mindful serenity that tends to attract the most attention among modern Western practitioners. It makes a great deal of sense that the Hanshan poems would frequently resort to anger, because they draw upon an earlier Buddhist rhetoric of condemnation as well as upon Chinese secular forms of critique. From these sources grows a stance of righteous indignation, the sort of position that has been associated in the West with the genre of satire. Related to this, we find laughter as well—not genial laughter, but the laughter of scorn, employed as a skillful means to educate the benighted.

Two Buddhist traditions contribute to the expression of anger in the Hanshan corpus. On the popular side of things we have minatory literature: warnings against sinful activity that will result in the generation of bad karma and rebirth in the "three evil paths" (the animal realm, hungry ghost realm, and hell realm). This fire-and-brimstone tone can be seen in the Tang-era poems attributed to the legendary Wang Fanzhi that were discovered at Dunhuang. In earlier chapters we have seen this tone emerge when Hanshan talks about the inevitable bad karma generated by living the life of a householder, especially if one eats meat.

Second, the Chan culture that was evolving at the same time the Hanshan poems were composed often embraced antagonism and violence in order to compel self-reflection, personal striving, and the breakthrough characteristic of satori. Literature espousing this type of aggression was popular in the Linji/Rinzai tradition of Zen, the lineage to which Hakuin belonged. Those who have read Hakuin know that he often takes on a particularly stern and unforgiving voice when attacking tendencies of Zen practice with which he disagrees; it may have been a similarly cranky quality in the Hanshan poems that he found attractive. For Hakuin, no one benefits from leniency or a failure to enforce correct doctrine rigorously. It is possible, then, to see indignation and fury as qualities suitable for popular Buddhist rhetoric as well as for elite Zen discourse. Anger is also connected to the "antinomian" strain in the Chan/Zen tradition, with its enlightened practitioner who deliberately acts in an offensive or contemptuous manner in order to jar believers out of their conventional (and, consequently, lazy) moral stance.

From the secular point of view, Hanshan is also inheriting a long-standing tradition of poetry meant to criticize social ills. Literary historians trace this genre to a kind of folk poetry expressing the common people's outrage at government policies (usually taxation and military conscription) that emerged around the second or third century CE and which came to be imitated by educated poets shortly thereafter. Such verse, usually referred to as "music bureau" poems (*yuefu*, after the government office supposedly tasked with the purpose of recording them for the emperor's consideration) tended to evolve into nonpolitical forms; the label could be applied vaguely to any poem that seemed folkish in style. Still, educated Confucian males continued to return to this early tradition when protest of public policies was called for (in the Tang, this is seen most prominently in the work of Du Fu [712–770] and Bai Juyi [772–846]). The Hanshan poems draw upon this tradition of righteous anger as well.

However, the Hanshan corpus deviates in interesting ways from this precedent. It is worth noting that while mainstream literati poets like Du Fu and Bai Juyi wrote social protest poems, they wrote them within an implicit autobiographical frame—later readers assumed that specific policies of the time triggered strong emotions in the poets, who then felt a compelling need to express themselves. Later readers were usually not so much interested in the critique of the policies expressed in the poems as they were in the uprightness of the poets in choosing to write about such topics. In this light, protest poems remain focused on a hermeneutics that embraces self-expression and the desire of a reader to know the poet. As we have seen, many modern readers have chosen to read Hanshan in such a light, and they too would prefer to see the subjects that earned his wrath or sorrow as somehow intimately connected with his own life story; it makes him more human. However, it is much more likely that the anger in the Hanshan poems is a quite deliberate pose, not an expression of personal emotion. The poems, as a manifestation of a bodhisattva-like perspective on the evils of samsara, are meant to elicit our own indignation rather than to demonstrate the authenticity of the emotions of a human poet: premodern readers often kept Hanshan's identity with Mañjuśrī uppermost in their minds. Critiques in such a reading are thus not so much a form of self-expression as a form of fictional staging (once again, a skillful means) meant to elicit our moral response.

Hanshan's targets are various, as are his methods. We will begin by looking at a particularly unusual method: the use of animal parables to lampoon folly. Then we will look at the groups that most often arouse his anger and contempt: scholars, the wealthy, and Buddhist monks.

Animal Parables

Though the use of animals to illustrate moral principles is not uncommon in traditional Chinese literature, it is rather unusual in elite poetry, probably because of the expectation of autobiographical self-expression.[1] Hanshan's occasional use of the form provides us with further evidence of the nonconventional nature of his verse. We have already seen a number of these poems: the parrot of HS 12, the deer of HS 293, and the dog and deer of HS 152. In HS 39 we encounter yet another parable, one that satirizes Daoist alchemical practices in a novel way:

白鶴銜苦桃,	White crane holds a bitter peach in his beak;
千里作一息。	He rests once every thousand miles.
欲往蓬萊山,	He wants to go to Penglai Mountain,
將此充糧食。	And this he took as his provender.
未達毛摧落,	But feathers snapped and fell before he arrived,
離群心慘惻。	And his heart grieved as he lost his flock.
却歸舊來巢,	Home he returns, to his nest of old,
妻子不相識。	Where wife and children fail to know him.

Hanshan plays with conventions of Daoist literature, in which Transcendents *(xian)* are often said to ride cranes or to have the power to turn into them, especially after they have cultivated the alchemical and hygienic arts that grant them eternal life. The crane here, obviously a fanciful substitute for a real Daoist practitioner, aspires to immortality, and so he is set on traveling to Penglai, the mythical isle of the Transcendents located somewhere in the ocean east of China. Peaches too are traditional symbols of immortality, cultivated by the Queen Mother of the West, a Daoist goddess residing on Kunlun Mountain. However, this crane carries with it on its journey a "bitter peach," not a peach at all, but an entirely different fruit that merely resembles it.[2] This gives us a hint that his quest is doomed to failure, much like the merchant-adventurer's quest of HS 199.

As the crane flaps home at the end of the poem, we are left to wonder what exactly is the meaning of the last line: why are his wife and children unable to recognize him? Hanshan seems to be playing on a number of folktale themes. A reader might be reminded of a popular Daoist story that had been in circulation since at least the fourth century CE, and which was well known to Tang poets:

> Dingling Wei was a native of Liaodong. He studied the Way at Lingxu Mountain. Afterwards he transformed into a crane and returned to Liaodong, where he roosted on the ornamental pillar by the city gate. At that time a youth drew his bow, preparing to shoot him. The crane then flew off. It hovered in the air and recited:

有鳥有鳥丁令威，	"There's a bird, there's a bird, Dingling Wei!
去家千年今始歸。	He left his home for a thousand years, and only now comes home.
城郭如故人民非，	The city's the same as of old, but everyone's different.
何不學仙塚壘壘。	Why not study Transcendent arts? Tomb is piled upon tomb."

> He then flew high up into the sky.[3]

Dingling Wei masters the arts of immortality while studying on a magic mountain that shelters him from passing time. As a result, when he emerges in his crane form, he discovers that centuries have elapsed. This is, of course, a fairy-tale motif found in many cultures: in China, it includes the story of Liu Zhen and Ruan Zhao, who have a brief love affair with mountain goddesses at Tiantai and then go home, only to discover that ten generations have passed.[4] Even more famous is the Japanese example of Urashima Tarō, who spends several days at an undersea dragon palace and then turns into an old man upon his return to shore. In the case of Dingling Wei, however, the passing of time only accentuates his own triumph over death; he departs this world forever, warning that those who remain should study Daoism as well, or be trapped in a world where "tomb is piled on tomb."

On the other hand, attacks on Daoist alchemy were common in poetry, and they occur a number of times in the Hanshan corpus.[5] This crane poem places such an attack within a powerful narrative frame and undermines the trope found in the Dingling Wei story by inverting it. The crane labors to achieve immortality and to join the gods on Penglai, but has to return home an aged failure whom his family fails to recognize. This poem also echoes another, rather melancholy Hanshan verse, HS 134:

昨夜夢還家，	Last night I dreamt I went home again,
見婦機中織。	And saw my wife weaving at her loom.
駐梭如有思，	She stopped her shuttle, as if lost in thought;
擎梭似無力。	Held it there, as if too weak to go on.
呼之迴面視，	I called to her—she turned her head to look—
況復不相識。	And she didn't know that it was me.
應是別多年，	I guess we've been parted for so many years,
鬢毛非舊色。	And my hair's not the color it was.

We are not told why the narrator has been away from home for so long, but his return here, possible only in a dream, is like the crane's: both poems speak to the fear of failure and of growing old, of being separated from a home life that should have provided meaning. Both suggest ambitious men who have lost families because of this ambition. Their change into unrecognizable entities also speaks to the inevitability of Impermanence, which the crane has failed to halt with his Daoist practice.

HS 34 is the most peculiar of the animal fables:

兩龜乘犢車，	A pair of turtles in a calf-drawn carriage
驀出路頭戲。	Drive out to the road to have some fun.
一蠱從傍來，	A *gu*-beast then comes up beside them,
苦死欲求寄。	Desperately wants them to give him a ride.
不載爽人情，	Inhumane not to let him climb up;

始載被沈累。	But if they do, big trouble for them!
彈指不可論,	Snap your fingers, don't bring it up.
行恩却遭刺。	If you're kind, you'll suffer harm.

The *gu* was a legendary monster said to be created by humans for the sake of poisoning their enemies. It required placing a hundred venomous creatures into a jar and leaving them alone for a lengthy period of time. They would then devour each other; the victor, the *gu*, was particularly deadly, since it had consumed its poisonous companions. It would be then fed to unsuspecting victims, within whom it would take up a parasitic existence, eating its way from the inside out. Certain families supposedly made a living raising these creatures and selling them to assassins. A variant text reads "scorpion" for *gu*, but the latter seems more appropriate if Hanshan wants to create the most extreme dilemma for the poor respectable turtles. There is also a possible pun in line four: *ku si*, "bitter death," an idiomatic expression that can simply mean "desperately," here has a slightly more poignant resonance, granted the petitioner. One might also note that in the last line, the expression *zao ci* can bear two meanings. It can mean "suffer harm/injury," which would imply that the *gu* will bring physical harm to the carriage drivers. However, it can also mean "receive criticism," which would suggest that the turtles will suffer society's condemnation for daring to be kind to a social pariah.[6]

Regardless of how the last line is read, one can easily interpret this poem as an attack on altruism, or at least on wrong-headed altruism. However, if readers desire to see its message as consistent with the Buddhist compassion common in other poems, they might seek ways to make it less hardheaded and hardhearted. Hakuin suggests that we have a criticism of naïve bodhisattvas here; he also goes to great lengths to explain other elements of the poem:

> This poem instructs practitioners by telling of a bodhisattva at the initial stage of his development, when the strength of his capacities is still slight. From ancient times turtles have been symbols for *prajñā* [wisdom]. The Biography of Shitou in *Eulogies for the Orthodox Lines [of the Five Houses]* says: "His Eminence Shitou one day had a dream that he was traveling through a deep pool on the back of a turtle with the Sixth Patriarch [Huineng]. When he awoke, he interpreted: 'The magic turtle was *prajñā*. The pool was the Sea of the Sages.'"[7]

> Moreover, the two turtles represent the twin teachings of *samādhi* [meditation] and *prajñā,* as well as the performance of the twin bodhisattva vows to benefit oneself and others. When a bodhisattva whose capacities have matured carries out these twin vows, he rides a great carriage drawn by a white ox in order to profit all sentient beings. But now because the bodhisattva in question has not yet perfected his capacities, the poem speaks of driving a "calf-drawn carriage." "Driving out to the road" is the equivalent of "entering the market with extended hands."[8] "A *gu*-beast then comes up beside them" represents a single condition of external disturbance.[9] Because the practitioner who receives it is still weak, he will be unable to manage it and instead will generate emotions that will bring harm to the Way. This is the "big trouble." "If you're kind, you'll suffer harm" is like someone who wishes to rescue another who has accidentally fallen into the water. Because his strength is weak, he will end up drowning with him.[10]

The moral of the poem is not that helping others will endanger oneself, but rather that an inexperienced bodhisattva will not have the capacity needed to really do good. Hakuin draws rather cleverly on other elements of the Buddhist and Zen traditions, alluding to the superior ox-carriage of the Burning House parable, as well as the famous ox-herding pictures, and tying these to the poem's "calf-drawn carriage" in order to emphasize the relative naiveté of the turtle-bodhisattvas.

It should be noted that none of these fable poems alludes back in any clear way to the poet's own condition; rather, they all seem to satirize a general vice or an unfortunate life situation. As we shall see, this distanced, satiric perspective continues in other poems.

Hapless Scholars

Elite Chinese literature was largely the product of educated males interested in participating in the governance of the state, who often wrote of their frustration in failing to achieve eminent positions. We have already noted this theme in the "blasted tree" poems of chapter 5. When elite writers consider the difference between the poor and lowly as opposed to the wealthy and high-ranking, they usually place themselves self-righteously in the former category, suggesting that in a corrupt world only those who are impoverished can claim a moral high ground. For them, inequality of wealth is not a societal ill per se; rather, the wrong people are wealthy.

The Hanshan poems occasionally take this position as well. One prominent example is HS 187—which is nonetheless striking for an ambiguous ending that fails to show a clear preference for the nobility of failure:

客難寒山子,	A guest scolded Master Hanshan:
君詩無道理。	"Your poems make no sense at all."
吾觀乎古人,	"But I've observed the men of old:
貧賤不為恥。	To be poor and lowly is no shame."
應之笑此言,	He answered: "I find your words amusing.
談何踈闊矣。	And your speech is really wide of the mark!
願君似今日,	I think it best for you to be modern:
錢是急事爾。	Money's really the important thing."

Behind this poem is a context of changing circumstances in the Tang dynasty. As the government-administered civil service examination became more widespread, a large group of moderately affluent men aspired to office through the examination route. However, their chances for success often depended upon the favorable attitude of examination administrators, who were often familiar with the talent or connections of examinees beforehand and could make sure that the "right sort of person" passed. One way for a man to get noticed was to establish a reputation as a writer gifted in fashionable genres of literature—of which regulated verse was a noted example. In this case, the visitor chides Hanshan for his failure to write poetry in a form that would provide him with a successful career and the wealth that would come from official advancement. He is contemptuous of Hanshan's suggestion that poetry as a form of moral expression for its own sake has any value, sounding much like a modern career guidance counselor leading an idealistic student away from a major in the humanities. What is disturbing about this poem—and makes it unusual in comparison to similar debates in other Chinese texts—is that Hanshan has no answer. Ultimately, the poem's silence implies, anyone who does the right thing as far as poetry is concerned had better be ready for a life of poverty.

However, this embrace of noble failure is unusual in the collection as a whole. Much more common is Hanshan's contempt for young men who desperately try to pass the examinations and fail, setting themselves up for a lifetime of uselessness. He stands at the very beginning of a satiric tradition in Chinese literature that would last for over a millennium, and which would culminate in such works as Wu Jingzi's great eighteenth-century novel, *An Unofficial History of Scholars* (Rulin wai shi). What's more, from a Buddhist perspective, the theme potentially has an additional element of critique: the pursuit of worldly studies for the sake of wealth and power is useless in comparison to embracing the Dharma.

Four of Hanshan's poems in particular lay out a pathetically amusing career for a scholarly youth. HS 113 begins the sequence by giving the youth's reaction to his first exam failure:

書判全非弱,	I did well in Judgments and Penmanship,
嫌身不得官。	But I failed because they hated my looks.
銓曹被拗折,	The Civil Board sure cut me off;
洗垢覓瘡瘢。	They scrubbed me down to look for scars.
必也關天命,	But if it's all because of fate,
今冬更試看。	This winter I think I'll try again.
盲兒射雀目,	If a blind guy shoots at a sparrow's eye,
偶中亦非難。	Eventually he'll score a hit!

Anyone who wants to read this poem autobiographically, imagining that it comes from early in Hanshan's life when he still sought an official position, is missing out on a cleverly conceived fictional vignette. This poem captures perfectly the frustration of any student who has failed an examination but still holds out hope for the "next time."

Tang examinees were judged in several categories. One of the essay assignments was often a "judgment" *(pan)*, asking the examinee to express his judicial opinion on a legal matter. Calligraphy was evaluated as well, as was personal deportment. Here the examinee explains to his hearer that he did well enough on the written part, but that the part he had less control over, his personal appearance, killed his chances. He then complains about how picky the Board of Civil Office was in evaluating him, using a slangy metaphor in the process. But he proceeds to decide that it isn't the examiners who are really to blame, but his own fate, and that he can always try again. The last couplet is particularly poignant: it may be acceptable as a proverb to indicate that anything can happen at least once, but as a rule on which to base exam performance, it seems rather questionable.

Next comes HS 120. Our examinee has taken the examination several times now and is starting to become rather pathetic:

箇是何措大,	Who is that poor old bookworm there
時來省南院。	Who's come to take the South Court exam?[11]
年可三十餘,	He must be over thirty now,
曾經四五選。	And this is his fourth or fifth time!
囊裏無青蚨,	No "blue beetle" cash in his sack,
篋中有黃卷。	His satchel full of yellow books.[12]
行到食店前,	And when he passes the food shop,
不敢暫迴面。	He doesn't dare to turn his head!

The poet outlines a number of comic traits by which an impoverished scholar can be known: he is growing a bit too old to take the exams, his purse is empty, and he is carrying a pile of books around with him. We see a satiric method in use that is quite common in Western literature as well, the descriptive caricature. The balance and brevity of the four-couplet poem works quite well for this type of writing: an opening couplet mentions the target, middle couplets define him with a few brushstrokes, and the conclusion ends with an action that epitomizes his nature. Rather than feeling sorry for him in his hunger, we are meant to feel amusement—he has brought this on himself by continuing to remain obsessed with his hopeless examination goals.

The next poem, HS 129, uses another satiric weapon, sarcasm:

雍容美少年,	How stately is the lovely youth
博覽諸經史。	Who reads broadly in Classics and Histories!
盡號曰先生,	For all will call him "doctor,"
皆稱為學士。	And everyone names him "scholar."
未能得官職,	He's yet to get an official post,
不解秉耒耜。	And he cannot guide a plow.
冬披破布衫,	All winter he wears a tattered shirt:
蓋是書誤己。	I guess his books have fooled him.

The opening begins with a series of clichés that make us expect a poem in praise of an ideal type. Perhaps only the emphasis in the second couplet that he is *given* titles by those who admire him (instead of asserting that he *is* those things) drops a hint to us that this is show and not reality. We then swiftly learn that he has not achieved the one position that this book-learning is supposed to acquire for him, and that he has no practical skills. The poem ends with the same bald disenchantment of HS 13, the poem in which the beautiful woman is turned into a piece of pressed sugar cane. For Hanshan, learning acquired with the expectation of achieving wealth and power is undependable, because it is connected with vanity and arrogance. The fine titles of "doctor" and "scholar" are applied to a starving man in a tattered shirt. Perhaps reading the sutras (or Hanshan's poems themselves) would have been more useful.

Finally, HS 99 gives us a whole community of worthless poets:

蹭蹬諸貧士,	Struggling along, those poor scholars,
飢寒成至極。	Hungry and cold beyond endurance.
閑居好作詩,	Nothing to do, so they like writing verse:
札札用心力。	They grind away with all their brains.
賤他言孰采,	They're nobodies—so who will notice?
勸君休歎息。	But I suggest you don't sigh about it!
題安餬餅上,	Write your verse on a sesame cake:
乞狗也不喫。	Even a dog wouldn't take it from you.[13]

Our starving poets are clinging to the cultural capital of their education by writing poems, in the hope either of attracting patronage, or simply of achieving some fame among their peers. But because they have no particular social status, no one is interested in what they have to write. The satirist offers them a sarcastic consolation: disabuse yourself of any hope of winning an audience, for even dogs won't eat your unsolicited poems; they're too indigestible. In light of the self-consciousness of the collection as a body of "useful" poems, as we saw in chapter 2, this verse has a double edge. It can be seen as the poet's response to the critic in HS 187: it is in fact secular regulated verse that proves to be profoundly useless, while Hanshan's poems, though misunderstood and scorned, provide true wisdom and advantage to the "elite," understanding readership.[14]

In the Tang era, it was still fairly common to treat examination candidates with sympathy; the unhappiness and trauma caused by failure was a powerful theme in Tang literature. Consequently, the degree of contempt expressed in these poems is somewhat surprising, and suggests a poet who saw himself as outside literati circles. He is not necessarily dismissive of education, as HS 129 might suggest to some; rather, he detests the connection Tang literati made between education and worldly ambition.

The Evils of Wealth

Though Hanshan may satirize scholars who embrace poverty in order to pursue an unlikely success, he tends to see the divide between rich and poor in starkly realistic terms. He understands full well the sufferings caused by poverty. In HS 174, for example, he portrays the starkness of indigence: "A storage jar often empty of rice / And a kettle that tends to collect dust." In contrast to this stage of constant want, the wealthy hoard their wealth, indifferent to the sufferings of others. This is somewhat different from the standard Buddhist rhetoric addressed to the rich: typically, they are reminded that their wealth is a result of good karma in a previous life, and are warned that if they do not show compassion in this existence (and earn good works by giving generously to the poor and the church), they will be reborn in a life considerably less pleasant. However, this usually doesn't involve a condemnation of the rich *per se*; wealth inequality is part of the natural order. The following Wang Fanzhi poem is typical:

世間日月明,	Sun and moon glow bright in the world;
皎皎照眾生。	They shine upon all living things.
貴者乘車馬,	The high-born ride in horse-drawn cart,
賤者膊擔行。	While the lowly walk shouldering burdens.
富者前身種,	Wealth was planted in a former life,
貧者慳貪生。	Poverty arose from stinginess.
貧富有殊別,	The poor and wealthy have their differences,
業報自相迎。	In response to karmic repayments.
聞強造功德,	He who listens well earns future merit,
喫著自身榮。	Glorying in what he eats and wears.
智者天上去,	The wise will ascend to a heavenly realm,
愚者入深坑。	While the foolish fall into a deep pit.[15]

It would be difficult to find a more simplistic view of karma than the one expressed in this poem: not only is rebirth in Heaven or in Hell determined by one's previous life, but so are wealth or poverty, starving or eating well. The poem warns against stinginess as a principal karmic cause for future suffering, so that one can read it mostly as a warning directed at those who are close-fisted in the present. Still, it is difficult to avoid the conclusion that this poem accepts the status quo, as exemplified by the metaphorical sun and moon of wisdom that shine and illumine our futures from above: karmic rules regulate all human activity with predictable accuracy, and the way things are is a manifestation of that rightness.

In comparison, many of Hanshan's poems bring a welcome cynicism to this complacency. For example, HS 126 describes a man forced to borrow grain from his neighbors:

新穀尚未熟,	The new grain has yet to ripen,
舊穀今已無。	And the old grain is now used up.
就貸一斗許,	I go out to borrow a measure or two,
門外立踟躕。	And I dawdle outside their gate.
夫出教問婦,	The man comes out, tells me to ask the wife;
婦出遣問夫。	The wife comes out, sends me back to her man.
慳惜不救乏,	Stinginess won't help the needy,
財多為累愚。	And too much wealth just makes you stupid!

The humor of this poem lies partially in its tone of intimacy—the speaker is addressing a fellow member of the lower orders, and both of them are showing their unmitigated contempt for the arrogance of the rich. No obsequiousness here!

In HS 151, a man fallen on hard times castigates a friend for his selfishness and ingratitude:

是我有錢日,	Back in the day, when I had cash,
恆為汝貸將。	I always gave you what you asked.
汝今既飽暖,	And now that you're all fat and warm,
見我不分張。	When you see me you won't share.
須憶汝欲得,	You've got to know that when *you* wanted,
似我今承望。	It's just like *me* who's begging you now.
有無更代事,	Sometimes you have stuff, sometimes you don't—
勸汝熟思量。	I think you'd better think hard about that.

This is one of the most doggerel-like of the Hanshan poems, yet it conceals an effective barb. While Wang Fanzhi posits a stable world of karmic justice, Hanshan emphasizes a world in flux, where Impermanence makes things wildly unpredictable. Identities and statuses collapse amid the constant change, and the differences between "you" and "I" are redefined from moment to moment.

Other satires on the wealthy are fictional vignettes, typically in the same style as the poems on poor scholars. HS 104:

富兒會高堂，	Wealthy lads meet in the high hall,
華燈何煒煌。	Where ornamental lamps glow bright.
此時無燭者，	Just then a man without a candle
心願處其傍。	Comes, hoping to stay at their side.
不意遭排遣，	Who would have thought they'd throw him out;
還歸暗處藏。	He goes home to sit in the dark.
益人明詎損，	It's no less bright to help someone—
頓訝惜餘光。	Surprise! They begrudged the extra light.

Hanshan is partially rewriting an anecdote from the Han-era *Biographies of Virtuous Women* (Lie nü zhuan):

> A woman of Qi, Xu Wu, was an impoverished wife from the eastern sea district of Qi. She would participate in candlelit work sessions held by a neighboring wife, Li Wu, in which women would engage in spinning in the evening hours. Xu Wu was the poorest, and she was unable to contribute to the cost of candles. Li Wu said to the association members, "Xu Wu has failed to contribute candles. I move that we exclude her from the group."
>
> Xu Wu then said, "What are you saying? Because I'm poor and am unable to contribute candles, I've always started my work early and have stopped later than the rest of you. I've done the straightening up and have set out the mats, serving in attendance on everyone else. I take the thinnest and most worn-out mat, and I always sit in the lowest place. And that's all because I am poor and do not contribute any candles. Now if this room had one more person in it, the candles wouldn't be any darker for all that, and if you took one person away, they wouldn't get any brighter. Why should you begrudge the abundant light within your walls and not let a poor lady accept some of it? Wouldn't it be permissible for you to be gracious in recognition of my labors, and for all of you to extend your kindness to me on my behalf?"
>
> Li Wu could not respond to this, and so they allowed her to remain in the group and said nothing more about it.[16]

There is a significant difference here between the poem and its source. In keeping with its role as a conduct book for females, the *Virtuous Women* tale emphasizes a moral and ethical balance: Xu Wu does not deserve light simply because she is a human being; she does so because she takes up her share in the distribution of women's labor. She is a member of the "deserving poor" and does not hesitate to launch into a self-righteous defense of her position. In the Hanshan poem, we have instead a poor man who wants to enjoy the light given off by a party of the wealthy. Their only possible reason for throwing him out is sheer mean-spiritedness; they do not have even the excuse of Li Wu, who at least could claim that Xu Wu was not contributing the necessary capital to make their enterprise a success. Hanshan is not interested in determining who deserves what in society's economy. He is simply concerned with compassion, human dignity, and the casual cruelty of the rich. The focus of this poem is not merely their selfishness, but also the shame they inflict on the poor man.

In most of these poems we see a sharpness of wit and a disregard of conventional social niceties. Because the Hanshan corpus is likely to come from a non-Confucian source, we rarely sense the disapproving Confucian moralist behind his poems: there is no hint of belief in a social moral order that *should* be functioning, if only the right people were in power or the emperor were heeding the call to virtue.[17] This gives the poems a refreshing edge that is missing from most elite Tang poetry that purports to deal with social problems. Perhaps only Du Fu was able to achieve the same quality of genuine anger and sarcasm untouched by sanctimony.

The Guileless Fool

Words for "fool" or "foolish" (*yu*, *chi*, or the compound *yuchi*) occur forty-three times in the poems. Many of the poems I have discussed so far include condemnations of the foolish, and by this point it may be redundant to discuss them further; anyone perusing the collection can discover many more examples for herself.[18] However, before discussing anticlerical poems, we need to touch on the occasional verse that portrays the ideal practitioner as a sort of guileless fool, or at least as someone who escapes the pitfalls of excessive cleverness. This ideal has its origins in the early Daoist classics, in which simplicity or stupidity is held up as an ideal quality. Here, the fool appears as a sort of variant on the antinomian trickster considered in the preface. For example, HS 289 seems to be narrated by a sort of wise simpleton who maintains his purity:

我住在村鄉， A tiny town is where I live,
無爺亦無孃。 Without a dad, without a mom,
無名無姓第， Without a name, without a clan,
人喚作張王。 And people call me Zhang or Wang.[19]
並無人教我， And no one's ever taught me things,
貧賤也尋常。 And poor and base I'll always be.
自憐心的實， But I love the Real that's in my mind—
堅固等金剛。 It's firm and tough as diamond.

The narrator lacks all of the things that give someone an identity in medieval China: parents, clan affiliation, education, wealth, and status. Like the withered tree examined in the last chapter, the speaker's identity is brought down to its most essential element, the Buddha Nature—which is in fact the only thing that actually exists. Though the narrator is not laughing explicitly at the foolishness of others, the critique is implied.

Another, less radical poem, HS 25, has the narrator locating himself in a sort of intermediate space between secular fools one the one hand and overly clever believers on the other. Perhaps the latter are Buddhist cultivators who depend too much on doctrine and philosophical interpretations of the scriptures:

智者君抛我， Wise Ones, you have cast me off;
愚者我抛君。 Foolish Ones, I have cast you off.
非愚亦非智， Neither a fool, nor am I wise:
從此斷相聞。 From now I will hear no more of either.
入夜歌明月， When night comes I sing the bright moon;
侵晨舞白雲。 And at dawn I dance the white clouds.
焉能拱口手， How am I to still my hand and mouth,
端坐鬢紛紛。 Meditate with my hair undone?

This poem is rather attractive for biographical readers: the speaker seems to be rejecting life both as a member of secular society and as a monk, thus making him resemble the preface's description of Hanshan. He also reinforces the concept of nonduality by denying identification with either camp. In the second half of the poem, he claims to celebrate nature rather than engage in formal meditation: how can he mediate properly as a monk without a shaved head? He is too restless to turn himself into a piece of dead wood, like the sage of HS 155.

A less lovely but "biographically" interesting poem is HS 275:

憶得二十年,	I remember twenty years ago,
徐步國清歸。	When I wandered back to Guoqing Temple;
國清寺中人,	And the Guoqing Temple monks
盡道寒山癡。	All said that I was a fool.
癡人何用疑,	Why should they hold a fool in doubt?
疑不解尋思。	They fear he won't know how to think.
我尚自不識,	But if even I don't understand,
是伊爭得知。	I hardly think that *they* would know.
低頭不用問,	So I lowered my head, no use to ask—
問得復何為。	For what could come out of asking?
有人來罵我,	People came to abuse me then,
分明了了知。	And that's when I understood it at last!
雖然不應對,	And though I gave them no reply,
却是得便宜。	I benefitted from it all.

There are some problems in interpreting this poem. I will give my own reading here, while acknowledging that others may disagree on some details.

This poem describes Hanshan as developing his own sense of wisdom somewhat passively, under the assault of outside forces. He is not the confident, antinomian troublemaker portrayed in the preface. The verb "return" *(gui)* in line 2 seems to imply that the speaker is actually a monk at the Guoqing monastery, or at least is living there on a semiregular basis—again, somewhat at odds with the preface's account. In any event, his time there proves to be a disaster: his fellow monks think him a fool, and suspect him of being unable to understand any of the Dharma. At this point, however, he starts to suspect *their* authority: if he can't "get it," he doubts that anyone else is "getting it" either. There is a nice ambiguity in line 7, which could mean either "If even I don't understand [it] myself" or "If even I don't understand myself." He may think that his fellow monks neither comprehend him nor comprehend his own capacity for understanding. His reaction to this is to turn passive-aggressive: he refuses to ask any questions of his superiors, because he has ceased to have any faith in them or their answers: he will receive no benefit from them.

What *does* bring him illumination, however, is the abuse he receives from his fellow monks, who think he is a fool. Xiang Chu argues that the poem is meant to embody the Perfection of Forbearance *(kṣanti)*, much like the *jātaka* tale of Khantivādi discussed in the last chapter.[20] Perhaps, but this is very much at odds with at least the perceived personality of Hanshan—we cannot imagine him putting up with abuse from anyone. Rather, there is a sort of koan dynamic going on here. The abuse of the monks provides him with a challenge that forces him to confront his own understanding; this in turn results in a kind of satori. His response, ultimately, is silence and departure. As HS 25 phrases it, "From now on I will hear from neither [the Wise or the Fools]." He is now the outsider who can challenge the world that surrounds him, both the secular world with its greedy householders, impoverished scholars, and vain fools, and the monastic world. This is one of the classic ways in which his antinomian stance inverts the direction of humor. Poems like HS 221 (translated in chapter 5) visualize how the ignorant see him, and how they laugh at him or think him mad: "When people these days see Hanshan, / All of them say he's a madman." But the joke's on them—the very persona he projects and that they find risible is a test, and the laughter of ignorance is countered with the laughter of wisdom.

Anticlerical Satire

SD 24 provides us with a sheep allegory:

躑躅一群羊,	Wandering about, a flock of sheep;
沿山又入谷。	Following hills, entering valleys.
看人貪博塞,	But their shepherd's fond of gambling games,
且遭豺狼逐。	So they end with wolves on their trail.
元不出孳生,	They were never meant to be their prey
便將充口腹。	But end up filling maw and gut.
從頭喫至尾,	From their head down to their tails,
飩飩無餘肉。	They're gobbled up with nothing left.

It is unlikely that the poet merely wanted to give us a warning about lazy shepherding. This is pointing to some deeper meaning. But what?

If one is reading as Hakuin would, one might conclude that the poem describes inattentiveness in meditation, which will result in the disturbance of one's practice with disastrous results. This might have been a quite likely interpretation among serious believers. However, a Western reader might happen to think of Christian imagery involving pastoral care, the obligation of priests to look after their charges. This theme emerges occasionally in the

Western literary tradition, even in satiric contexts.[21] There are good reasons to see SD 24 as a similar anticlerical satire, in this case on Buddhist monks.

It is worth recalling the social position of the sangha during the Tang dynasty. How might a devout lay Buddhist of the time characterize the role of the sangha in relation to the larger world, as opposed to each member's private cultivation of the Way? Certainly the sangha's main role involves ritual: sutra recitations for the well-being of the living and dead, as well as the performing of ceremonial rites for the protection of the state and for the prevention of natural disasters. The transference of merit would certainly be significant as well: monastic activities could be pledged to the benefit of sentient beings (or, in practical terms, of the lay believers who paid for the activity). A number of occupations not necessarily Buddhist in origin came to be associated with the sangha also, such as medicine; certainly in many cases devout and educated believers would be invited to attend sermons on the dharma or to discuss doctrinal issues. There was also a significant monastic presence at public festivals, usually of a ritual nature, the most obvious being the Ghost Festival in the summer, when the sangha's power was channeled for the salvation of lay ancestors who had been reborn in one of the evil paths.[22] Monks in turn were generally supported by one of three groups: the government, wealthy families and the nobility, and the general population.

This seemingly ideal system was almost immediately subject to abuse. Gifts and support from both rulers and elites put a massive amount of wealth at the disposal of monasteries, which then engaged in a number of profitable enterprises: money-lending, the expansion and exploitation of agricultural lands, milling, and textile industries. As Jacques Gernet has discussed at great length, this made the economic power of the sangha during the Tang omnipresent, as well as a matter of great concern: not only among anti-Buddhists, who were concerned over the exploitation of the empire's resources by a faction that they saw as fundamentally alien, but also among many believers, who saw such activity as a self-evident violation of the Buddha's original guidelines for monastics.[23] This situation produced numerous critiques of the priesthood that sound quite familiar to readers of Western medieval literature. Gernet quotes at length a passage from an apocryphal Chinese scripture that purports to describe the world in the "latter days of the Dharma," when the Buddha's teachings are in decline. It is obvious that contemporary abuses are being described:

They will clothe themselves in religious habits but their conduct will be unscrupulous like that of laymen. Some will engage in commerce in the marketplace in order to enrich themselves. Others will traffic by the roadside for a living. Others again will ply the trades of painters and artisans. Others will devote themselves to the arts of divination and physiognomy and predict good and evil fortune. They will inebriate themselves, disturb the peace, sing and dance, and make music. Some will play chess and the board game *liubo*. There will be *bhikṣu* who will preach false teachings to please the people. There will be those who shall pretend to be devotees of Dhyāna [meditation] even though they be incapable of concentrating their minds. They will prophesy the future on the basis of texts that falsely claim to be canonical. Some will practice acupuncture and apply moxa. They will proffer all kinds of potions and cures in exchange for food and clothing. Under these conditions, laymen will have no respect for the Law.[24]

Among the vices castigated here are gambling games like *liubo*—very likely the game played by the incompetent shepherd in SD 24. It is this attack on frivolous activities that likely makes this poem an anticlerical assault. Throughout the Hanshan and Shide poems, we see a constant concern with monastics not fulfilling their roles and perpetrating fraud. For example, HS 286:

世間一等流，	There's a kind of person in the world
誠堪與人笑。	Who really has to make you laugh:
出家弊己身，	"Leaves the household," brings harm to self;
誑俗將為道。	"To con the people" is his Way.
雖著離塵衣，	Though he wears the garb that transcends dust,
衣中多養蚤。	His garb is the breeding ground for lice.
不如歸去來，	Better far just to go back home,
識取心王好。	Discern the virtue of the King of Mind.

Here, the poet cleverly juxtaposes "leaving the household" *(chu jia)*, the standard term for becoming a monk, with the non-Buddhist phrase "go back home," a locution that took on strong secular eremitic connotations after it was used as the title of a poem by Tao Qian. Rather than join a religious order, wouldn't it be more valuable to go into personal reclusion and cultivate the Buddha Nature (the King of Mind) within oneself? At least when you are cultivating the Way as a hermit, you will not turn the deception of the common people into the goal of your practice! The poem also ironically alludes to clerical garb: though it marks its wearer as someone who has transcended the dust of samsara, it has become filthy with vermin—the poor hygiene of monks became an increasing topic for satire in later Chinese writing.

A number of Shide's poems elaborate on specific aspects of clerical abuse. SD 37 alludes to the habit wealthy families had of supporting monks as unofficial, private chaplains:

後來出家子,	These latter-day household leavers
論情入骨癡。	Are stupid right down to the bone.
本來求解脫,	At first they looked for liberation
却見受驅馳。	But now just rush from place to place.
終朝遊俗舍,	All day they frequent laymen's houses,
禮念作威儀。	Making a show of their chanting rites.
博錢沽酒喫,	When they get their money, they go buy wine,
翻成客作兒。	Acting just like some hired hand.

In Shide's view, the monks' defining spiritual mission—which obtains its efficacy from their freedom from social obligations and pressures—has been incorporated into a patron-client system. In the end, such monks are no better than hired hands, drawing a salary and spending it as any member of the working class might, as they rush back and forth indulging in the very excesses that destroy their practice. Not only their spiritual but also their economic independence is threatened. The opening line suggests that this represents a falling away from a supposedly earlier period when monks were more virtuous: we are living, it implies, in a period characterized by the decline of the Dharma.

These critiques probably helped to advance Hanshan's reputation among Zen believers in later centuries. As the Chan movement in the Song dynasty attempted to interpret its own past, it tended to create and adapt older narratives in ways that supported the distinctiveness of its own school. Eventually this evolved into the romantic version of Chan origins that is still very much part of modern attitudes toward the sect. Supposedly rejecting the desire for wealth and power that characterized the large, urban-based Buddhist groups and embracing a monastic code that emphasized economic self-sufficiency, Chan was a "purer" form of Buddhism that returned to its ascetic (and often rural) roots and was less prone to the vagaries of imperial and aristocratic patronage. The work of more recent Chan scholars has largely shown this vision to be a later creation: Chan's adaptability after the Tang owed a great deal to the patronage of local elites and the reputation that Chan abbots had for administrative competence.[25] Nonetheless, when one reads many of the Hanshan and Shide critiques of the clergy, one can see the idealized attitudes that contributed to later romantic historiography. As semi-outsiders to institutionalized Buddhist practice as embodied in the monks at the Guoqing Monastery, Hanshan and Shide seem to be embracing many of the attitudes that would become cliché assumptions about Zen among Western believers: the dismissal of hollow ritualism; the detestation of financial remuneration for ritual services; and the claim that the Buddha Nature can be manifested by anyone, not just religious specialists. For such readers, it would seem clear that Hanshan and Shide were true prophets of the Zen movement.

We should not let this later and inaccurate perspective prevent us from seeing the broader frame of the poems' critiques. All of these issues were noted by Tang intellectuals, both Buddhist and non-Buddhist, and do not necessarily form a list of grievances distinctive to the Chan movement.

HS 231, for example, seems to be an attack on an antiritualist:

心高如山嶽,	Mind higher than a lofty peak,
人我不伏人。	A striving will that cannot bend;
解講圍陀典,	Able to lecture on Vedic lore,
能談三教文。	Can discuss Three Doctrines texts;
心中無慚愧,	A mind that has no shame at all:
破戒違律文。	He breaks the Precepts and the Rules.
自言上人法,	He speaks of a Law for higher men,
稱為第一人。	Is termed the greatest one of all.
愚者皆讚歎,	The fools all praise his name and sigh;
智者撫掌笑。	The wise will clap their hands and laugh.
陽燄虛空花,	He's a flame or a spot before the eyes,[26]
豈得免生老。	He'll not avoid rebirth and age.
不如百不解,	Better to not understand it all,
靜坐絕憂惱。	Sit quiet and sever your worries.

The attack here is on monastic arrogance; the subject of the poem is an ambitious monk who has mastered doctrines of all kinds, both obscure Indian thought (Vedas) and "the Three Doctrines" (Confucianism, Daoism, and Buddhism). This intellectual competence has led him to believe that he is above the ordinary monastic regulations and that he is privy to a superior Dharma that applies only to himself.

In short, he is a potential antinomian, the sort of "anti-monk" that many have praised Hanshan himself for being. But rather than interpreting this monk's attitude as a sort of necessary corrective to the routinization of the Buddha's message, the poet simply sees an egotist who deceives the fools who listen to him. Perhaps the reason the poet does not approve this as genuine, constructive antinomianism is that the preacher is still operating within the rules of Buddhist cultural capital: he is playing a game whereby he can win attention and glory from wealthy patrons and possibly even the emperor. He is not deliberately violating the precepts because he wishes to demonstrate the dualistic trap into which precepts can lead, and which prevents us from being truly liberated; rather, he is asserting that he personally is above the precepts. Obviously, this sort of mania violates one of the most basic principles of all Buddhism, the nonexistence of the Self—it is perhaps for this reason specifically that he is still subject to karmic suffering and rebirth, as the poem suggests. Nonetheless, the poem does touch on the profound unease the Buddhist tradition had with antinomianism in general, and the difficulty it had in differentiating constructive opposition to its rules on the one hand from self-aggrandizing display on the other (the sort of practice later condemned as "wild fox Zen").

We will close with HS 277, a longish satire on monks, one of two poems (HS 276 and HS 277) that some have mistaken as one very long poem. Its focus is on monks who engage in secular activities, particularly those who exploit the common people:

又見出家兒,	I've seen all those household-leavers:
有力及無力。	Both those with strength and those without.
上上高節者,	The very best, conduct restrained:
鬼神欽道德。	Both gods and ghosts admire his power.
君王分輦坐,	Princes grant him a carriage seat,
諸侯拜迎逆。	And lords will bow to him in greeting.
堪為世福田,	Fit to be the age's Merit Field,
世人須保惜。	The age's men must cherish him.
下下低愚者,	The very worst, most ignorant
詐現多求覓。	Makes great display to gain his wants.
濁濫即可知,	You see at once his muddy thoughts:

愚癡愛財色。	Foolish, in love with wealth and pleasure.
著却福田衣,	He wears the robe of Merit Fields,
種田討衣食。	Plants *real* fields, looking for clothes and food;
作債稅牛犁,	Lends money, takes ox and plow in tax;
為事不忠直。	Crooked and shady in all he does.
朝朝行弊惡,	He practices evil every day,
往往痛臀脊。	And is often beaten for his crimes.
不解善思量,	He can't consider carefully:
地獄惡無極。	Hell's sufferings will have no end.
一朝著病纏,	If you catch a passing illness once,
三年臥床席。	You'll end bedridden for three years.
亦有真佛性,	Yes, he has the true Buddha Nature,
翻作無明賊。	But acts just like an ignorant thief.
南無佛陀耶,	All give praise to Lord Buddha!
遠遠求彌勒。	May you seek Maitreya afar.

In contrast with the main topic of the poem, lines 3–8 describe the ideal, a virtuous monk. He is described as a Merit Field, that is, a source of good karma for all sentient beings. As such, he is a sort of living treasure that must be protected, just as the sangha is one of the Three Treasures of Buddhism.

Much more enthusiasm is spent on the description of the quintessential bad monk, however. Though he may make a show of piety in order to gain his desires, those who look carefully will see through this and realize that he is an endless source of craving. His chief acts of wickedness involve the acquisition of wealth through the exploitation of the peasant class. Though he wears monastic robes that are supposed to make him a "Field of Merit," he is much more interested in real fields that he can have cultivated for their agricultural output. He lends money at usurious interest, and takes oxen and plows as interest or collateral. His continuous wickedness does indeed earn beatings from the authorities (either monastic or secular), but this is not enough to make him think of the evil consequences of his actions, which will doom him to a Hell realm. The somewhat obscure metaphor of illness elaborates on this: even the smallest wicked action can have much greater karmic consequences. The poem ends with a sort of invocation to the Buddha and to Maitreya, the Buddha of the future, perhaps with the hope that their mercy can bring enlightenment to such wicked clerics.[27]

The depth and quantity of anticlerical sentiment in the collection suggests that the monastic orders were a major focus of popular satire in the Tang era (as they very obviously became in the vernacular fiction tradition of later centuries). It might be worth noting as a final comment, however, that much of this satire could actually be classed as a variation on one of Hanshan's principal satiric targets: the wealthy. Though obviously greed is particularly heinous when it arises within a monastery, it is essentially the same sin, whether in the secular world or in a religious community. And like his critique of the secular wealthy, Hanshan's attack on monks is not connected to the mainstream ideological position of Chinese literature as expressed by Confucian literati. Rather, it comes out of a general indignation directed toward social injustice and the exploitation of the powerless.

PART THREE

Reading Buddhists

CHAPTER 7

WHO GETS TO CLIMB THE MATTERHORN?

As we have seen, the poetic voice in the Hanshan poems can be taken as originating with the bodhisattva Mañjuśrī, who is relating a series of fables meant to instruct us in the nature of suffering in samsara and how we might transcend it. Such a reading is rooted in the believer's response to the text; it does not need to imagine a wholly human Hanshan writing of his own experiences. When we are confronted by Buddhist-oriented texts written by actual historical individuals, however, we may wonder whether this same perspective is still possible—especially when those writers are quite obviously attempting to convey their own private experiences. The instructive fictionality of the fables seems to be replaced by autobiography, and the modes of self-expression and confession threaten to overshadow the text's potential to serve as a skillful means that might lead to salvation. This is particularly apparent in the Buddhist-themed works of the Beats; it was precisely their desire to speak honestly about themselves and about their own responses to the society around them that led them to read Hanshan in such a way as well—to the detriment of his poems.

And yet, as chapter 2 argues, a Buddhist way of textual interpretation might take as one of its givens the possibility that the act of reading actually helps us in transcending our illusory sense of self, by allowing us to think as Other. To interpret in such a manner would allow us to reach the fundamental "storehouse consciousness" *(ālayavijñāna)* that underlies the text. That level is not dependent on the historical or biographical specifics of its author for its meaning, though it might take those specifics as part of the text's own causes and conditions. Even an intensely autobiographical work by a modern writer can, when read in that manner, continue to convey a more general knowledge of the experience of samsara. In addition, problematic aspects that such a narrative might contain (internal contradictions, imperfect awareness of the Dharma, and failure to achieve satisfactory progress in practice, for example) do not render the text useless. After all, any account within the bounds of samsara is necessarily imperfect. Our abilities as skillful readers—as Buddhist *zhiyin*—will ultimately confirm its utility. Thus, the way we have been reading Hanshan, which deconstructs him as a biographical Self, might in turn prove useful in our recognizing the universality of any experience in an explicitly autobiographical text.

One case in point is Kerouac's *The Dharma Bums*, the very novel that played such a prominent role in introducing Hanshan to modern American readers. To read the book "as a Buddhist" provides us with some particularly striking insights into the nature of Buddhist faith and practice—the more striking because its portrayal of Buddhism itself is deeply flawed and plagued with contradictions. As we shall see, the narrator's own experiences suggest an attempt to reenact the spiritual pilgrimage of Hanshan, to see the mountain as a literal and figurative dwelling place that will bring him peace and transcendence. Ultimately, that attempt will prove to be futile, not least because it is subject to the same Buddhist critiques that Hanshan applies to human activities in his own verse.

Such an analysis can only work if it grants Kerouac's quest validity in Buddhist terms. Many readers have in fact looked askance at Kerouac's Buddhism, and have wondered if his version of Buddhism is too skewed to deserve that designation. However, recent scholars of Kerouac have seen his beliefs as more complex and nuanced.[1] Admittedly, his understanding was limited by what was available to him in English translations at the time, and like many American Buddhists he largely devised a practice based on his reading and not on study with a recognized member of an Asian sangha. However, to use that as an excuse to dismiss the Buddhist implications of his writing is to treat his efforts with a patronizing superiority they do not deserve. It is important to remember that 1950s enthusiasts had discovered an idealized Buddhism in their reading: a system that promised a sense of fulfillment far beyond that of Western religion, which they considered spiritually bankrupt. Their thinking included very little discussion of the problems of real believers, of the social issues that sangha and laypeople have struggled with for two millennia, or of the intermingling of pious popular devotion on the one hand and philosophical complexity on the other. Many of the Beats were only marginally aware that Buddhism had altered radically from country to country and from culture to culture, and that no one national tradition (or scholarly orientation) had a right to "speak for" Buddhism. The result is often an embarrassing naiveté concerning the practice of the faith in its various forms on the one hand, combined with a highly intelligent awareness of the capacity of Buddhist ideas to question and refigure the concerns of the postwar West on the other. Both factors fueled a romantic rejection of modernity, producing nostalgia for a mythical timeless Asia where an idealized faith supposedly actually existed and functioned; where crazy Zen masters wandered the countryside, bringing enlightenment wherever they went; and where economic simplicity bred a culture of contentment, free from the consumerist pressures of capitalist America.

But could an actual, functioning society absorb such idealistic norms? And could Buddhism succeed in America as long as its believers held practice to such impossibly high standards? To understand this problematic is also to recognize that Buddhism could not become more than an ideal in the writings of the Beats in general or of Kerouac in particular—moreover, an ideal that tended to lose its rigor and distinctive characteristics when it came into conflict with their other ideals, such as freedom from societal constraints and celebration of sensual pleasures.[2] Kerouac remained profoundly uncomfortable with the orientation he developed toward the faith and also constantly questioned his own capacity to live up to it; he was incessantly caught in a dualistic trap, unable to reconcile his tendency toward self-mortifying asceticism on the one hand and self-indulgent excess on the other. By 1960 he had largely left Buddhism behind and retreated to a pessimistic and conservative Catholicism until his death in 1969. Some of the possible reasons for this philosophical and spiritual failure are visible in *The Dharma Bums* itself. Though it is usually read as a celebration of the Buddhist worldview and its inherent superiority over the spiritual emptiness of postwar America, in fact, much of the novel sees Buddhism as a contested space: no one is in agreement about what it is exactly, what it should be, or how it should be practiced. In the midst of this debate Hanshan stands, an elusive model of an ideal Buddhist saint from a distant mythical past: an aspirational figure who, for Kerouac at least, was beyond reasonable imitation.

Buddhist Competition

The structure of *The Dharma Bums* is exceptionally straightforward. In the first section (chapters 1–12), Ray Smith arrives in San Francisco after hitching rides and riding trains from Mexico City. There he immerses himself in bohemian artistic life and makes close friends with the lumberjack-poet-scholar-Buddhist Japhy Ryder. Japhy invites Ray on a hike to climb the Matterhorn, a tall peak in the Sierra Nevada; the climb itself takes up chapters 7–12. In the second part (chapters 13–23), Ray hitchhikes to the East Coast, winters with his mother, sister, and brother-in-law at their house in North Carolina, then hitchhikes back to San Francisco to rejoin Japhy. The third part (chapters 24–34) mirrors the first part: after living with Japhy for several months and enjoying the company of his artist friends, Ray sees Japhy off to Japan (where he will formally study Zen), then proceeds to Desolation Peak in the Cascades range of Washington State, where he serves as a fire-spotter for two months in complete isolation. His experiences there are meant to form the climax of his spiritual journey.

Like Kerouac's most famous novel, *On the Road*, *The Dharma Bums* centers upon the narrator's friendship with a charismatic younger man who mysteriously seems to possess some secret that will make life understandable and worth living in the face of an inevitable mortality. The major difference is that Japhy, based on Gary Snyder, represents an answer that involves intellectual seriousness and self-discipline, as opposed to the sociopathic excess exemplified by Dean Moriarty, the hero of the earlier novel. The intimacy between the two men is shadowed by Ray's own insecurities and jealousies. At the beginning of the novel, Ray presents himself as a Buddhist seeker:

> I was very devout in those days and was practicing my religious devotions almost to perfection. Since then I've become a little hypocritical about my lip-service and a little tired and cynical. Because now I am grown so old and neutral. . . . But then I really believed in the reality of charity and kindness and humility and zeal and neutral tranquility and wisdom and ecstasy, and I believed that I was an oldtime bhikku in modern clothes wandering the world (usually the immense triangular arc of New York to Mexico City to San Francisco) in order to turn the wheel of the True Meaning, or Dharma, and gain merit for myself as a future Buddha (Awakener) and as a future Hero in Paradise. (5)

Ray's vision of Buddhism is largely drawn from the rhetoric of mainstream Mahayana scriptures. At the heart of these scriptures is the ideal of the bodhisattva, the believer who vows to bring all sentient beings to enlightenment. In the passage above, Ray gives a somewhat skewed version of the Six Perfections, a Mahayana listing of the six virtues cultivated by an aspiring bodhisattva: generosity, discipline, forbearance, zeal, concentration/meditation, and wisdom. Tellingly, the one item missing from his list is discipline.

Nonetheless, Ray's vision of Buddhism privileges compassion above all, an essential part of which is humility—the recognition that others may be as far along on the path to enlightenment as oneself, and the desire to learn from them. In the opening scene, he meets a bum riding the boxcars who expresses a devotion to Saint Teresa, with her continuing compassion for the creatures of the earth. Ray acknowledges this as true piety, and the bum as one of the "Dharma bums," a sort of shorthand for down-and-out types whose outlook on life defines them as bodhisattvas in the rough. The vision of Saint Teresa strewing the world with roses is not far removed from Indian Mahayana imagery, which may explain why Ray afterwards engages in a meditation on the infinity of the universe and of its sentient beings as he eats a meal of franks and beans that evening on a beach in Santa Barbara. For Ray, his Buddhist meditation is inextricably linked with the sublimity of Emptiness, with seeing the Buddha's power expand beyond our own frame of reference into infinite stretches of space and time.

Trust in the infinitude of the Buddha's and bodhisattvas' mercy is obviously quite close to Christian belief in God's mercy, and in this early scene Ray is seeing them as much the same—his concept of ritual practice and devotion is often indistinguishable from Christian piety. This makes a collision with Japhy's rather different take on the faith inevitable. Japhy is probably the first person Ray has met who actually knows more than he does about Buddhism, and Ray must decide whether Japhy is a potential authority and teacher from whom he can learn, or someone whose opposing ideology threatens the life practice he has developed so far. His first description of Japhy's outlook highlights at least one of the sources of potential contention. He emphasizes Japhy's knowledge of Buddhist lore: "I warned him at once I didn't give a goddamn about the mythology and all the names and national flavors of Buddhism, but was just interested in the first of Sakyamuni's four Noble Truths, *All life is suffering*. And to an extent interested in the third, *The suppression of suffering can be achieved*, which I didn't quite believe was possible then" (12). Ray claims to be hostile toward mythology, an odd assertion, since his own personal expression of meditative ecstasy often inclines to the florid and sublime; he is much fonder of mysticism than Japhy. The motivation behind this response does not lie in a concern about whether Buddhism should include mythological elements. Rather, Ray is made profoundly uneasy by the fact that Japhy is a more advanced student of Buddhism than he is, and it touches his feared inadequacies. Finally, and most extraordinarily, Ray expresses interest in only the first and third of the Noble Truths. He omits the second, which states that the origins of suffering lie in desire and craving; and the fourth, which gives a blueprint for removing that craving by following a series of disciplinary practices, the Eightfold Path. In other words, Ray ignores the Truths that involve self-analysis and hard work. These are precisely the ones that preoccupy Japhy: the efforts that are necessary to bring contentment in this world, and how they can be implemented.

Ray's characteristic response to Japhy is an odd combination of schoolboyish submissiveness mixed with protest. He expresses hostility to classical Zen, Japhy's sect of choice, condemning it for its excessively cerebral take on enlightenment, while labeling himself both a "serious Buddhist" and a "Hinayana coward" (13). This claim is weirdly contradictory, and betrays a sort of passive-aggressive petulance: in fact, Hinayana is not a proper name for a Buddhist sect at all, but a dismissive term used by Mahayanists to denigrate believers of inferior views; his use of the term here mirrors this Mahayana contempt, but also is worn as a badge of honor. Ray resents the whole Zen mentality, which would ostensibly place intellectual breakthroughs derived from meditation and koan practice above acts of piety and compassion. What perturbs him is the antagonistic, confrontational, often brilliantly intuitive aspects of Zen as exemplified by Japhy; in the 1950s this philosophical and intellectual form of Zen was embodied by the teachings of D. T. Suzuki, rather than Chan/Zen as it was actually practiced in East Asia. Ray fears that Japhy will see his own perspective as inferior, superstitious, and unliberated. But he also finds Japhy's charisma and self-confidence highly seductive. As the novel goes on, he reluctantly accepts many of Japhy's Zen ideas and views him (at least sometimes) as his roshi.

Accordingly, Ray's idealized interpretation of Japhy's personality is heavily influenced by an artistic tradition that tends to portray Zen monks in a distinctive way. We learn a good bit about Japhy's physical appearance throughout the novel: his backwoods way of walking, his slightly bowlegged stance, and, most important, his resemblance to cliché portrayals of amused Chinese sages (11). Shortly after their first meeting, Japhy introduces Ray to

Hanshan himself, and Ray's equation of the two is inevitable. This is made quite explicit toward the end of the novel, right before Japhy's departure for Japan, when Ray has a dream in which he imagines Japhy as Hanshan, envisioning him as a disreputable hobo visiting an ancient Chinese marketplace (208). Japhy is literally outside time, and he embodies a form of Buddhist practice identified with the idealized classic Chan masters of a millennium ago. However, this timeless quality of Japhy's threatens to place his ideals out of reach for someone like Ray, who cannot escape from the pressures of his modern life.

Contrast this with Ray's own insecurities about his beliefs and his inability to teach others; though he is ten years older than Japhy, he feels inarticulate and immature next to him. At one point, he pathetically resorts to his Buddhist teachings in an attempt to reassure Rosie, a young woman who is likely suffering from paranoid schizophrenia. When (not surprisingly) she refuses to listen to his sermon, he reacts with despair; none of his friends and family take his commitment to Buddhism seriously, he concludes, and they insist on treating him as a naïve child (111). That evening, Rosie plunges to her death from the roof, fleeing from the police she is convinced are about to arrest her. Ray believes that her grisly end is a sign of his own personal failure as a proselytizer.[3]

Mountain Pilgrimage

Japhy's forms of practice and enlightenment are even more out of Ray's reach because they are inextricably bound up with the wilderness and environmentalism—most specifically, with mountains. If we step outside the novel for a moment and note some distinctive aspects of the small group of Hanshan poems that Gary Snyder himself chose to translate, we can see this even more clearly. Yuemin He has noticed the tendency of Snyder to emphasize mountain reclusion poems at the expense of the many other themes in the Hanshan corpus.[4] But there is another factor worth noticing. Out of the twenty-four poems that Snyder translates, twenty-one mention Hanshan in the text of the poem itself (Cold Mountain as a location is mentioned eighteen times; Hanshan as a name the poet applies to himself, three times). However, in the 313 poems of the collection, only thirty poems mention the place-name Cold Mountain, and only nine poems refer to the poet by the name Hanshan. This means that when Snyder was selecting poems to translate, he consistently chose poems that actively perpetuated the idea of a specific recluse named Cold Mountain who lived in a place of the same name. The overall effect of his short anthology is to create an assertive poetic ego who is repetitively explicit about his abode and its indivisible connection with his identity as a Buddhist recluse. Gone is the sense of the Hanshan corpus as a lively and detailed representation of human experience, as a toolbox of skillful means; it is instead limited to one countercultural path that embraces nature and reclusion, privileging the aspect of Hanshan that was dismissive of ordinary communities.

It may not be fair to bring this external detail into a discussion of the fictional narrative of *The Dharma Bums*, but granted that Ray reads translations of Japhy's that are essentially Snyder's, it is reasonable to argue that the fictional Ray is making a series of equations in his head: Japhy *is* Hanshan who *is* Cold Mountain. Japhy's identity as a lumberjack raised in the Pacific Northwest becomes a part of his spiritual identity as well. Through this series of equivalences, we end by seeing Japhy as a sort of Buddhist shaman who draws his power from mountains specifically, and who has combined his concept of Buddhism with American naturalism. Underlying these equivalences is the assumption that an ecological sensitivity to Nature is a timeless and universal quality, something that the Tang dynasty Hanshan would have possessed as well as Japhy. Early in the novel, Ray and Japhy discuss HS 28, which would become Snyder's Cold Mountain poem 8 (we have already looked at it in chapter 4).[5] The poem is in the voice of a pilgrim climbing Cold Mountain, likely Hanshan himself. He passes through difficulties and mysteries to obtain the heights. Once there, he invites a fellow practitioner to join him, one who can "transcend the bonds of the world." This is precisely Japhy's invitation to Ray, and will lead to the climb of the Matterhorn in chapters 6–12. As a naturalist-mountaineer-shaman-monk, Japhy has the required knowledge to lead Ray to proper enlightenment.

But mountains are a problem for Ray, because Ray is very much not a naturalist, though he claims to view nature positively. As we shall see in the Matterhorn chapters, he actually is subject to a genuine terror in its presence. This terror emerges often in Kerouac's heroes, perhaps most strikingly in Jack Duluoz's sublimely vertiginous descriptions of the California coastline in *Big Sur*. Throughout *The Dharma Bums*, Ray is attracted to quiet spaces as settings for meditation, but only when they are not too far from human presence: the meadow near his sister's house in North Carolina, for example, or the stretch of desert near the railroad yards in El Paso. Though Kerouac could describe nature with stunningly vivid language, his characters need to have people around them. *On the Road* consists mostly of descriptions of people Sal Paradise meets throughout the country; what fascinates Sal is generally not the terrain itself, but the effect that terrain has on personalities, how it makes a Texan different from a Coloradoan from a Californian from a Mexican. Moreover, Kerouac's form of Buddhist practice—with its constant preoccupation with compassion, concern, and prayer for others—must remain rooted in human society to work. In *The Dharma Bums*, Ray needs to talk constantly about what he is feeling. To accept Japhy's form of eremitism, in which monastic practice becomes a form of mountaineering, means cutting himself off from much of what gives his life purpose. This does not mean, however, that he can practice successfully in the city either; beginning with *The Dharma Bums*, Kerouac creates a series of autobiographical heroes who are constantly trapped between their feeble attempts to find peace in nature and the temptations of an urban existence that drives them further into the vices that will destroy them. Ultimately, Japhy's successful cultivation of a wilderness Buddhism creates for Ray a sort of excuse for his own failure.

Many of the tensions outlined here—Ray's sense of inferiority around Japhy, his competitiveness, his uneasiness around Nature—are figured beautifully in the Matterhorn chapters. It would be easy to see these as superseded by the novel's climax at Desolation Peak, as if the Matterhorn climb were merely a dress rehearsal for the more important performance. But the Matterhorn section is outstanding in its own right, combining vivid natural description with subtle character study; it also genuinely wrestles with Buddhist issues in a way that the ending does not.

The section opens with detailed preparations for the climb. Here, Japhy's position as naturalist-expert takes over, as he provides detailed justification for everything that they take on their hike. Ray essentially makes no distinction between Japhy's role as roshi and his role as mountaineer—he submits to his teacher in both areas, expressing a sort of wide-eyed admiration at every bit of wisdom, even if he disagrees. Exact quantities of food are analyzed and discussed: Japhy explains what bulgur is, which foods are needed for energy, and how good homemade chocolate pudding will taste under the stars. As Ray accompanies Japhy to his shack in preparation for their departure, Japhy continues to lecture on life in the Pacific Northwest and urges Ray to take a summer position as a government fire lookout. He also discourses (as he does throughout the novel) on the shallowness of bourgeois existence, and Ray notes how bohemian and peculiar the two of them must look to others as they walk along. This pose of self-conscious exclusivity occurs several times in this section: Japhy desires to mark them off from commonplace American society, as though they were members of an ascetic fraternity committed to a different way of life, a society consisting of the *zhiyin* of Hanshan.

Japhy's attitude here may point to some of the paradoxes present in Hanshan's poetry itself, which are exacerbated by Japhy's own interpretations about the relationship of Buddhist practice to isolation, to Nature, and to friendship. In chapter 4, we saw that Hanshan rejects various forms of association (even with Shide and Fenggan), arguing that true enlightenment can only occur through acting alone, though he might be tempted by the companionship of the like-minded. Hakuin in turn wanted to see Hanshan reintegrated into a higher, loftier community of bodhisattvas, one that transcended the limitations of more mundane eremitic groupings. Japhy very much wants to create this community; his affection for Ray is a tentative movement toward it. Bohemian friendship has the potential to establish deep spiritual roots: "Chatting of mysteries on a moonlit night, / Or probing principles in a sunlit dawn" (HS 280). But a Shide poem, SD 10, warns that a true *zhiyin* relationship is difficult, especially when there are differences in understanding and interpretation. The fact that there are so many innumerable paths to enlightenment guarantees that we rarely travel together:

有偈有千萬,	There are gathas—millions of them—
卒急述應難。	You can't explain if you're hasty.
若要相知者,	But if you want an understanding mind,
但入天台山。	Then go off to Tiantai Mountain.
巖中深處坐,	Sit in seclusion on the cliffs,
說理及談玄。	Talk principles, discuss mysteries.
共我不相見,	Though if we two don't see eye to eye,
對面似千山。	It's like a thousand hills between us.

Japhy is assuming that Ray and he are traveling the same path up the mountain, but Ray thinks in terms of dualities, constantly dwelling on each quality that makes him different from his friend, and whether it makes him better or worse.

At this point, the third central character in the narrative arrives: the college librarian Henry Morley. He will drive them to the mountain in his car and join them in the climb. It would be easy to dismiss Morley as an inessential clown, a piece of comic relief, but his presence is absolutely vital, and in the end will become as important as Ray's and Japhy's—he plays a sort of Fenggan to Japhy and Ray's Hanshan and Shide. Morley seems to possess two key characteristics: a habit of babbling eruditely but incomprehensibly about everything, and a stubborn desire to do things the way he wants, even if doing so violates the rules of Japhy's mountain expertise. Japhy is exasperated when Morley insists on bringing a string of useless items: a can of chop suey, a rubber air mattress, and a pickax. As they set out for Yosemite and the mountain, Ray regales the reader with further examples of Morley's incomprehensible, stream-of-consciousness monologues, with their references to contemporary politics, medieval literature, and European art history. Morley seems in all respects the exact opposite of the focused and antitraditionalist Japhy.

They stop at a hunting lodge for a drink late at night. Japhy deplores the existence of the hunters around them and boasts of how he will wander the hills of Japan visiting ancient sages and temples. Morley says that he is "neutral" to Buddhism, though he likes some of the art. They depart and arrive at a spot several miles from the foot of the trail. There they will sleep by the car until dawn and then begin the climb. They discover to their dismay that Morley has forgotten his sleeping bag, and all of them suffer a horrible night trying to keep warm with just two sleeping bags divided between them.

In the morning, Morley begins to yodel, a recurring habit of his. However, Japhy quickly corrects him, telling him that "Hoo" is the proper (Native American) way to call in the mountains (50). For him, everything has its proper (non-Western) ritual, even mountain-yelling. This ritualization continues when they begin the climb (after breakfast and Morley's acquisition of some blankets from a local family): Japhy solemnly draws a magic mandala in the sand at the foot of the trail, which he claims will aid them in their expedition and even predict the future. They all put on their proper clothing and equipment and set off. Before they have proceeded four miles, however, Morley realizes that he has failed to drain the crankcase in his car. If it freezes over during the night, it will ruin the radiator and leave them stranded. He returns, letting them go on without him, and promises to catch up as soon as he can. It may be significant that we learn later that the night remained balmy, making Morley's diversion completely unnecessary—at least in mundane terms. In fact, Morley's temporary departure gives Ray and Japhy time to spend by themselves, and may thus serve as a sort of skillful means.

Japhy and Ray begin to climb in earnest, discussing mostly Nature and Literature. Japhy impresses Ray with his theories on haiku and his intimate naturalist's knowledge of birds and plants. As they continue, Ray feels alternately sad and elated, and increasingly sees his trip as a sort of pilgrimage. At one point, Japhy points out some "ducks," distinctive piles of rocks set out by earlier climbers to mark convenient shortcuts for those who come after them. An attentive reader might notice an echo here of a conversation Ray and Japhy had earlier with a student named Rol Sturlason, an enthusiast of Japanese Zen rock gardens, who suggested that the mysterious arrangements of rocks enabled the meditator to achieve enlightenment (23–24). Ray and Japhy are beginning to move into a sacred and spiritual space. This emphasis intensifies as Japhy describes to Ray the path ahead of them, which will challenge all of their efforts. He compares successful mountain climbing to Zen: one has to learn how to place one's feet instinctually, rather than to think laboriously about it.

They finally stop for the night in a cave with overhanging rocks that frighten Ray. Japhy continues to lecture him, this time on the rituals of the Japanese tea ceremony and on geology. Ray in turn impresses Japhy with a compassionate prayer that he has composed for all sentient beings, and Japhy gives his approval as roshi, while taking the opportunity to lecture him on the importance of Nature and isolation in improving his practice (69). The two express their momentary concern for Morley, who has failed to reach them by nightfall. (As it turns out, he is doing fine by himself, and manages to catch up to them the next morning.) As the night wears on, a great contentment descends upon Ray, and he comes to appreciate the gentler qualities of Japhy, in particular his generosity and willingness to share his wisdom with others. He vows to turn over a new leaf and share Japhy's free and wandering life. He now seems completely committed to his roshi and his words of wisdom.

The next day, they set out at noon and face the final ascent of the peak late into the day. When they reach the last stretch, Morley (whose stamina has astonished Ray) decides to give up and remain resting by a small mountain tarn at the foot of the peak. Ray and Japhy start out together. Ray is soon frightened by the increasingly precipitous climb. "It was terrifying to look down and see Morley a dreaming spot by the little lake waiting for us. 'Oh why didn't I stay with old Henry?' I thought. I now began to be afraid to go any higher from sheer fear of being too high. I began to be afraid of being blown away by the wind" (82). Japhy continues to coax him upwards step by step. Ray follows until he makes the mistake of looking around, and panics. He manages to crawl onto a sheltering ledge and refuses to budge. Meanwhile, Japhy continues leaping upwards like a mountain goat. And here an even stranger terror overcomes Ray, one that ceases to be simple fear for his life and instead becomes a sort of supernatural dread—a dread that includes a fear of the very Void to which Buddhist teaching is supposed to inure him:

> I nudged myself closer into the ledge and closed my eyes and thought "Oh what a life this is, why do we have to be born in the first place, and only so we can have our poor gentle flesh laid out to such impossible horrors as huge mountains and rock and empty space," and with horror I remembered the famous Zen saying, "When you get to the top of a mountain, keep climbing." The saying made my hair stand on end; it had been such cute poetry sitting on Alvah's straw mats. Now it was enough to make my heart pound and my heart bleed for being born at all. "In fact when Japhy gets to the top of that crag he *will* keep climbing, the way the wind's blowing. Well this old philosopher is staying right here," and I closed my eyes. (83–84)

Ray has failed to follow his teacher to the highest place. He hears Japhy yodeling and sees him dancing in joy on the peak. But this brings him no real satisfaction, nor does it convince him to leave the place where his old philosophy (not his recent trust in his roshi) suggests he remain.

When you get to the top of a mountain, keep climbing. Beyond the possible significance of this line as a "Zen saying," it has some resonance in Chinese belief in general, though not in the way we might think.[6] Mountains are terrifying, if necessary, locations for spiritual practice in the Chinese Buddhist tradition; monks who found monasteries on mountains often have to defend themselves against local spirits, and there are always demons nearby to interfere with the practitioners' calm. Moreover, mountains are the connecting point between the world of the mortals and that of the Transcendents in Daoist religious belief. Those who are successful in the pursuit of immortality can quite literally step off a mountain and ascend into the Heavens. But as Chinese tales often emphasize, proceeding to that point takes an extraordinary amount of courage, perseverance, and faith. Read, for example, a tale concerning Zhang Daoling, one the founders of the Celestial Masters sect of Daoism (Tianshi dao), and his followers Zhao Sheng and Wang Zhang:

> Daoling led all his disciples to climb a steep cliff at Cloud Terrace. Below it there grew a peach tree, as thick around as a man's arm, that

grew out from the face of the rock. It hung over an unfathomable gulf. The tree bore many fruit. Daoling said to his disciples: "If any of you are able to obtain those peaches, I will inform him of the essentials of the Way." Over three hundred of them crouched down and gazed down at it; but all fell to trembling and broke out in sweat. None dared stare down at it for long, and each sooner or later retreated back from the edge and apologized for his failure. Only Zhao Sheng said, "What danger is there when the spirits will protect me? Our divine master is here, and surely will not let me perish in this ravine. Since our Master has something to teach us, there must be some way to acquire these peaches." He then threw himself over the cliff and cast himself upon the top of the tree without losing his footing. He filled the fold of his robe with peaches; but the face of the stone cliff was too steep and he had no way to climb back up and return. He then threw each peach up one by one, two hundred and two in all. Daoling divided them among his disciples, one apiece. He ate one himself and reserved one for Sheng. He then stretched out his hand and pulled him up. Everyone saw his arm grow over twenty feet long. He pulled at him and Zhao suddenly was there again.

After Sheng had finished eating the peach Daoling had saved for him, Daoling looked over the edge of the ravine and said jokingly, "Since Sheng's heart was upright he was able to throw himself on top of the tree without losing his footing. I'm going to try doing that myself. I should be able to get a big peach!" Everyone remonstrated with him. Only Zhao Sheng and Wang Zhang were silent. Daoling then threw himself into the air; but instead of alighting on the peach tree, he disappeared.

The disciples looked all around them. The area above them stretched to Heaven itself, and the area below them was bottomless. They found there was no longer a road by which they could leave. All moaned in terror and wept grievously. Only Zhao Sheng and Wang Zhang said, after some time had passed: "Our Master is our father. How can we be content after he has thrown himself off a fathomless cliff?" Both of them jumped. They landed right in front of Zhang, who was sitting cross-legged on a couch surrounded by a curtain. He laughed when he saw them: "I knew you two would come." He then instructed them in the Way, and they departed after three days. They returned then to their former dwelling. The disciples continued to fear and lament. Afterwards

> Daoling, Zhao Sheng, and Wang Zhang all ascended into the sky in broad daylight. The disciples all looked up and saw them. They continued to gaze after them until they vanished into the distant clouds.[7]

Ray is terrified that the cute little motivational proverb might prove to be literally true. And he has no courage to follow his master into the sky. The Zhang story really does not tell us what happened to all of the stranded disciples. Perhaps they remained clinging to their ledge.

At this point, however, Ray seems to have an extraordinary insight amidst his terror—and this salvages something from his failure:

> I looked down at the small lake where Morley was lying on his back with a blade of grass in his mouth and said out loud "Now there's the karma of these three men here: Japhy Ryder gets to his triumphant mountaintop and makes it, I almost make it and have to give up and huddle in a bloody cave, but the smartest of them all is that poet's poet lyin down there with his knees crossed to the sky chewing on a flower dreaming by a gurgling *plage*, goddammit they'll never get me up here again." (84)

Morley has been mostly the butt of jokes so far; but at this moment of clarity, Ray realizes that he is the only one of them who has taken the entire climb with complete indifference. For Morley, climbing a mountain is fine; not climbing a mountain is also fine. He will arrive at a place when he's ready. He forgets things, and goes back to get them, without being particularly bothered. He speaks nonsense that no one really understands. And earlier, at the end of chapter 10, he spoke what is probably the most authentic Zen koan in the entire novel:

> "Well Morley you ready to climb Matterhorn?"
> "I'm ready just as soon as I can change these wet socks." (79)

We have a sort of *panjiao* working itself out, a gradation of learning according to capacity: Ray at the lowest stage, a "gradualist" frightened of a final leap of faith (a "Hinayana coward," in fact); Japhy, who still takes the triumph of the mountain seriously, as if he had actually accomplished something (a position the Diamond Sutra would have warned against); and Morley, who finds it unnecessary to climb the final stretch of mountain at all.

Ray does have another dramatic emotional shift when he sees Japhy running down the side of the mountain. But since Japhy's return means a return to earth, Ray does not experience the terror he felt when he was convinced that Japhy would walk into the sky; instead, supernatural awe overcomes him once again and he feels elation. And to the previous proverb he now appends a much more consoling and reassuring proverb: "It's impossible to fall off mountains." The two run down together to the lake and Morley. Ray puts his terrestrial proverb up against Japhy's celestial one. As he expresses the awe he felt, Japhy answers with an odd touch of elitism:

> "Dammit that yodel of triumph of yours was the most beautiful thing I ever heard in my life. I wish I'd a had a tape recorder to take it down."
>
> "Those things aren't made to be heard by the people below," says Japhy dead serious.
>
> "By God you're right, all those sedentary bums sitting around on pillows hearing the cry of the triumphant mountain smasher, they don't deserve it. But when I looked up and saw you running down that mountain I suddenly understood everything."
>
> "Ah a little satori for Smith today," says Morley.
>
> "What were you doing down here?"
>
> "Sleeping, mostly." (86)

The Linji/Rinzai school of Zen practice often used sudden shouts to shock the student into comprehension or enlightenment. But Morley responds to this technique with yet another koan: he, the master of yodeling, sleeps through a yodel supposedly too marvelous for ordinary people to hear.

The other interesting moment here is Morley's recognition of Ray's satori. In traditional Chinese Chan and Japanese Zen, it is the abbot's responsibility to interview monks who believe they have had a genuine moment of awakening and confirm whether it was in fact a breakthrough. Morley is the master acknowledging what Ray has accomplished, not Japhy. The Matterhorn narrative has carefully built up an idealized teacher-relationship between Ray and Japhy, only to undermine it in a series of striking moves: the collapse of Ray's faith in his roshi in the final stage of the ascent; the distraction provided by the seeming idiot Morley, whose comic presence undermines the solemnity of the climb; and Morley's final transformation into true Zen master and Japhy's superior. This does not bode well for a continuing teacher-pupil relationship between the two main characters, nor even for a continuing friendship.

Falling off the Mountain

They stumble down the mountain in the middle of the night, their path lit only by moonlight; and Ray almost immediately loses the serenity of his satori, as if it could only exist and thrive within the isolation of the mountaintop. He also loses patience with the drudgery of going downhill, and in his peevishness he mentally rejects all of Japhy's ideas (90). He increasingly notices things that put his teacher in a less than flattering light. That very evening, he is amused to discover that Japhy is too shy to go into a restaurant where the people are better dressed than he. So much for the anarchist who expresses contempt for the bourgeoisie!

From this point in the novel, Ray increasingly sees his roshi with a jaundiced eye, in spite of his protests to the contrary. Optimistically, one could see this as a gesture of independence, that his enlightenment on the Matterhorn (Cold Mountain) marks the end of what Japhy can teach him, and that he can now be fully independent. However, it soon becomes clear that what it really indicates is backsliding and the failure of what Hakuin referred to as "post-satori practice." In Hanshan's terms, Ray fails to find the Cold Mountain beyond Cold Mountain, the site where he can stop the source. Again, this underlines the tension Hanshan articulated between traveling the path alone or in company. Japhy was hoping to inspire Ray to adopt his own emphasis on mountain-pilgrimage as a guide to practice, and that Ray's embrace of solitude would cement their friendship and join them in a community—that they would be alone together. But Ray is too much in love with the world.

Even before this change of mood, Ray had already shown impatience with the political aspects of Japhy's thought, particularly his argument that embracing an environmental, anarchistic Buddhism would lead to "a rucksack revolution." In contrast, Ray's spiritual concerns are entirely personal: he is concerned with his own salvation as well as that of those for whom he prays, and he does not think that Buddhism can have broader social implications. It turns out that his and Japhy's concepts of "Dharma bum" are perhaps not so similar. For Japhy, bums are forerunners of social change; they exemplify the "beat" qualities that will defeat middle-class complacency and draw our attention to what really matters. They are in fact Hakuin's community of bodhisattvas. All that is required of the bums of the future is that confidence and mental discipline that will allow them to wander the world, bringing spiritual joy wherever they travel. For Ray, bums are . . . well, bums:

human beings who have suffered, who have proved themselves unable to function in society, and who yet have some spark of spirituality that shines through their suffering. His vision of Dharma bums is an idealized transformation of Christian humility and self-abasement projected onto the American underclass.

Ray's self-confidence about his practice continues to erode after the Matterhorn climb. He asks Japhy to help him buy proper supplies for a possible future sojourn in the desert, or at least for his hitchhiking trip back to North Carolina for Christmas. Almost immediately, they quarrel over Christianity: Ray wants to see Jesus's teachings as compatible with Buddhist thought, Japhy remains skeptical. Then Rosie's suicide—which demonstrates to Ray his utter inability to reach out successfully to another suffering being—strikes another blow to his self-confidence.

Ray returns to hitchhiking and to his old habits. We briefly have a resumption of the type of narrative detail that filled *On the Road*: eccentric tramps, restless truck-drivers, visits to whorehouses, confrontations with cops. One particular event demonstrates his increasing distance from Japhy. Before the Matterhorn climb Ray had shown anxiety about thrombophlebitis in the veins of his feet, fearing that the change in air pressure would worsen his condition. However upon returning, he finds that his condition has cleared, a fact he attributes to the climb (94). Shortly later, at a party, Japhy mentions Hakuin's famous essay, *A Chat in a Boat in the Evening* (Yasen Kanna), in which the Zen master describes a supposed visit to a three-hundred-year-old hermit who teaches him a form of hygienic meditation (100–1).[8] Both of these anecdotes suggest a future for Ray in which Buddhist practice (especially mountain reclusion) will have the potential to heal him and to cure his addictions and unhappiness. However, when Ray takes off across the country, he briefly meets an ex-Marine bum, who, like the "little bum" at the beginning of the novel, is also carrying a slip of paper with a spiritual message: in this case, a quotation from the Dīgha Nikāya, one of the Buddhist Pāli scriptures. Taking this as a sign of the bum's goodness, Ray engages him in conversation, and the talk turns to medical treatments. The bum advises him that his thrombophlebitis can be treated by standing on his head for three minutes a day. Ray does so, and his condition clears up completely in three months; he dubs his savior a Dharma bum (118). There is no mention at all that just a few days before Ray had been claiming that the ascent of the Matterhorn had cured his condition. He has already dismissed Japhy's guidance in favor of insights he gleans from the bum-oracles he meets on the road.

The irony of all this is that once Ray abandons the mountain as a place of spiritual pilgrimage and tries to practice down among the people he loves, he cannot find peace. Hitchhiking across the country is the closest he can come to resembling Japhy's rucksack revolution bhikkus—but 1950s America is not ancient India. Every place he goes to camp there are cops watching him suspiciously: "sleek, well-paid cops in brand-new cars with all that expensive radio equipment to see that no bhikku slept in his grove tonight" (121). Ray has plunged into the very hellish capitalist world that Japhy despises, but seems unable to make the connection between his own continuing suffering and the potentially political impact of his Buddhist beliefs on this world.

There is something particularly poignant about this because for all Ray's talk of compassion and all his desire to offer up prayers for all living creatures, Buddhism is something he has embraced in order to find his own salvation, to find a refuge from his perpetual restlessness and his fear of death. He recognizes on some level that his broader bodhisattva aspirations are inextricably linked with his personal obsessions, and that he cannot heal others until he heals himself. This also makes his strangely ambivalent attitude toward Japhy quite moving: part of him desperately wants to embrace Japhy's self-confident transcendence—a transcendence he largely accepts, like a humble disciple, whenever Japhy can haul him off into the wilderness—but another part of him wants to find ways of belittling him, to reject his advice, and to claim the superiority of his own bum-centered egoism.

Mountain and Self

When Ray finally does leave for his stint as a fire-spotter on Desolation Peak, he must at last confront an enforced period of meditation completely by himself, as a genuine Buddhist hermit. And yet here once again Ray lets his interest in people, in freedom, and in restlessness derail the narrative from the important matter at hand. When he sets out for the Cascades, it takes him eight pages just to get there (after a series of digressions on the interesting types who give him rides) and another eleven pages to describe his training as a fire-spotter and his trip up to the cabin; a bare ten pages are devoted to the two months of his actual experience, the novel's seeming climax. This might be understandable if he communicated to us the idea that the truth he discovered was incommunicable, and if the narrative trailed off into an ungraspable mysticism. But in fact he is quite descriptive, and these ten pages are filled with ordinary actions and banal details.

One might argue that, in Zen fashion, he is practicing the Way through a mindful attentiveness to daily activities. But in fact his life at Desolation Peak as he describes it focuses on his emotional reactions to everything around him, at a time when (supposedly) he should be meditating in order to transcend the illusory nature of the Self. In these ten pages he uses "I," "me," "my," "mine," and "myself" 172 times. Of course, foregrounding personal experience in as straightforward and as honest a way as possible is an essential element of Kerouac's style. But this heavy reliance on the first-person does suggest something about Ray's inability to transcend his immediate responses to the stimuli around him. Perhaps most telling is his use of the possessive, which is applied to pretty much everything within his visual range: not just parts of his own body ("my bones," "my teeth," "my head," "my hair") and his possessions ("my hat," "my clothes"), but also, surprisingly, parts of the cabin itself and the things that belong to it, and presumably, to the Forest Service ("my door," "my house," "my attic," "my mop"). This possessiveness stretches to all of the outdoors: after naming all of the nearby mountains and creeks, he states: "And it was all mine, not another human pair of eyes in the world were looking at this immense cycloramic universe of matter" (235). Later, he says "my ridge," "my mountaintop," and even "my chipmunk." He is also in a constant stage of restlessness, and he tells us of this in substantial detail. He cooks various items, he stands on his head, he tries to find things that will amuse him. He complains of boredom. He notices the animals around him, some of which bother him, some of which don't. He sings to himself, dances about, and notices self-consciously to himself that he is happy (236).[9]

Moreover, when Ray does have experiences that lead him to spiritual awareness, they tend to undermine the practice of Buddhism, and suggest that he is actually moving away from Buddhist insights rather than coming closer to them. Beyond that possessiveness he expresses toward the landscape (an echo of Japhy's strange elitism when he conquers the top of the Matterhorn), he seems able to relate to the world about him only as an objective space "out there" to which he must find some way to respond. Beautiful as all of this is, it still is threateningly Other, a Void that must be filled with a knowable deity: "But night would come and with it the mountain moon and the lake would be moon-laned and I'd go out and sit in the grass and meditate facing west, wishing there were a Personal God in all this impersonal matter" (237). Later, he relates a strange vision:

> Standing on my head before bedtime on that rock roof of the moonlight I could indeed see that the earth was truly upsidedown and man a weird vain beetle full of strange ideas walking around upsidedown and boasting, and I could realize that man remembered why this dream of planets and plants and Plantagenets was built out of the primordial essence. Sometimes I'd get mad because things didn't work out well, I'd spoil a flapjack, or slip in the snowfield while getting water, or one time my shovel went sailing down into the gorge, and I'd be so mad I'd want to bite the mountaintops and would come in the shack and kick the cupboard and hurt my toe. But let the mind beware, that though the flesh be bugged, the circumstances of existence are all pretty glorious. (238)

In his thoughts about the insubstantiality of the world, he coincidentally echoes the opening of HS 236:

> Humans born in this world of dust
> Are just like bugs in a bowl.
> All day they travel round and round
> But never get out of the bowl.

A fitting description of the frivolity of existence—but why this should show how people remember that the world "was built out of the primordial essence" is less clear (existence fashioned out of primal nothing suggests a certain cosmogony not completely typical of Buddhist belief). Todd Giles has also argued persuasively that Ray's inverted position suggests *viparyāsa*, or "upside-down thinking," a Buddhist technical term that indicates a fundamental error in perspective; Giles shows how the image pervades Kerouac's poem-cycle "Desolation Blues," a more pessimistic description of his time on Desolation Peak.[10] Though Ray seems to recognize the absurdity of human activity by turning it literally upside down, he cannot help but partake of that perverted perspective as well. Finally, the passage dwells on how simple mistakes would throw him into a rage totally out of proportion to their importance, making him want to "bite the mountaintops," in a combination of two of the principal "poisons" of Buddhism, desire and anger. He wants to consume the mountains, turning them into part of the Self, the mountains that he claims are "his." He only recovers from this state when he realizes that though the "flesh be bugged" (a reworking of the Christian adage "the flesh is weak"—again, a very un-Buddhist idea, separating flesh from mind), "the circumstances of existence are pretty glorious" (seemingly a reaffirmation of the reality of samsara, also quite un-Buddhist).

The book's final evocation of Hanshan enforces both the idea that Hanshan and Japhy are one and the same, and that they are ultimately becoming inaccessible to Ray as teachers. As Ray departs the mountain for good, he has his most mystical moment: a vision of Japhy once more as the Chinese bum he had dreamed of before his departure. "It wasn't the real-life Japhy of rucksacks and Buddhism studies and big mad parties at Corte Madera, it was the realer-than-life Japhy of my dreams, and he stood there saying nothing. 'Go away, thieves of the mind!' he cried down the hollows of the unbelievable Cascades" (243), thus evoking the cry of the magical Hanshan from Lüqiu Yin's preface. Ray praises this dream-Japhy, "realer-than-life," thanking him for guiding him to Desolation Peak, "where I learned all." He tells vision-Japhy he must return to the immoral world below. Ray then looks up to the sky and cries, in a reassertion of desire, "I have fallen in love with you, God. Take care of us all, one way or the other" (244).

This is a heartbreaking moment, even within the context of the novel: the struggle for enlightenment in terms of Zen practice has been displaced instead onto a vision of an idealized Japhy, who has transformed into a higher being. The fact that he is no longer the *actual* Japhy—the one that Ray knew, interacted with, and learned from—suggests that he, like a Buddha or an advanced bodhisattva, is no longer manifesting his *nirmaṇakāya*, or "transformation body," the body shown to ordinary human begin in samsara, but rather his *sambhogakāya*, or "enjoyment-body," the sublime, magical form manifested to advanced believers or in dreams and visions. In Ray's mind, this is a Japhy to be worshipped, not one whose advice must be heeded—conveniently so, since Japhy's idealization allows Ray to ignore the real Japhy. Then, in a last gesture that renounces Buddhist faith completely, Ray cries out: "I have fallen in love with you, God."

It is not so much that these visions and responses on Ray's part are unprecedented from a Buddhist perspective: they represent what Japanese Buddhists sometimes designate by the term *tariki*, or "[dependency on] another's strength," an acknowledgement that one cannot achieve enlightenment on one's own, that one must depend on the benevolent mercy of a bodhisattva like Kannon or a Buddha like Amida, who presides over the Pure Land. Ray has surrendered autonomy and acknowledges that he can no longer find enlightenment on Japhy's terms, though he can beg for mercy from the beings that manifest themselves through him. In the end, this makes his particular form of faith largely indistinguishable from the stern Roman Catholicism of his childhood. Traditional East Asian believers thought that Hanshan was Mañjuśrī; Ray thinks that Japhy is Kannon. Or possibly the Virgin Mary. No matter how many mountains he climbs, he will never find Cold Mountain again.

Ray is still a fictional character in a novel; the narrative puts a brave face on what ultimately was a spiritual disaster for Kerouac. Todd Giles has written of the despair evident in "Desolation Blues"; the entire first section of Kerouac's novel *Desolation Angels* gives a depressingly thorough account of how tedious and maddening the author actually found his stay on the mountain to be. And yet Kerouac could never quite remove himself from the idea that the wilderness would rejuvenate his spirit in some vital way; in *Big Sur*, his autobiographical hero continues to shuffle back and forth between eremitism and urban dissipation, and neither life can save him in the end. Nonetheless, the Buddhist reader can learn much from Kerouac's problematic construction of Beat Buddhism and from Ray's complex relationship with his hermit-roshi. Failure too can serve as a skillful means.

Gary Snyder: In Search of the Real

The poets Gary Snyder and Jane Hirshfield, like Kerouac, can be highly confessional and autobiographical. Yet they too provide insight into the Dharma that transcends their specific experiences. Perhaps their main difference from Kerouac is their self-awareness in talking about the autobiographical realm; gifted with a more sophisticated knowledge of Buddhism, they convey much more successfully the subtleties and difficulties involved in expressing matters of practice and faith. Like Kerouac, they cannot be defined exclusively as "Buddhist writers," and they explore many other themes in their work (for example, environmental issues permeate much of Snyder's writing). Nonetheless, they commonly employ Buddhist rhetoric or arguments in working through larger ontological and epistemological issues. In this way, both write poetry that is infused with a sort of spirituality and also with (for lack of a better term) a kind of didacticism. This approach to verse does not have to result in over-simplification, new-age clichés, or sanctimony; in their poems, it is marked by a sense of sympathetic urgency that addresses fellow sentient beings and demands that they come to a fuller awareness of their position of suffering in samsara. As Rilke's oft-quoted phrase has it, "*Du mußt dein*

Leben ändern" (You must change your life). It is this perceived role for poetry that ties much of Snyder's and Hirshfield's work to Hanshan's.

We have already met a fictionalized version of Snyder in the person of Japhy Ryder, the young Buddhist believer who attempts to reform Ray Smith in *The Dharma Bums*. Snyder's renderings of twenty-four Cold Mountain poems have become part of the canon of modern American poetry, though they also remain outstanding as translations: sharp, witty, and comfortably straddling the space between classical Chinese and modern American English. These translations also provided model and inspiration for many of his other poems. Snyder's work employs techniques found both in Hanshan and in Zen writers in general: a sense of combative confrontation, a vernacular speech that seeks to address a nonelite readership, images that critique duality and that point to an intuited world that transcends our samsaric senses, and a use of natural images (which Hanshan and the Zen tradition drew in turn from traditional Chinese poetry).[11] Many of Hanshan's themes appear in Snyder's work as well, themes that he works out with a much more realistic sense of the complexities of living in samsara than Japhy seemed to possess. One of the most common issues is how one can reconcile a commitment to transcendence—which for Snyder means embracing the natural world and living in harmony with it—with the frustrations of a householder's life. In the Hanshan corpus, such a reconciliation was ultimately impossible, but Snyder makes the continuing attempt the theme of some of his most powerful works.

Snyder's first collection of verse, *Riprap*, begins with a poem that quite clearly shows the influence of Chinese poetic structure, Chinese nature imagery, and Hanshan's way of forming an argument:

MID-AUGUST AT SOURDOUGH MOUNTAIN LOOKOUT

Down valley a smoke haze
Three days heat, after five days rain
Pitch glows on the fir-cones
Across rocks and meadows
Swarms of new flies.

I cannot remember things I once read
A few friends, but they are in cities.
Drinking cold snow-water from a tin cup
Looking down for miles
Through high still air.[12]

Though Snyder breaks the lines of this poem to reflect the natural rhythms of speech, he works with the framework of an eight-line poem in the Chinese style.[13] As with most traditional Chinese verse, the title reveals the occasion for composition. After this, the structure of the poem resembles that of a Chinese octet. The first section (equivalent to the Chinese first couplet) provides setting and time (looking down on the valley; commenting on the weather at the time of writing). The second section (second and third couplets) gives details about the environment (glare of pitch against the cones, swarms of flies) as well as a comment about his reading and friends. Snyder's description here is deliberately ambiguous; his position on the lookout is liberating, but it also isolates him from human society. His comment about friends specifically echoes a lament for the dead in HS 296, lines 3–6:

故人無來往，	Old friends no longer come to visit;
埋在古冢間。	Buried they are, in ancient mounds.
余今頭已白，	And I: with my hair already white,
猶守片雲山。	Still keep to this cloud-fragmented hill.

Snyder is obviously not in mourning or complaining of old age (both quite standard themes among Chinese poets, but hardly appropriate for a young writer at the beginning of his career), but the gesture is much the same. The ending (fourth couplet) gives a summary that grows out of the earlier description and response to the scene, as the poet looks down from a mountaintop, a conventional stance in many traditional Chinese poems. However, Snyder puts a specifically Buddhist inflection on the poem, as his speaker drinks the pure water of Enlightenment and imagines that the false distinctions of samsara have been erased. One might recall the opening of HS 287 (discussed in chapter 5): "High up, on the top of the peak: / Infinite in all directions." Snyder's final lines imply a note of exhilaration that suggests that the speaker's separation from friends and books is largely a positive thing, something that brings him closer to satori. This is a very "Japhy" poem, fully reflecting the fictional character's concerns and perspective.

But this poem is perhaps the closest Snyder comes to imitating traditional Chinese verse; in other places, he plays with some of its characteristic structures and images without necessarily replicating the form. More importantly, he shows a sensitivity to the human world that Japhy never demonstrated. Another poem in *Riprap*, "Kyoto: March," shows a sort of dialectic in progress between nature and humanity, between Snyder's Chinese antecedents and his own poetic voice:

> A few light flakes of snow
> Fall in the feeble sun;
> Birds sing in the cold,
> A warbler by the wall. The plum
> Buds tight and chill soon bloom.
> The moon begins first
> Fourth, a faint slice west
> At nightfall. Jupiter half-way
> High at the end of night-
> Meditation. The dove cry
> Twangs like a bow.
> At dawn Mt. Hiei dusted white
> On top; in the clear air
> Folds of all the gullied green
> Hills around the town are sharp,
> Breath stings. Beneath the roofs
> Of frosty houses
> Lovers part, from tangle warm
> Of gentle bodies under quilt
> And crack the icy water to the face
> And wake and feed the children
> And grandchildren that they love.[14]

Here, the poet keeps himself out of the poem except as a selective observer. The Chinese style comes through in the finely balanced descriptions of nature that are placed paratactically, one after another. All is quite lovely; the evocation of such harmony may show the influence of traditional East Asian painting as well. However, Snyder quite deliberately breaks this Chinese rhythm at the end as he moves from outside to inside and encounters people waking in the morning. We close with a run-on sentence meant to imitate the bustle of people rising from the warm, safe spaces of their beds and going about their family-centered lives. It is an interesting moment in Snyder's early poetry—poetry that is usually centered very much on a male response to the environment, particularly in its Frostian celebrations of working men. These lines are the first hint of what will become one of his great themes in later volumes, the intimate relationships between family members: wives and husbands, children and parents, the world of the householder. "Kyoto: March" feels like a critique or counternarrative to the magisterial and austere imagism of Chinese nature poetry, reminding us that there are people with their own lives under the trees and across the rivers.

This note reemerges most strongly in the collection *Axe Handles* (1983); the poems here evoke a poet trying to balance the pressures of a life within samsara—that is, with obligations both public and private—against the need for spiritual transcendence. One of the masterpieces of the collection, "True Night," plays off the sense of familial intimacy we saw at the end of "Kyoto: March" and makes it a source of anxiety, setting it against the poet's complex relationship with nature and with animal life.[15]

The poem opens with the poet in deep sleep, like a knife resting in its scabbard or a child resting in a womb:

> Sheath of sleep in the black of the bed:
> From outside this dream womb
> Comes a clatter
> Comes a clatter
> And finally the mind rises up to a fact
> Like a fish to a hook
> A raccoon at the kitchen!
> A falling of metal bowls,
>   the clashing of jars,
>   the avalanche of plates!
> I snap alive to this ritual
> Rise unsteady, find my feet,
> Grab the stick, dash in the dark—
> I'm a huge pounding demon
> That roars at raccoons—
> They whip round the corner,
> A scratching sound tells me
>   they've gone up a tree.
>
> I stand at the base
> Two young ones that perch on
> Two dead stub limbs and
> Peer down from both sides of the trunk:

Roar, roar, I roar
you awful raccoons, you wake me
up nights, you ravage
our kitchen

We have a moment of "sudden awakening" here, but it is more a parody of satori than satori itself. Coming out of sleep, in this poem, is not so much an escape *from* as an emergence *into* danger, "like a fish to a hook." To emphasize this, the raccoons' business in the kitchen evokes the language of catastrophe, of disasters that humans cannot control but which are nonetheless part of the natural world of Impermanence. As the raccoons root through the dishes, there is "falling," "clashing," "avalanche," all in the service of their "ritual." This is the way raccoons are supposed to act. The poet's house would seem to be a safe space, domesticated, invulnerable to the forces of nature around it—a bit of illusory permanence, like the dwellings of Hanshan's householders. But the natural world *will* enter—it is only natural for it to do so—in the person of raccoons. In response, Snyder turns himself into a wrathful Buddhist deity, a *vidyarāja* who rushes in to drive out the *kleśa* that threatens the household's peace of mind.

All of this is a comic reversal of Snyder's customary approach to nature: the elevated embrace of wilderness, the exhilarating experiences in lofty places that can lead to a communion with the Real behind the illusions of samsara: "Looking down for miles / Through high still air." Rather, he is awakened out of a place of tranquility into chaos, a chaos that arises from Nature itself. There is a Daoist wisdom here, an analysis typical of Laozi and Zhuangzi: the delineation of categories out of a previously undifferentiated awareness creates both evil and good, and the espousal of one form of behavior guarantees the creation of a form of behavior opposed to it. If we didn't live in houses with kitchens, there would be nothing for raccoons to invade. In that sense, we are invading ourselves. Though Snyder starts out as a storming *vidyarāja*, he ends as an aging, impotent householder, yelling at two juvenile delinquents who mock him from the safe branches of a tree. He has failed to climb Cold Mountain, so Cold Mountain has come to him.

Not surprisingly, this is the turning point, as Snyder suddenly opens himself up to the night, free for a moment from the inside/outside categories that the house—his house—has created. He is open to the Truth as well, even if that Truth is difficult to face:

As I stay there then silent
The chill of the air on my nakedness
Starts off the skin
I am all alive to the night.
Bare foot shaping on gravel
Stick in the hand, forever.

Long streak of cloud giving way
To a milky thin light
Back of black pine bough,
The moon is still full,
Hillsides of Pine trees all
Whispering; crickets still cricketting
Faint in cold coves in the dark

I turn and walk slow
Back the path to the beds
With goosebumps and loose waving hair
In the night of milk-moonlit thin cloud glow
And black rustling pines
I feel like a dandelion head
Gone to seed
About to be blown all away
Or a sea anemone open and waving in
cool pearly water.

Fifty years old.
I still spend my time
Screwing nuts down on bolts.

It may in fact turn out that the raccoons' attack was an incentive to satori, equivalent to the blow of the master's stick: it has brought the poet into a new moment of awareness. He now develops a meditative sensitivity to his surroundings. The eye that sees with descriptive intensity is restored, as he merges with the world around him: "Bare foot shaping on gravel / Stick in the hand, forever." Gravel, stick, foot, hand—all are one thing, independent of causality, no longer driven by purpose. Everything is white or black: pale moonlight and clouds, black trees. Even the sounds are bare, reduced to the faint sound of crickets, who remain in their natural abode, doing cricket things, "cricketting." The speaker too decides to return to his cave, but things have changed. He moves slowly, meditatively, goose bumps marking his sensitivity to his surroundings. In his renewed sensitivity to the outside world he notices his own hair, blowing loose in the night, extending its tendrils into its environment. Two images occur to him. First, the wild hair turns his head into a dying dandelion, about to dissipate into the world with the first wind. Second, it becomes a sea anemone, hair-tentacles reaching out for nourishment. He goes on reaching out to things, hungry for union with the world around him, yet exhausted, wondering if his own physical self will soon disintegrate and join the cosmos in a final, literal way. He is thinking of growing old. Then, in the most poignant lines of the poem, he asserts: "I still spend my time / Screwing nuts down on bolts." The declaration is poignant because Snyder's poetry often gives us the record of an extremely self-confident man who, above all, knows how to do things. His is a poetry of competence: he knows how to log, how to hike, how to live in the wilderness, how to repair things, how to live successfully in Nature. That we must not lose the ability to do things that connect us to the world is one of his great themes. The collection *Axe Handles* itself includes many moments that highlight this competence: the title poem, for instance, where he is teaching his son how to throw a hatchet; or "Fence Posts," where he humorously lectures us on the most economical way to built a fence. "Working on the '58 Willys Pickup" embraces the joy of fixing a truck, and ends with a paean to people who both are scholars and have practical skills.[16]

At this moment, though, the poet grows tired of constant business and busyness, the requirements of the householder's life, the things to which he must constantly attend. There is a bit of the yearning associated with Brahmin men, the desire to leave the family once one grows old and go off to live in the forest and attend to spiritual matters. But for the time being he has to return to the Burning House:

> At the shadow pool,
> Children are sleeping,
> And a lover I've lived with for years,
> True night.
> One cannot stay too long awake
> In this dark

Dusty feet, hair tangling,
I stoop and slip back to the
Sheath, for the sleep I still need,
For the waking that comes
Every day

With the dawn.

As long as he has a family to look after and a public life to live, the poet must postpone the final merging with nature. He returns to the shadow pool, the sheath of darkness, the "true night." This night bears at least two meanings here. It is first the "night" that all of us must acknowledge in order to live our human lives, the night of required sleep, of temporary oblivion that enables us to prepare "For the waking that comes / Every day / With the dawn." But it is also the return to samsara, the temporary disavowal of the taste of enlightenment that this special experience has brought with it. That samsaric dulling is the "true night," in comparison to which the current moonlit night is actually illumination—though it is an illumination hard to sustain: "One cannot stay too long awake / In this dark." In the end, the householder's life triumphs.

Illumination as a sort of disillusion is quite unusual in Snyder's work, but it provides a compelling shadow to the more assured voice in most of his other poems. Snyder evokes in many ways a Chinese poet of great self-confidence, Su Shi (1037–1101), a Confucian thinker, statesman, prolific writer, and lay Zen Buddhist. Su Shi often exemplifies the poetic voice of the Song dynasty, which the Japanese scholar Yoshikawa Kojirō once characterized as "the transcendence of sorrow."[17] Yet Su Shi's stylistic optimism often is an explicit technique employed to keep anxieties and depression at bay. Snyder's "True Night" bears a resemblance to one of Su Shi's most famous poems, a lyric *(ci)* written to the tune "Transcendent by the River" (Lin jiang xian):[18]

夜飲東坡醒復醉，	At night I drank at Eastern Slope, sobered, then got drunk again.
歸來彷彿三更。	Then I came home, I guess, around midnight.
家童鼻息已雷鳴，	My serving boy was snoring now, already thundering away.
敲門都不應，	I knocked on the gate. No answer.
倚杖聽江聲。	I leaned on my cane and listened to the river.

長恨此身非我有，	I've always hated that this Self never belonged to me.
何時忘卻營營。	When can I forget this endless bustle?
夜闌風靜縠紋平，	The night grew late, the wind was calm, the river ripples smoothed.
小舟從此逝，	I'll depart from here in a little skiff,
江海寄餘生。	Lodge what's left of life in lake and river.

Unlike Snyder, Su Shi is trying to get in, not get out, but as in "True Night," a comic situation (the sleeping servant boy cannot be wakened to let in his master) forces a moment of self-reflection and stillness on the poet. In the second stanza, the poet recognizes his failure to escape from the compulsions of the world (at the time of its composition, he was exiled by imperial command to a remote district in Hubei). His final fantasy of departure remained a fantasy; he never succeeded in becoming a retired wanderer.

But how can one regain the experience of satori, how invigorate one's sense of transcendence while still functioning in a modern world? In one of the best poems in Snyder's most recent collection, *danger on peaks* (2004), he gives us a sort of reversal of "True Night," a renewal of the poet's search for the source. "Really the Real"[19] is a forty-six-line narrative that describes Snyder and the Korean poet Ko Un engaged in a spiritual pilgrimage: in this case a bird-watching expedition, departing from University of California, Davis. As so often happens, things never appear when you seek them. You have to be patient.

The first fifteen lines give us the car's itinerary as the two poets leave Davis, sketching a world of interstate highways and bleak American exurban communities:

Heading south down the freeway making the switch
from Business 80 east to the I-5 south,
watch those signs and lanes that split
duck behind the trucks, all going 75 at 10 am
I tell Ko Un this is the road that runs from Mexico to Canada,
right past San Diego—LA—Sacramento—Medford—Portland—Centralia—
Seattle—Bellingham, B.C. all the way,
the new suburban projects with cement roof tiles
neatly piled on unfinished gables,

turn onto Twin Cities Road, then Franklin Road
pull in by the sweet little almost-wild Cosumnes River
right where the Mokulumne meets it,
(*umne* a Miwok suffix meaning river)
walking out on a levee trail through cattail, tule, button-brush,
small valley oaks, algae on the streams. Hardly any birds.

These fifteen lines are spoken in one continuous breath, rushing past location after location, until the first full stop in line fifteen, followed by the three-word sentence fragment: "Hardly any birds." As a voice of authority about the North American West Coast, Snyder lectures Ko Un on the road system. Snyder has, the poem reminds us, traveled these roads or their predecessors from his youth; some of the competence we saw him considering in *Axe Handles* comes from his familiarity with this human network that reaches out to community after community, from Canada all the way to Mexico. This is the world of Kerouac's novels—and, for that matter, the world of certain of Snyder's poems, like "Night Highway 99" from *Mountains and Rivers without End*, a long rhapsody that exhausts human experience through telling of people that the speaker has met while hitchhiking.[20] In this shorter journey, Snyder and Ko Un are first condemned to follow the barren interstate, with its bordering suburban projects. Relief comes as they move off the numbered highways and turn to named roads, and then from roads to a different directional ribbon free of human artifice: the river. Here we have a world of Native American naming, and the two men's first attempt to get behind the façade of Western civilization. Snyder indulges in a touch of etymology here in naming the Mokulumne, as a way of guaranteeing a world that antedates Western civilization. Yet his fondness for the Cosumnes is chastened by the adjective "almost-wild." They are not quite there yet. And true enough, they are disappointed in the climax of this first stage of their trip by an absence of birds—a quest with nothing at the end:

Lost Slough, across the road, out on the boardwalk
—can't see much, the tules all too tall. The freeway roar,
four sandhill cranes feeding, necks down, pacing slow.
Then west on Twin Cities Road til we hit the river.
Into Locke, park, walk the crowded Second Street
all the tippy buildings' second stories leaning out,
gleaming bikes—huge BMW with exotic control panel

eat at the Locke Gardens Chinese place, Ko Un's choice,
endless tape loop some dumb music, at the next table one white couple,
a guy with a beard; at another a single black woman
with two little round headed clearly super-sharp boys.

Their earlier breathless quest having ended in failure, the poem falls back into a calmer narrative mode. However, this is not the lyrical descriptive style characteristic of much of Snyder's nature poetry, but a wryer, observational style, taking note of detail and at times making implicit judgment. The lines suggest a certain impatience and frustration with the failure to find what he is looking for. A few desultory and lackluster descriptions lead to a return to the car and to civilization. The town of Locke possesses historical interest, and its role in the poem is somewhat ironic. The first town ever to be founded by Chinese immigrants, it is registered as a National Historic Landmark District. However, it has dropped from a peak population of six hundred to a present one of seventy, with virtually no residents of Chinese ancestry; consequently, eating at the local Chinese restaurant smacks a bit of tourism. This may be why the poet tells us "Ko Un's choice"—he wants to distance himself from a selection that he himself would not have made. And, true to this state of mind, his jaundiced eye notes a series of inauthentic or problematic elements: motorcycles, a luxurious (pretentious?) BMW, annoying piped-in music, and diners who stand out for not being Chinese. The poet notices race—not in any flamboyant way, but simply to make a note of it in describing the diners—yet taking note of it at all is a sign of living in the samsaric world, where the social construction of race is an element in our interactions with others.

The two return once more to their car and head south, into more remote regions. At first, the experience they look for continues to elude them; they continue to be surrounded by the marks of civilization (and of property):

Out and down to Walnut Grove til we find road J-11 going east
over a slough or two then south on Staten Island Road. It's straight,
the fields all flat and lots of signs that say
no trespassing, no camping, no hunting, stay off the levee.
Driving along, don't see much, I had hoped, but about to give up.
Make a turn around and stand on the shoulder, glass the field:

And this last-ditch scanning with binoculars finally provides what the speaker wants.

flat farmland—fallow—flooded with water—
full of birds. Scanning the farther sections
hundreds of sandhill cranes are pacing—then,
those gurgling sandhill crane calls are coming out of the sky
in threes, twos, fives, from all directions,
circling, counter-spinning, higher and lower,
big silver bodies, long necks, dab of red on the head,
chaotic, leaderless, harmonic, playful—what are they doing?
Splendidly nowhere thousands

And back to Davis, forty miles, forty minutes
shivering to remember   what's going on
just a few miles west of the 5:
in the wetlands, in the ongoing elder   what you might call,
really the real,   world

For the first time, the poem veers into a lyrical ecstasy as the birds rise in all of their glory. The language here is breathless, but not with the breathlessness of travel that characterized the opening. Here, it is the voice of a poet overwhelmed and brought to the edge of wordlessness: "what are they doing? / Splendidly nowhere thousands." The poem has entered a nowhere that is everywhere, a moment of transcendence that only means itself. At this point, the language ends without punctuation, and we have the only stanza break in the entire poem. The climax of the ecstasy goes unrepresented in language; only the after-impressions remain. Phrases become fragmented and slow, as if the exhausted poet cannot summon the energy to go into any further detail.

Few poems in Snyder's corpus so clearly identify the experience of enlightenment as a communion with the natural environment—his search here is finally successful. Most vividly, though, the poem conveys the idea that the search can only succeed when it ceases to be self-conscious. That keeps it strongly within the Zen tradition, particularly the tradition of koan practice characteristic of Hakuin and his successors. The speaker's return to ordinary life in the last stanza also suggests something more fruitful and satisfying than the ending of "True Night"—an ability to hold on to satori and to develop it into a prolonged affirmation. In the end, his encounter with the birds (in their wild, rushing, undifferentiated flood) is like Hanshan's search for the true source in HS 40, and Hakuin's discussion of it:

> Those who can distinguish the path will arouse their spirits and will personally go to seek for the water in the place where it arises. But where does this water arise? What place acts as its root? He will seek for it everywhere, until both the place he seeks and the mind that seeks for it disappear in one stroke. At this time, when falsity melts away and iron mountains crumble, he will split the steep cliffs with his hands; and only then will he again attain a state of peace. . . . And yet, though one seeks it to its end, the water as before will continue to flow without exhaustion.

Jane Hirshfield: The Attractions and Sorrows of Samsara

For any American poet who considers herself a practicing Buddhist or simply is influenced by Buddhist concepts and themes, Buddhism is mainly a way of seeing reality. That way may seem quite different from the world of much modern American poetry, which is still often flavored by Judeo-Christian perceptions and assumptions—Snyder's path largely illustrates such differentiation. More frequently, however, American "Buddhist poets" display an ability to fuse multiple traditions, Asian and European, letting each illuminate the other in unprecedented ways. Jane Hirshfield is a poet of extraordinary versatility who writes very much within a Western tradition—certainly much more so than the Beat poets. Yet no matter how much she evokes Western images and traditions, her work is strongly colored by her awareness of the Buddhist viewpoint, though she could hardly be called a "Buddhist poet" or a "Zen poet" as her most important identity.

Hirshfield's work inherits Hanshan's task, even if her work does not show any explicit engagement with his poetry, in one key way: much of her work is written in a sort of "didactic" mode (*not* didactic in a negative sense) that tends to create a bifurcation in her poetic voice. Quite often, there are two Hirshfields who address us: a suffering, lyric "I" who relates her own experiences in a confessional manner; and a slightly distanced, enlightened "I" who draws our attention to the larger Buddhist issues implied by that suffering. The second Self (or non-Self) has learned lessons from experience, and wishes to impart them to the reader. This is also what distinguishes her work from both the mainstream works of traditional Chinese poets and from the confessional strain of American verse with which we are familiar since Plath and Lowell: she is not merely trying to convey experience, but to obtain some distance from it. Yet this is also not Wordsworth's aesthetic distancing of experience in order to make it universal, not a poetics of powerful feelings "recollected in tranquility." Rather, it is the universalization of experience in order to make of it a source of learning. Hanshan's poems attempted to co-opt the self-expressive function of traditional Chinese verse, in which the reader is the *zhiyin*, set on "knowing" the individual poet through his writing; but that co-optation filtered experience through figurative language *(biyu)* as a skillful means: the bodhisattva-poet, as the simulacrum of an individual, presents experience in order that we all may partake of that experience, recognize its commonality, and learn from it. This creates a bifurcation in Hanshan's work, an alternation between a more naïve, suffering persona and a sermonizing persona. Hirshfield never sermonizes, at least not in the way we commonly think of the term; but she does have an ability to objectify her own experiences in order to draw bigger lessons from them.

The following Hirshfield poem performs just such an act of distancing. We just saw Ray Smith in *The Dharma Bums* uneasily flitting about his cabin at the top of Desolation Peak, looking for some form of serenity. One of his fundamental failures was his inability to surrender the Self; he placed a claim of ownership on everything around him, from mountain to chipmunk. Hirshfield's poem serves as an uncannily appropriate commentary on Ray's predicament:

> One night eating potatoes pan-fried,
> the next night baked, two nights later, mashed.
> A hummingbird drives at the evening fuchsia,
> still sunlit this far north.
> Because I have seen this before, I think:
> *My hummingbird is drinking.* And later, *my four-point buck*—
> who also likes the red flowers.
> If the hummingbird is thinking, *my pendant fuchsia*,
> *my watching human*, I will not know it.
> Then in broad evening brightness the raccoon
> races its shadow across the mown grass.
> Not *my raccoon*—it's Eleanor and Richard's, next door.
> Each of us racing with him, making our own
> for a little while, as travelers do, what is no one's.
> Every third morning here I wake from another nightmare,
> and still I find myself thinking: *paradise, bliss.*[21]

Hirshfield is ill at ease in her cabin as well, though she is considerably more honest about it than Ray was. The simple, tedious potato fare establishes a routine in her cabin-life, which allows her to make a transition to considering the way in which her observations of nature are becoming a force of habit too: the hummingbird is hers, she thinks, "Because I have seen this before"—thus asserting that we claim possession of things simply because we become familiar with them. But the poem is clear: we have no right to do this. She flips the perspective and wonders if the hummingbird is making the same assumption, also acknowledging that she has no way to see the world from the hummingbird's point of view. Then the raccoon shows up (like Snyder's in "Real Night," a potential mark of disruption), and assigns it to the neighbors. But the raccoon's racing reminds her of the way we spend our lives dashing about, temporarily claiming things as our own simply to give us the illusion of some stability, because we are perpetual travelers. As Chinese poets often (and Hanshan sometimes) phrase it, we "lodge" *(ji)* ourselves in this world as temporary sojourners: "Our lodging in this world is for a moment" (HS 146, line 5).

In spite of her familiar relationship with local nature, the speaker has a nightmare every three days. Three days of potatoes, one night of nightmare, as if she were keeping to a routine. Yet the Self that is in the midst of this will not surrender the idea of vacation, still claiming, through it all, that she has attained some sort of paradise, some sort of bliss, perhaps some sort of nirvana. The poet who looks back at the experience is more critical: she titles the poem "Self-Portrait in a Borrowed Cabin," evoking both Impermanence (the cabin is our momentary lodging) and the illusory Self that brings about our possessiveness and our unease.

Hirshfield is a great poet of samsara: she has an uncanny knack for finding language that expresses what causes our suffering in this world, from minor inconveniences to fear of death and aging to grand historical tragedy. She explores this theme by drawing on a wide variety of techniques, many of them reminiscent of earlier poets, all of which demonstrate her artistry and her ability to refine "confessional" experience into something more profound. There is Dickinson in her deliberately skewed aphorisms, the modern Polish poets in her laconic narratives and engagement with things, and classical Japanese poetry in her imagistic precision. But there are many other voices present as well, all of which she forges into her own distinctive style. Though specific Buddhist allusions emerge occasionally in her verse, she mostly keeps Buddhist perspectives to the level of theme. Behind them all is a much less grand narrative than we find in Snyder's work: she often describes the world as fragmented, flawed, incomplete. It is as if she recognizes that our modern experience of the samsara/nirvana dichotomy is the product of a fallen age, in which only bits and pieces can give us the deeper insight that we crave. The poems' breakthroughs and insights are thus comparatively modest.

One way to think through her poems is to imagine them from the perspective of the "three marks of conditioned existence," that is, the three characteristics that define our life in samsara: Impermanence *(anitya)*, suffering or dissatisfaction *(duḥkha)*, and Non-self *(anātman)*. These in turn can be contrasted with the momentary glimpses of nirvana to which she occasionally gives us access.

First, the poems acknowledge Impermanence. Everything is in a state of flux, they assert, and we only deceive ourselves if we imagine that we will remain the same or that we can possess anything forever—or even until the end of our lives. This is expressed powerfully in a poem that borders on allegory; here she writes not about her own experiences (as she does most often), but as a concerned observer, much like Hanshan writing about a blasted tree:

ON THE BEACH

Uncountable tiny pebbles
of many colors.

Broken seashells mixed in with whole ones.

Sand dollars, shattered and whole,
the half-gone wing of a gull.

Changed glass
that is like the heart after much pain.
The empty shell of a crab.

A child moves alone in the grey
that is half fog, half wind-blown ocean.

She lifts one pebble, another,
into her pocket.
From time to time takes them out again and looks.

These few and only these. How many? Why?

The waves continue their work of breaking
then rounding the edges.

I would speak to her if I could,
but across the distance, what would she hear?
Ocean and ocean. Cry of a fish.

Walk slowly now, small soul, by the edge
of the water. Choose carefully
all you are going to lose, though any of it would do.[22]

The poem begins by laconically itemizing a list of objects: we do not know yet where these objects are, only that they are typical examples of beach detritus. They seem to have no particular meaning, yet they have a history suggested by the only phrase that breaks with objective description: "Changed glass / that is like the heart after much pain." This phrase makes us realize the nature of beach detritus—all these things were once different, perhaps whole and living, but have been handled roughly by the force of the sea. The mollusks that inhabited the shells are long dead; the gull that may have feasted on them has died as well, mysteriously, leaving behind a wing. These are objects that indicate destruction and death.

We now pull back and see a child walking in the midst of all this, lost in a grey indistinguishable space, picking and choosing some of these fragments to be treasured (for what child visiting the seashore doesn't collect examples of such interesting trash?). She makes them her own, these curious objects that have suffered the ocean's turbulence, pulling them out of her pockets constantly to admire them. This innocent act is weighted with a kind of darkness: because she is a child, she cannot know the degree of suffering the objects have undergone, nor the dangers of the sea that has inflicted the suffering: she is like the children in the Burning House, merely diverted by the things around her, even as the ocean continues to torture them, "breaking / then rounding the edges." The poet herself is the bodhisattva of this scene, reading reality from outside samsara. Why does the child pick one object over the other? What makes a human want to possess one thing and not another? Can someone blind to the true nature of the world truly understand the objects she claims to possess? The poet, curious but also compassionate, considers attracting the child's attention, perhaps to ask why she chooses the pebbles that she does, or to warn her about the dangers of the sea. But she concludes that the sea of samsara would drown out her voice; at most, her shouting would be mistaken for the "cry of a fish," a bit of fanciful delusion in the mind of the child. In the end she can do nothing but apostrophize her, warning her to be careful and telling her to pay more attention to what she chooses to call her own. Moreover, she emphasizes a central principle underlying Impermanence: once you own something, you will lose it at some point in the future, inevitably. And yet it also doesn't matter what the child chooses, since it is all the same anyway, all beach detritus. The quest motif here is delusory—it is not the search for a real treasure, a *maṇi* gem that would stand in for our already-possessed Buddha nature. Rather, these are gems of samsara, misleading bits of flotsam that we collect, possess, and make part of our illusory Selves.

"On the Beach" is written very much in parable mode—though it may be based on a real experience, its actions are meant to create a drama that contains larger allegorical truths. In such a drama, the poet must inevitably hold a symbolically superior position, as someone who can see through samsara and who has a greater degree of wisdom than those who wander through its dangerous gray spaces.

The second mark of samsara is suffering and dissatisfaction. Here we are our own worst enemy. Our concerns express themselves in the false reality we create for ourselves, where everything around us becomes a source of pleasure or pain. Yet the pleasures, because of Impermanence, turn to pain when they leave. And to think about suffering is to think about desire as well. Suffering is one of the forces that makes us human, and yet helps to ensure that our experience as humans is one of dissatisfactions and disappointments.

Hirshfield is forthright in writing about suffering, desire, and their role in defining our humanity. Like Impermanence, they are qualities best understood when they are acknowledged and embraced, rather than shunned. "The Adamantine Perfection of Desire," for example, begins "Nothing more strong / than to be helpless before desire," and ends with an aphorism: "The living cannot help but love the world."[23] In other poems, she takes a more measured look at desire and discontent; in a number of them, she emphasizes how both enjoyment and suffering are aspects of the same world, though we are too blind to understand either, or to judge our own actions wisely. Here is "Bees":

In every instant, two gates.
One opens to fragrant paradise, one to hell.
Mostly we go through neither.

Mostly we nod to our neighbor,
lean down to pick up the paper,
go back into the house.

But the faint cries—ecstasy? horror?
Or did you think it the sound
of distant bees,
making only the thick honey of this good life?[24]

Like Snyder's, many of Hirshfield's poems play out within domestic space, but her domestic space is often closer to that of middle America: a place of residence placed amid other places of residence, a community of self-contained and often alienated presences. As in the parable of the Burning House, however, these sites are traps, and we may only know Truth if we finally choose to depart from them—to "leave the home," like a Buddhist monastic. And yet if such a spiritual "departure" is only temporary, it has merely a momentary effect on our awareness, especially if the action that occasioned it has become routine (perhaps this is what Snyder worries about when he reenters his house in "True Night"). In "Bees," the poet imagines an allegory wherein we are constantly confronted with two paths, one leading to a gate of karmic reward, the other to a gate of karmic punishment, to delight or to suffering. Yet the poem admits that most of our actions have little serious consequence—rather than choose to go through either gate, we withdraw into the safe space of our own dwelling, and our own consciousness. And, the poet asserts, rather than decipher the noise that comes from beyond the two gates, we mistake it for some comforting guarantee of our future pleasures. Though obviously subtler, this poem engages a Buddhist evangelistic tone not too different from that found in certain didactic poems of Hanshan's and Shide's—for example, SD 35:

常飲三毒酒,	Always you drink three-poisoned ale,[25]
昏昏都不知。	Dark in your minds, and unaware.
將錢作夢事,	Spending your money to make your dreams,
夢事成鐵圍。	Dreams that turn to an iron cell;

以苦欲捨苦,	Use suffering to cast your suffering away,
捨苦無出期。	Never a time when you'll really be free.
應須早覺悟,	You must awaken as soon as you can,
覺悟自歸依。	And once awake, take Refuge.[26]

The third mark of samsara is the absence of a Self. All three marks of contingent existence overlap, of course. It is often because we desire things that are Impermanent that we then suffer; the source of our desire is often rooted in our false belief in a Self that can possess things and derive pleasure from them. When Hirshfield addresses the issue of the Self specifically (rather than how it manifests itself as a seeking or suffering being), she is often fascinated by the way Self attempts to assert its autonomous existence by insisting that it is different from others—in other words, by how our sense of having Selves emerges because we accentuate the differences between our own experiences and feelings and those of others around us (like a child picking up debris on a beach). However, these created Selves are subject to Impermanence, and we soon realize that we create Selves that differ from the Selves of our past and present. By making the Self into Other, Hirshfield accentuates the degree to which there is no coherent entity that maintains a predictable continuity over time.[27] In the poem "Dream Notebook," she carries the dispersal of the self even further: as she looks at the descriptions of dreams she recorded in a dream journal many years before, she realizes that the distance between her present self and the self that kept the journal is as vast as the one between her dreaming and waking selves.[28]

Another essential deconstruction of the Self involves recognizing its assembly out of contingent, ephemeral phenomena—an idea nicely illustrated by the short poem "Lighthouse":

Its vision sweeps its one path
like an aged monk raking a garden,
his question long ago answered or moved on.
Far off, night-grazing horses,
breath scented with oat grass and fennel,
step through it, disappear, step through it, disappear.[29]

The obvious Buddhist content here is the image of the monk using his rake to create patterns in the sand of a traditional Japanese Zen garden, to which the poet compares to the perpetual turning of the lighthouse beam. The monk repeats a gesture that seems directionless but may have some benefit for those who can read a deeper lesson behind his actions, just as the lighthouse simply repeats its own movement, showing a path, without conscious thought or specific direction. It is up to the beholder (the ships) to interpret the light and its significance. The nature of the monk's question remains unclear, but if it was a koan that resulted in his own awakening (or a question that was transcended and rendered useless when he became enlightened), then his repeated action represents his confident dwelling within a state of purposelessness—he has become what the Zen master Linji called "a person of value with no affairs" *(wushi shi guiren)*.[30] Still, there is also a touch of sadness and impermanence in mentioning that the monk is "aged," just as lighthouses themselves mostly seem part of our own past and are now tinged with a maritime nostalgia. We can also detect the play of a tension common in Buddhist texts between the idea of light as a vehicle of sensory perception as deceptive as any of the senses, as opposed to light as the illuminator of the Real—as we saw, for example, in Zen masters' discussion of HS 51 in chapter 5. Accordingly, the lighthouse is both an instruction for practice, something that explains the topography around it, as well as a source of light meant to transcend mere utilitarian purposes. It is then not merely the Dharma as experienced from within samsara—a temporary raft that can be abandoned once the river is crossed—but actual True Thusness itself, as opposed to illusory conceptions of the Self as real.

The most powerful image of the poem, however, is not the lighthouse but the group of horses: as the repeating beacon flashes past them, they appear to step into the light and back out of it, though it is really the light that is moving. The poem makes visible our inclination to grant autonomy and independence of action to sentient beings without seeing that it is really the karmic phenomena around them that are doing the moving. Moreover, the scene's continual shifting between illumination and darkness is a reminder of impermanence and the illusory nature of Being; the lighthouse of True Thusness exposes this fact to our awareness. There is a similarity here to the opening stanza of "Preface," the first poem in the collection *Spring and Asura* (Haru to Shura) by the modern Japanese poet and devout Buddhist Miyazawa Kenji (1896–1933):

> The phenomenon that we know as "I"
> is a single blue glow from that posited

organic alternating current lamp,
compound body of all transparent ghosts,
and while with scene and all together it
works and works away at its flickering,
so truly it continues in its presence,
this single blue glow from a
karmic alternating current lamp
(the light it lingers, the lamp is lost)[31]

Miyazawa compares the Self to an alternating-current lamp that flickers so rapidly it gives the illusion of constancy, though its light is actually the result of a sequence of discrete phenomena. However, this light of the Self flickers "with scene and all together"—in accord with Miyazawa's love of nature and his emphasis on the Mahayana doctrine that there is no solid boundary between our selves and the rest of the world, so that our connection with the world (both social and natural) compels empathy and compassion. This same element of empathy comes through in Hirshfield's verse, as simple and objective as it is, both in its portrayal of the lone, aged monk and through the image of the continually nightlit horses.

But Hirshfield's poems are not only concerned with the marks of samsara but also with satori, the moment when one can see through samsara into the possibility of nirvana. Sometimes Hirshfield uses the composition of poetry as an analogy for Buddhist practice. Such a viewpoint sees the act of writing as a form of meditation—an act that may or may not lead to inspiration as a sort of flash of satori.[32] But as in Snyder's verse, Nature also plays a powerful role in allowing her to visualize existence free of the sufferings of samsara. Though she is not set on creating an all-encompassing Buddhist philosophy of the Wild, as Snyder is, she does see the natural world (and animals specifically) as providing an emblem for the Real and for the spontaneous, fragmented and momentary though it may seem. It is important to note that this intellectual reorientation is characteristic of modern Buddhism: in a premodern world, where Nature may seem threatening in so many different ways, there is much more ambivalence about it, as we saw in Hanshan's view of mountains. In traditional Buddhism as well, the lives of animals have often not been viewed positively, but instead are said to comprise one of the Three Evil Paths of rebirth. Human intelligence, on the other hand, has been praised for its ability to think rationally about the escape from samsara, something animals are considered to be incapable of doing.[33] For Hirshfield, though, as for many modern Buddhists, animals can be emblems of spontaneous being, untroubled by the emotional anguish that often signifies our own suffering. In some ways, she writes of them as Hanshan does, using them as the ground for implicit fables that reveal the human condition; unlike him, she never reduces animals to a mere metaphor, but grants them dignity:

AGAINST CERTAINTY
There is something out in the dark that wants to correct us.
Each time I think "this," it answers "that."
Answers hard, in the heart-grammar's strictness.

If I then say "that," it too is taken away.

Between certainty and the real, an ancient enmity.
When the cat waits in the path-hedge,
no cell of her body is not waiting.
This is how she is able so completely to disappear.

I would like to enter the silence portion as she does.

To live amid the great vanishing as a cat must live,
one shadow fully at ease inside another.[34]

The dark is the Other, the sense of alienation from things, the discriminating consciousness. The solution is to join with it in some way and eliminate discrimination—but how? The poet longs to have the cat's whole-hearted concentration and intensity, which can accomplish just that, and which also means no decisions to make and no *language* to use. In spite of its power as a medium for communication and for poetry, language becomes wearisome for us as it constantly marks the articulation of discriminating thought. Withdrawing into shadows and becoming one with them can mark a form of transcendence, a merging with the unselfconsciousness of the natural state.

This discourse of Nature/nirvana is illustrated rather well by Hirshfield's view of cats and dogs. Her cats are fundamentally Other, though she views them sympathetically. In one poem, "A Small-Sized Mystery," she emphasizes their strangeness and our inability to make them more than themselves, to imbue them with greater symbolic significance.[35] Dogs, however, are different. There are many dogs in Hirshfield's verse. Not only do we learn much about her own dogs, but she constantly turns to dogs to provide metaphors for our relationship with reality. Dogs are transitional animals: they seem somehow to have inherited our own insecurities and anguish, yet the simplicity of their actions and the transparency of their emotions invite us to see them as a sort of clarifying mirror for ourselves. Where we are likely to overcomplicate our own lives or elevate our emotions to something far more high-minded than they deserve, dogs remind us of what is more basic in us. Dogs do not simulate their feelings or conceal how their feel. In watching dogs, she does not perceive them as alien and fully incorporated into an environment free of samsaric anguish, but rather as better and more honest versions of our passionate selves. Perhaps this is the best model to which we can aspire in our present existence.

In one poem, Hirshfield imagines our ego in the form of a watchdog: it preserves the chaos of our emotions, guarding them and assuring their existence within samara; it prevents the "thieves" of enlightenment from stealing these false feelings that our false Selves think they actually possess. Our ego-dog means to serve us, but it may actually get in the way of the frightening yet exhilarating breakthrough of satori:

THE PROMISE

Mysteriously they entered, those few minutes.
Mysteriously, they left.
As if the great dog of confusion guarding my heart,
who is always sleepless, suddenly slept.
It was not any awakening of the large, not so much as that,
only a stepping back from the petty.
I gazed at the range of blue mountains,
I drank from the stream. Tossed in a small stone from the bank.
Whatever direction the fates of my life might travel, I trusted.
Even the greedy direction, even the grieving, trusted.
There was nothing left to be saved from, bliss nor danger.
The dog's tail wagged a little in his dream.[36]

These moments of enlightenment sneak past the guard dog, who, finally, falls asleep. The poet admits that her satori is modest, not a grand, permanent enlightenment—it has come and gone. But for a few moments she feels complete and utter contentment. This is what it means to realize that samsara is nirvana. And even her dog of confusion is happy.

AFTERWORD

JANE Hirshfield's modest view of enlightenment brings my readings to a close. We have moved from the verse of Hanshan—a body of poems that can be constructed as coherent Buddhist verse in the minds of interpreters and readers like Hakuin—to writers who are quite self-conscious about their debt to Buddhist ideas. Thus, "Buddhist poetry" (or, more broadly, "Buddhist literature") is not always defined by authorial intention (though it can be), but emerges instead through a reading tradition: a community that finds usefulness in a text because it sees it illustrating certain Buddhist truths in a way that is salutary for believers.

In this sense, it is useful to see Buddhist poetry as a continuing skillful means that may contain elements of both intentionality and happenstance. Is the text a method employed by a bodhisattva, hoping that a message of salvation will reach the reader? Or is the reader discovering a salvific truth through the act of reading, in which she draws upon her own inclinations toward enlightenment, upon the Buddha Nature within her attempting to manifest itself? If, as I have suggested in chapter 2, the Buddhist reading of poetry is a way of attempting to eliminate the false distinction between Self and Other, then the distinction between external instruction and internal realization may not exist either. In this sense, writers like Snyder and Hirshfield—and even Kerouac—are bodhisattvas engaged in a skillful means for the benefit of sentient beings; as are in fact the readers of their works the moment that they take them seriously as "Buddhist texts." Hanshan drew upon the breadth of traditional Chinese literary and cultural experience in order to represent the full range of samsaric experience for his readers, relating to them, as the Buddha had, the *avadānas* that explained their past lives and the lessons that they might draw from them. Modern writers continue the same process, converting personal experience into a representation of the personal predicament of all sentient beings—intensely specific but universal at the same time. It is the Buddha preaching:

> The Buddha with a single sound preaches the Dharma,
> While each sentient being understands in accordance with its kind.

And that, precisely, is what literature is from the Buddhist perspective.

Perhaps we should close with a more homely metaphor though, something more Zen-like. Hanshan's poetry is also like the fly-whisk of a Zen abbot—its handle may be carved from exotic Indian sandalwood or from modest Chinese timber, but that is really of no importance. What matters is how the abbot employs it, as he lets the sweep of his hand or the flick of his wrist expose the ignorance of others. Like the sword of Mañjuśrī, it cuts through discriminating thought, bringing enlightenment to those who heed it. HS 83:

白拂栴檀柄,	White fly-whisk, sandalwood handle:
馨香竟日聞。	A scent that lingers through the day.
柔和如卷霧,	Gentle and soft as curling mist,
搖拽似行雲。	Then shaken forth like moving cloud.
禮奉宜當暑,	It's offered up to banish heat,
高提復去塵。	Then lifted high to drive off dust.
時時方丈內,	And sometimes, in the abbot's room
將用指迷人。	He'll point it at the wayward ones.

NOTES

Introduction

1 Kerouac, *Dharma Bums*, 19–20.

2 Snyder, *Riprap and Cold Mountain Poems*, 40.

3 Kerouac, *Dharma Bums*, 21.

4 Kerouac here is evoking a line of thought concerning Chinese characters and poetry that goes back to Ernest Fenollosa and Ezra Pound, one that is compelling though inaccurate. See Haun Saussy's essay "The Prestige of Writing" in *Great Walls of Discourse*, 35–74.

5 For this point, see Yuemin He, "Gary Snyder's Selective Way." This is not to deny the sensitivity to nature that runs through Chinese poetry in general and often emerges in the poetry of Buddhist believers. However, our present way of viewing nature as an unqualified good in itself would have made little sense to medieval Buddhists. For them, nonurban spaces held value mostly because they provided places away from the distractions of society, allowing for successful Buddhist practice.

6 There is little modern Japanese scholarship on the Hanshan poems, other than commentaries on the poems, the most distinguished of which remain Iriya, *Kanzan*, and Iritani and Matsumura, *Kanzan shi*. Numerous articles exist on the cultural influence of Hanshan on Japanese art and literature, but they are beyond the scope of this study.

7 Mair, "Script and Word," 272.

8 See for example Sharf, "The Zen of Japanese Nationalism."

9 See Lenfestey, *A Cartload of Scrolls*.

10 *Cold Mountain: Han Shan*, minutes 12:14–14:13.

11 For a thorough discussion of this issue, see Heine and Wright, eds., *Zen*

Ritual, especially the essay by T. Griffith Foulk, "Ritual in Japanese Zen Buddhism," 21–82.

12 "One who is deluded calls on the Buddha's name, seeking rebirth in the other realm; while the one who is enlightened will cleanse his own mind. For that reason, the Buddha says, 'The Buddha Land is pure when one's own mind is pure.'" *Liuzu dashi fabao tan jing*, T. 48, no. 2008, 352, a20–21.

13 Watson, trans., *Cold Mountain*, 13–14. Watson is referring mostly to prewar Japanese commentaries, though it is likely that his critique is in fact aimed at Hakuin's commentary, which probably set the tone for later ones.

14 For a survey history of American Buddhism and its intellectual roots, see Seager, *Buddhism in America*.

15 There were in fact premodern Daoists who believed that Hanshan was a Daoist poet. While the poems use explicitly Buddhist language much more frequently than Daoist language, they do leave room for Daoist interpretations, especially granting the free exchange of rhetoric and terminology between Daoist and Buddhist circles during the Tang dynasty. Hanshan's language often inclines toward Zen rhetoric, but it is more connected with the concerns and imagery common to early Chan texts, probably due to a Tang-era Buddhist discourse that underlies both the poems and early Chan. Because later readers tended to read Hanshan with Zen eyes, however, it is natural that Zen issues will arise most often in this study.

16 Hakuin is given credit for revitalizing the main (Rinzai) school of Zen in Edo-era Japan and for reestablishing monastic discipline during a period of its decline; he is also considered the main authority for modern koan practice in the Rinzai school, and is probably more highly honored by the modern Rinzai clergy than any other figure in the tradition outside the original Chinese masters. For a summary of his career, see Yampolsky, *Zen Master Hakuin*, 11–27.

17 Mount Sumeru is the large mountain said to exist in the center of every world in Buddhist cosmology; the phrase is often used as a metaphor for impressively large mountains or immense things.

18 The Land of Constant and Calm Illumination was said in the Tiantai school to be the dwelling place of the *dharmakāya*, or Dharma Body, a manifestation of the Buddha that embodies the nature of reality itself.

19 Hakuin, *Notes on the Lectures on Cold Mountain's Poems at Icchantika Cave* (Kanzan shi sendai kimon) (1741), in *Hakuin Oshō Zenshū,* 4:14–15.

20 Other examples of the possibly positive aspects of fear or awe can be seen in HS 144 and 154. Depending on the context, mist and cold might also seem negative, representing suffering and ignorance, as in HS 67.

1. Who Was Hanshan?

1 Chen Yaodong gives a detailed list of early allusions to the poet and the poems in *Hanshan shi ji banben yanjiu*, 312–22, though many passages that he identifies as allusions are vague enough to be treated with skepticism.

2 Ouyang Xiu, *Ouyang Wenzhong gong wen ji,* 41: 2b–3b.

3 I take my text from *Hanshan zi shi ji*, 1a–3b.

4 A *li* is roughly one third of a mile.

5 "The three realms" is a standard Buddhist locution for the world of current suffering or samsara; they are the realm of desire, the realm of form, and the realm of formlessness. The "turning wheel" refers to our continual rebirths within samsara.

6 Though Hanshan is technically not a monk, the "insider-outsider" role he plays at Guoqing is similar to that of antinomian monks at other monastic centers.

7 Kieschnick, *The Eminent Monk*, 58.

8 Faure, *Rhetoric of Immediacy*, 115–18.

9 Not surprisingly, the Vimalakīrti Sutra was a popular text with lay believers. Its importance makes it a significant text for understanding the Hanshan poems.

10 The actions of the Tang Chan masters are analyzable outside the realm of "historical truth": scholars of Chan have increasingly noted the degree to which our vision of the Chan golden age has been filtered through the efforts of Song dynasty practitioners, who were creating an ideal out of an unobtainable past. See McRae, *Seeing through Zen* on this issue.

11 Faure, *Rhetoric of Immediacy*, 98.

12 Compare especially T. 14, no. 475, 539, b13–29.

13 *Jingang boreboluomi jing*, T. 8, no. 235, 749, a24–25. In Buddhist terminology, a mark *(xiang)* is the perceptible manifestation a phenomenon makes in the world of samsara; a Tathāgata ("one who has come thus") is a com-

mon designation (particularly common in Mahayana Buddhism) for a Buddha.

14 *Gātha* is a Sanskrit term that was first applied by Buddhists to verse passages in sutras. In the Chinese tradition, the term could be used to designate nearly any verse with Buddhist content.

15 Amitābha is the Buddha who has created a "Buddha Field," the Western Paradise or Pure Land, and has promised a rebirth there to anyone who invokes his name. He continues to be the most popular focus of devotion in East Asian Buddhism.

16 I use the term "Transcendent" in keeping with many modern scholars of Daoism to indicate the special class of Daoist practitioners *(xian)* who have achieved immortality through various disciplines of body and mind. This cross-fertilization of religious traditions is typical of Tang practice and narrative and does not necessarily put Hanshan's or Shide's identity as Buddhist figures in doubt. See recent discussions of this issue in Sharf, *Coming to Terms*. A "grotto heaven," a recurring motif in Daoist folklore, is a world located within a mountain, usually accessed by a cave.

17 The term "six bandits" turns up in the Hanshan corpus itself several times as a symbol for the six senses in Buddhism: sight, hearing, smell, taste, touch, and mind. "Bandits!" as a provocative shout also occurs in Chan texts such as *The Linji Record* (Linji lu).

18 *Huangbo duanji chanshi Wanling lu*, T. 48, no. 2012b, 386, a15. The image of a buddha or a bodhisattva as a magician conjuring sentient beings is a recurring one, especially in *prajñāparāmitā* literature.

19 *Huangbo Shan Duanji chanshi chuan xin fa yao*, T. 48, no. 2012a, 382, b26–27. This text has become famous to Western Zen enthusiasts through the John Blofeld translation, *The Zen Teaching of Huang Po*. I am not concerned here with whether Pei Xiu is the true author of the text; I am merely interested in illustrating the gap between an ostensibly ignorant narrator and a knowing transcriber or author.

20 For this issue, see especially Nugent, *Manifest in Words*. Scribal practice might also affect the transmission of the poems themselves, making dating based on historical linguistics problematic.

21 Yu's piece on the Hanshan collection can be found in Xiang, ed., *Hanshan*, 963–75.

22 Zanning, *Song gao seng zhuan*, T. 50, no. 2061, 831, b8.

23 Zanning, *Song gao seng zhuan*, T. 50, no. 2061, 777, b25–c1.

24 Yu Jiaxi points out that Zanning's supposition here is false—military officials could receive crimson insignia as well.

25 Zanning, *Song gao seng zhuan*, T. 50, no. 2061, 832, a29–b9.

26 Wu Chi-yu, "A Study," 398.

27 Wu Chi-yu, "A Study," 399.

28 Somewhat unusually, the Hanshan corpus also contains a large number of five-syllable octets that open with a rhyming couplet; though in mainstream Chinese poetry it is fairly normal for seven-syllable octets and quatrains to open with a rhyming couplet, rhyming couplets in five-syllable octets are relatively rare.

29 For those unfamiliar with early Chinese linguistics, the analysis of rhymes may seem to be a peculiar way to understand changes in pronunciation. But in a nonphonetic writing system, rhyme is one of the few ways we derive clues as to how the pronunciation of characters changed over the centuries.

30 Pulleyblank, "Linguistic Evidence," 165.

31 Another collection of poems, the Wang Fanzhi poems found among the Dunhuang manuscripts, can act as a comparison. However, these are unique in a different way, reflecting to most scholars' minds an even more "popular" level of composition, and dating would be an issue for them as well.

32 Pulleyblank, "Linguistic Evidence," 174. It is also noteworthy that Pulleyblank believes that his project entails locating the "real" Hanshan, as though this could give us some clue to an "authentic" figure: "Happily a study of the rhymes . . . helps one to separate the work of the original poet from the later accretions" (165).

33 Though this is open to debate, I would identify the following so-called Han-Shan I poems as reflecting content that might make them later: 1, 9, 25, 40, 51, 54, 105, 139, 166, 200, 202, 209, 210, 211, 213, 279, 280, 285. T. H. Barrett, while generally accepting the conclusions of Pulleyblank, also expresses some reservations on this score; see "Hanshan's Place in History," 126.

2. Who Was Hanshan, Again?

1 For issues concerning the cultural attractiveness of wall-writing, see Zeitlin, "Disappearing Verses," especially 75–79.

2 Zanning, *Song gao seng zhuan*, T. 50, no. 2061, 786, b28.

3 Zanning, *Song gao seng zhuan*, T. 50, no. 2061, 831, c29–832, a1. Since Zanning seems to have had access to the preface, which states that about three hundred poems were collected, I suspect that the number "two hundred" here indicates a textual error in transmission.

4 Xiang, ed., *Hanshan*, 970.

5 Tongbo Tabernacle (Tongbo guan) was a prominent Daoist temple at Tiantai.

6 *Taiping guang ji*, 274–75.

7 On this, see Owen, "Poetry and Its Historical Ground."

8 The term *zhiyin* derives from the ancient story of the zither-player Bo Ya and his friend, Zhongzi Qi. Whenever the former played, the latter could tell exactly what he had in mind through his music. Since then, *zhiyin* has been used for the sensitive reader who can divine the author's intent and personality behind the text.

9 The meaning of the term *bianwen* is open to debate. It is applied to a series of texts that survived in the Dunhuang caves in manuscript form and that sometimes bear this term in their titles. They are popular narratives, often religious in nature, composed in vernacular verse, prose, or a combination of both. For a discussion of the genre and some translations of typical examples, see Mair, *Tun-huang Popular Narratives*. Wang Fanzhi is the supposed author of a collection of just under four hundred poems in the Dunhuang corpus, all on popular Buddhist themes and written in a vernacular language usually less elegant than Hanshan's. See Xiang, ed., *Wang Fanzhi shi jiaozhu*.

10 Much of this tendency originated with Hu Shi, whose work on Buddhist texts in the Dunhuang corpus during the 1920s and again in the 1950s contributed greatly to this concept of literary progress (as well as to his belief that the Chan movement was a humanistic sinification of the Buddhist tradition). See McRae, "Religion as Revolution," 74–78. For the conceptualization of a vernacular literature movement in the Tang and Hanshan's place in it, see Xiang, "Tang dai de baihua shi pai."

11 Highly typical examples of biographical reading include Dai and Shen, "Qiong er gui yin"; Dai and Shen, "You dao ru fo"; Luo Shijin, "Hanshan de shenfen"; Zhang Tianjin, "Lüe lun Hanshan"; and Qian Xuelie, "Hanshan zi." Two English-language scholars who write on Gary Snyder's selective view of Hanshan, Yuemin He ("Gary Snyder's Selective Way") and Joan Qionglin Tan (*Han Shan*), still imagine a biographically coherent poet behind the collection. Most striking is He Shanmeng, who

manages to spin his readings of the poems into an almost three-hundred-page biography, *Yinyi shiren*. In the introduction he confidently tells us that Hanshan was born in 726 in Xianyang, and died at Tiantai on the seventeenth day of the ninth month of 830!

12 See Sun Changwu, *Chan si yu shi qing*, 238–46, and Hu Anjiang, *Hanshan shi*, 69–80. Hu's work probably holds the most skeptical attitude toward biographical approaches to Hanshan of any work published in China, and his summary of scholarly interpretations of the poet's life (69–102) is excellent.

13 See especially HS 275–77.

14 See Gregory, *Inquiry*, for a translation and detailed commentary.

15 See Sharf, *Coming to Terms*, and also Mollier, *Buddhism Face to Face*.

16 Barrett, "Hanshan's Place in History," 125–26. Barrett makes reference to similar points made by Stephen R. Bokenkamp in his review of Henricks's translations of Hanshan; see Bokenkamp, "Review."

17 See Owen, *Making of Early Chinese Classical Poetry*.

18 The three marks are Impermanence, dissatisfaction/suffering, and no Self.

19 Xiang, ed., *Hanshan*, 15–19.

20 Not surprisingly, a search of the Buddhist scriptures shows that the phrase was occasionally borrowed by Buddhist esoteric texts, though it is conventionally associated with Daoist magic.

21 *Shishuo xinyu jiaojian*, 318.

22 Mair, "Script and Word," 272.

23 This couplet refers to canonical commentaries on the *Shijing*, compiled by Mao Heng and Mao Chang in the Han dynasty, as well as to the later subcommentary composed by Zheng Xuan.

24 My translation is slightly tentative here. The poet is referring in line 7 to his inability to follow the rules of regulated verse, which prescribed specific tonal patterns. HS 288 also refers to this. As in that poem, the poet means to assert his own authenticity through a mock-modesty: unlike sophisticated (and false) elite poets, his verse is rough and dispenses with rules.

25 Bokenkamp, "Chinese Metaphor Again," 219; Wade-Giles changed to *pinyin*. His scriptural references here are T. 34, no. 1718, 63, b20–21 and T. 46, no. 1925, 690, b25ff.

26 Bokenkamp, "Chinese Metaphor Again," 217–18.

27 Hakuin, *Hakuin Oshō Zenshū*, 4:1.

28 McRae, *Seeing Through Zen*, xix.

29 *Miao fa lian hua jing*, T. 9, no. 262, 12b, 9–11.

30 Readers should not confuse the character "to know" 知 with the character "wisdom" 智, though they are close in pronunciation. The fact that they share a visual component, however, is significant.

31 *Weimojie suo shuo jing*, T. 14, no. 475, 548a, 9–15. Plural "dharmas" here (as opposed to the Buddha's teaching, the Dharma) refer to the impermanent phenomena that make up samsaric existence.

32 I refer here to the famous opening words of the *Laozi*.

33 *Weimojie suo shuo jing*, T. 14, no. 475, 538a, 1–4

34 Owen, *Traditional Chinese Poetry and Poetics*, 12–77.

3. Juxtapositions

1 *Quan Tang shi*, 1280. See also discussion of this poem in Owen, *Traditional Chinese Poetry and Poetics*, 134–37, to which I am indebted.

2 Owen, *Poetry of the Early T'ang*, 9–11.

3 *Zhenzhou Linji Huizhao chanshi yulu*, T. 47, no. 1985, 498, c11–17. Other Hanshan poems that use similar rhetoric to emphasize the need to act quickly include: HS 1 (discussed in chapter 2), 41, 210, 214, 232, 255, 269, and 272.

4 Other HS poems that mention "one hundred years" in similar fashion include 135 and 146. "The twelve divisions" derives from a bibliographic tradition of dividing Buddhist scriptures into as many categories, and serves as a stock term for the scriptures in general.

5 *Da ban niepan jing*, T. 12, no. 374, 453c, 26–28.

6 *Jingang boreboluomi jing*, T. 8, no. 235, 751a, 25–26.

7 For meat-eating, see specifically HS 56, 70, 74, 76, 95, 159, 186, 207, 233, 260, and 269; and SD 2, 4, 5, 12, and 39.

8 The use of the word "flesh" or "meat" to represent the corporeal self (and hence the ignorance of an unenlightened being) can be found throughout Buddhist writings; e.g., the term "eye of flesh" *(rou yan)* to refer to the lowest of the five forms of vision of which beings are capable (Hanshan alludes to it in HS 138.4). The term "foolish lump of flesh" occurs again at HS 240, line 6. Its use in HS 228 shows a vivid use of the dual meaning of *rou* as both ignorant corporeal body and as consumable being.

9 Mair, "Script and Word," 275.

10 This association was largely due to the influence of a rhapsody attributed

to Song Yu (fl. third century BCE), *Master Dengtu the Lecher* (Dengu zi haose fu), which describes a girl residing to the east of the poet who subjected him to her amorous advances.

11 Henricks, *Poetry of Han-shan*, 101.

12 Xiang, ed., *Hanshan*, 153–54.

13 There are in fact a number of miracle tales in the tradition that describe meditation states so deep and prolonged that vegetation actually grows up *through* human limbs. This poem does not describe such a phenomenon explicitly, but certainly hints at it. Hakuin cites an example from a meditation sutra, the Buddhadhyāna-samādhisāgara Sutra *(Fo shuo guan fo sanmei hai jing)*, T. 15, no. 643, 650, b29–c5.

14 Hakuin, *Hakuin Oshō Zenshū*, 4: 229.

15 I also think it unlikely that an editor of the late Tang or early Song would have thought of compilations in this way. Though associative sequence was already common by this time in Japanese anthologies (beginning with the *Kokinshū* [905 CE]), compilers of Chinese collections seem to have been uninterested in the technique. Later on, when biographically chronological imperatives become stronger in editorial work, artful juxtaposition became even less likely.

16 Henricks, *Poetry of Han-shan*: "My clothes are simple—worn for the purpose of dance" (209); Red Pine, *Collected Songs*: "unlined robes are good for dancing" (135). Though the *Hanyu da cidian*'s earliest citation for this usage is from the eleventh-century poet Mei Yaochen, it is not impossible that it was already common in Tang vernacular.

17 Xiang Chu's lengthy discussion of the odd use of the character *cui*, the last character in the fourth line, to mean "urging one to drink at a banquet" is likely correct (Xiang, ed., *Hanshan*, 360). Both Henricks and Red Pine are unconvincing. Henricks: "My wine is all gone—I sip because I sing" (209); Red Pine: "no wine means getting drunk on song" (135).

18 For example, HS 32, 47, 72, 94, 220, 274, 304; this does not include the many more references to death, burial, and mourning.

19 The Six Paths are the six possible realms of rebirth; the speaker is claiming that his awareness of Impermanence will allow him to escape rebirth altogether.

20 I doubt that charnel-ground contemplation was practiced in any substantial manner in China; it likely remained a literary trope derived from South Asian sources. Wilt Idema notes that most Chinese artists shunned portraying skeletons and seem to have only minimal exposure to their

anatomical details. As he further relates, however, skeletons eventually became a major motif in the religious literature of the Daoist Quanzhen sect, from the Yuan dynasty on. Idema, "Skulls and Skeletons."

21 See Graham, "Mi Heng's 'Rhapsody on a Parrot'" for translation and commentary.

22 *Fannao* occurs seven times in the Hanshan poems (65, 156, 210, 236, 253, 256, 293), five of them in conjunction with explicitly Buddhist vocabulary.

23 *Da ban niepan jing*, T. 12, no. 374, 436, b27–436, c1.

24 It was a poetic cliché to describe the delicate eyebrows of a beautiful woman as resembling the furry antennae of moths.

25 *Liezi yi zhu*, 127–28.

26 *Analects*, 7.14.

27 I follow Mair here in reading *jing* as meaning "carrying on an occupation," so that the phrase *xu jing* would mean "carry on in my parent's profession" (Mair, "Script and Word," 273). Hakuin agrees with this interpretation (Hakuin, *Hakuin Oshō Zenshū*, 4: 47). Others argue that *xu* should be amended to *du* ("to read"); Xiang accordingly interprets "*du jing*" as "reading the [Buddhist] scriptures" (Xiang, ed., *Hanshan*, 51). Much as I am partial to Buddhist interpretations of the poem, I doubt, granted the content of the poem overall, that an explicit reference to sutras is intended here.

4. At Home and Abroad

1 The phrase "hundred years" occurs eight times in the Hanshan/Shide corpus, and every occurrence except this one refers explicitly to the span of a human life.

2 The five *skandhas* ("bundles") are five different forms of psycho-physical phenomena that result in the false creation of the Self.

3 Hakuin, *Hakuin Oshō Zenshū*, 4: 223.

4 Even so, major monastic centers located in mountainous regions could still appear as liminal sites, where access to extraordinary forces was much more likely than elsewhere. See, for example, much of the visionary literature surrounding the Huayan center of Wutai, discussed in Cartelli, *Five-Colored Clouds*.

5 *Jingde chuan deng lu*, T. 51, no. 2076, 264c, 15. See Heine's koan commentaries in *Opening a Mountain*, which examine at great length Zen monks' relationship with mountain wilds.

6 For examples of conventional "time passing" laments, see HS 17, 19, 32, 46–48, 55, 64, 77, 121, 145, 251, 256, and 265.

7 This line alludes to the literary convention that a human life lasts one hundred years. See discussion of HS 184 above.

8 "Spring" here has a double meaning, referring to the season and serving as a poetic marker indicating the passing of a year. The poet is saying both that his dwelling is so high in the mountains that spring does not arrive there, and that he is unaware of the passing of the years.

9 The Three Forms of Existence are those that occur in each of the Three Realms: the realm of desire, the realm of form, and the realm of non-form.

10 Four Forms of Birth is a general term for the various ways in which living beings enter the world: by womb, eggs, dampness, or transformation.

11 The idea that there is no self—a principle universally held to be true by all Buddhists—is felt by members of Mahayana sects to be insufficient as compared to an understanding of the emptiness of all of existence.

12 The four universal bodhisattva vows are to bring limitless numbers of living beings to salvation, to bring to an end the numberless *kleśa* that afflict us, to master a limitless number of teaching methods to save others, and to perfect one's knowledge of the ultimate way of the Buddha.

13 In Tiantai Buddhism, "land of calm illumination" is a general term for any Buddha-land created by a Buddha; here, Hakuin may have in mind that our own land (the land presided over by the historical Buddha Śākyamuni) is in fact perfect, though our mental obstructions prevent us from seeing it as such. For example of this argument, see the first chapter of the Vimalakīrti Sutra.

14 Hakuin, *Hakuin Oshō Zenshū*, 4: 31.

15 *Jingde chuan deng lu*, T. 51, no. 2076, 240c, 19–23. HS 97 also alludes to this story.

16 *Fayuan zhulin*, T. 53, no. 2122, 330a, 23–26.

17 There are several references to "four dharma gates" in the Tripitaka, but none of them seem to apply to Hakuin's meaning here. I take it to refer to a scholastic conception of the different stages of meditation.

18 A *śravaka* is a "voice-hearer," one who achieves nirvana through listening to the sermons of a Buddha. Listening to a Buddha's sermons is one of the two inferior vehicles of practice from a Mahayana perspective.

19 To achieve "no outflowings" is to attain a state in which one no longer

produces actions that have karmic consequences and is associated with arhats, those who will achieve nirvana upon death.

20 A *pratyekabuddha* is "self-enlightened" and has no interest in aiding others; this is the second inferior vehicle of enlightenment, from a Mahayana perspective.

21 I interpret this sentence to mean: though you may be securely positioned and will not be washed away by the river, you are not dealing with the suffering of others (the sea of life and death).

22 A "word-head" *(huatou)* is the element of a koan that a master assigns to a student for meditation practice, meant to result in a breakthrough experience of intuitive understanding. This method was typical of the Rinzai (Linji) school and of Hakuin's own practice in particular.

23 Hakuin, *Hakuin Oshō Zenshū*, 4: 282–83.

24 *Miao fa lian hua jing*, T. 9, no. 262, 19, b1–b6.

25 See, for example, Bodhidharma's famous reply to Emperor Wu of Liang that his patronage of Buddhism had "no merit," as well as HS 173, which might be seen as the poet's commentary on just this story.

26 The two images are combined in the last couplet of HS 215: "How is this better than recognizing the true source *(zhen yuan)*? / Once you obtain it, you have it always."

27 Hakuin, *Hakuin Oshō Zenshū*, 4: 39–40.

28 Though I think that the following lines support a symbolic reading of this line, it is not impossible that the poet wants us to think of the one-chapter sutra as Hanshan's poems themselves.

29 *Weimojie suo shuo jing*, T. 14, no. 475, 537, a27.

30 The speaker mentions "three vehicles," but of course, in terms of the parable, there is (ultimately) only one vehicle.

5. Tropes

1 Owen, "Deadwood," 170.

2 *Da ban niepan jing*, T. 12, no. 374, 597, a23–27.

3 Parinirvana is the final entrance into nirvana upon one's physical death, as opposed to the state of enlightenment achieved while one is alive.

4 *Zhuangzi ji shi*, 43.

5 For the four bodhisattva vows, see chapter 4, note 12.

6 The seven qualities that characterize an enlightened being include zeal, joy, and ability to see past lives, among others.

7 "Eight Correct Paths" is another term for the Eightfold Path.

8 The "Four States of Fearlessness" are powers possessed by Buddhas or bodhisattvas that permit them to be fearless in any adverse situation.

9 "Entrances to the Dharma" serves as a general term for all of the teachings of the Buddha.

10 Hakuin refers to an imperfect or incomplete nirvana, unlike the nirvana of the Buddha or the nirvana which the bodhisattva seeks to bring to all living beings.

11 Hakuin alludes to taking a vow, as bodhisattva, to create a world when one becomes a Buddha that will aid living beings in finding salvation. The Pure Land is the classic example.

12 Hakuin, *Hakuin Oshō Zenshū*, 4: 16–17.

13 Hakuin, *Hakuin Oshō Zenshū*, 4: 190.

14 Heine, *Shifting Shape, Shaping Text*, 9.

15 *Miao fa lian hua jing*, T. 9, no. 262, 29, a6–17.

16 *Arhats* are those who have attained nirvana under the Buddha's instruction. In Mahayana Buddhism, they are usually seen to be practitioners of a lesser doctrine, inferior to bodhisattvas, who wish to aid all sentient beings.

17 For appearances of the ass in this context, see HS 59, line 6, and 75, line 2.

18 See, for example, *Longshu pusa zhuan*, T. 50, no. 2047a, 184, c9–11.

19 "Endless universe" is literally "the great thousand," a specialized Buddhist term representing a cosmos consisting of a thrice-multiplied thousand worlds (i.e., a billion).

20 T. 9, no. 278, 429, a3–4.

21 Xiang, ed., *Hanshan*, 138–43.

22 T. 48, no. 2008, p. 348, b24–25; 349, a7–8. I use the standard received text here, not the Dunhuang version. My translations are tentative and are meant merely to illustrate the riddle-competition nature of the exchange—the precise meaning of these quatrains has inspired a massive amount of commentary.

23 Hong Mai, *Rongzhai suibi*, 661.

24 Hakuin, *Hakuin Oshō Zenshū*, 4: 73.

25 *Hongzhi chanshi guang lu*, T.48, no. 2001, 59, c21–26.

26 *Wu deng hui yuan*, T. 80X, no. 1565, p. 378, c20–22.

27 *Zhanran Yuancheng chanshi yulu*, T. 72X, no. 1444, 778, a24–b4.

28 T. 19, no. 945, 111, a8–13.

29 *Quan Tang shi*, 1301.

30 A variant version reads *zhong* ("at the end") as *zhong* ("within"), and thus changes the line to "In this song there is no Zen." Though this sounds a bit more natural, I believe it misses the point of the poem, which is that one realizes, as the poem comes to its end, that no real Zen has been manifested—leaving the reader to carry on from that point with genuine practice.

31 The presence of these poems could be explained from a modern ethnographic perspective as simply reflecting the "popular poetry" nature of the collection's genesis—but such an option would not be available to most traditional readers.

32 The term *yiyang*, used here to describe the song, usually describes melismatic effects on a single sustained syllable.

33 For an example of the Indian tradition, see, for example, Ramanujan, Rao, and Shulman, trans., *When God Is a Customer.*

34 Bhiṣma-garjitasvara-rāja is the name of a primordial Buddha, praised in chapter 20 of the Lotus Sutra. Hakuin obviously picks his name here because its translation alludes to the majestic sound of a Buddha preaching the Dharma.

35 The Five Impure Ages are the five periods of decline that come about following the gradual decay of the Buddha's teaching. They are characterized by increased passions and delusions, human misery, and shortened life-spans.

36 Hakuin, *Hakuin Oshō Zenshū*, 4: 52.

37 See for example, Hakuin, *Hakuin Oshō Zenshū*, 4: 73; 4: 61.

38 The secular poetry that most closely corresponds to these poems are probably a number of lyrics by Li Bai, such as his *Lyrics for the Girls of Yue* (Yue nü ci) in *Quan Tang shi*, 1885.

39 Translation from Shaw, *Jātakas*, 110.

40 Khoroche, *Once the Buddha was a Monkey*, 195.

41 Pāpīyas is another name for Māra.

42 Kauśika is another name for Indra.

43 The "Five Desires" are those stirred by the senses of sight, hearing, smell, taste, and touch.

44 *Weimojie suo shuo jing*, T.14, no. 475, 543, a11–27.

45 *Weimojie suo shuo jing*, T.14, no. 475, 543, b12–b17.

46 See for example, the *Xian yu jing*, T. 4, no. 202, 359.

47 The eroticization of skillful means does explicitly occur at least once in

the Chinese tradition, in the popular legend of the "fish-basket Guanyin." In this account, Guanyin appears in a village in Shaanxi as a beautiful young girl and promises to marry whoever is most adept at memorizing sutras. When a certain Mr. Ma wins the competition, his new bride mysteriously dies on her wedding night. Later, a monk comes to the village and reveals that the girl was actually a manifestation of the bodhisattva. Readers' knowledge of this tale might encourage a similar reading of the Hanshan poem. See Yü, *Kuan-yin*, 419–38.

6. Satire

1 For a thorough examination of prose animal fables in the Tang, see for example, Spring, *Animal Allegories*.

2 See Xiang's note in *Hanshan*, 108–9.

3 *Xian Qin Han Wei Jin Nanbei Chao shi*, 1125.

4 Account found in *Taiping guang ji*, 310.

5 See also HS 68, 157, 220, 236, 248, 274, and 302.

6 Modern American readers may be struck by the resemblance of this poem to the popular fable of the scorpion and the frog, in which a frog agrees to carry a scorpion across a river on the promise that the scorpion will not sting him. The scorpion does so anyway, and both of them drown. Arata Takeda ("Blumenreiche Handelswege," 135–42) has demonstrated that the origins of this fable seem to be the Persian *Kalīlah wa-Dimnah*, an adaptation of the Sanskrit *Pañcatantra,* an influential collection of fables that came to be widely disseminated throughout Asia. Our current texts of the *Pañcatantra* lack this story. However, since both this Persian version and the Hanshan poem use a turtle rather than a frog, I rather wonder if an earlier South Asian version had found its way to China by Tang times.

7 *Wu jia zheng tong zan*, T. 78X, no. 1554, 578, a17–18. Shitou is the prominent Chan master Shitou Xiqian. "The Sea of the Sages" is not a Buddhist term; here it probably is a poetic term for the teachings (Dharma).

8 Hakuin derives this term from the classic Zen allegory of the ten oxherding pictures. "Entering the market with extended hands" indicates the tenth and final stage, when the newly enlightened believer reenters human society and spreads the teachings. Hakuin sees the turtles venturing forth as proselytizers.

9 Literally, "a single spot of objective-dust condition." "Objective dust" *(ke chen)* is the technical translation of the term *akasmāt-kleśa*, a disturbance

that intrudes upon one from outside, instead of being generated within the mind.

10 Hakuin, *Hakuin Oshō Zenshū*, 4: 61.

11 Examinations were held in a court established south of the Board of Civil Office.

12 "Blue beetle" was a medieval slang term for money, possibly derived from an early folk belief that if the blood from a mother beetle was smeared on one string of cash and the blood from one of her children on another, the two strings of cash would eventually find each other again. Books in Tang China tended to be written on yellow-hued paper. Hanshan uses the two terms here in order to create a parallel couplet that reinforces the theme of the poem: many books = no money.

13 My translation accepts Xiang's argument (*Hanshan*, 270–71) that *qi gou* means "offer to a dog" as opposed to "a begging dog"; this emphasizes that one is making an active effort to get the indifferent dog to eat the poem-cakes, just as the poets are trying to get readers for their poetry. However, "begging dog" would work in the line as well. A less likely (but tempting) choice would interpret the line to mean, "Even if you begged a dog, the dog wouldn't eat it."

14 Hanshan also makes this point in HS 288, when a scholar accuses him of being unable to write in the fashionable "regulated verse" form. The poet replies: "I laugh when *you* try to write poetry / Like a blind man praising the sun" (288, lines 7–8). Again, his laughter targets a lack of understanding on the part of the benighted.

15 Xiang, ed., *Wang Fanzhi shi jiaozhu*, 177–79.

16 *Gu lie nü zhuan*, *juan* 6, 29a–b.

17 Though the collection never refers explicitly to the doctrine of *mofa* ("the latter days of the Dharma"), the belief that society increasingly falls away from the Good following the departure of the Buddha, a Buddhist reader might see this implied. However, it is also clear that Hanshan sees the Confucian secular order itself as deeply problematic in relation to the Dharma.

18 See for example, HS 37, 54, 75, 86, 87, 96, 125, 136, and 243; SD 12 and 43.

19 Zhang and Wang are the two most common Chinese surnames.

20 Xiang, ed., *Hanshan*, 718–20.

21 See for example, lines 119–29 of Milton's *Lycidas*.

22 For a detailed examination of this festival during the Tang, see Teiser, *Ghost Festival*.

23 See Gernet, *Buddhism in Chinese Society*, especially his overview of Tang monastic power, 3–25.

24 Translation from Gernet, *Buddhism in Chinese Society*, 198. Original from *Xiangfa jueyi jing*, T. 85, no. 2870, 1337, b29–c6. I have altered the Wade-Giles romanization of *liu-po* to pinyin *liubo*.

25 See McRae, *Seeing through Zen*, 101–18 for an overview of the revisionist perspective; Poceski, *Ordinary Mind*, provides a detailed discussion of the rise of the Chan school in social and political terms during the mid and late Tang periods.

26 Flames and visual hallucinations (idiomatically called "sky-flowers") were cliché Buddhist metaphors for the Impermanent and unreal nature of reality.

27 Other translators see the last couplet as referring to the monk's useless devotion to Maitreya, but I think it much more likely that these lines act as a concluding benediction.

7. Who Gets to Climb the Matterhorn?

1 See for example, Johnston, "Dharma Bums"; Jones, *A Map of* Mexico City Blues; Giamo, *Kerouac, The Word and the Way*; and Giles, "upside down like fools."

2 Of course, this conflict resulted in a particular enthusiasm for the antinomian tendencies of the Mahayana tradition and of Chan more specifically, but the Beats tended to elevate this aspect of the faith to mainstream status, suggesting in some cases that antinomian behavior constituted typical Buddhist practice.

3 The Rosie incident portrays Ray in a particularly unsympathetic light—not only does he fail to treat Rosie's illness with the seriousness it deserves, he continues to see her horrible end as a judgment on his own abilities to communicate his privately held spiritual truths to others. It is a particularly painful example of how Ray can never escape his own ego enough to enact the compassion he feels is the most important part of his Buddhist faith.

4 He, "Gary Snyder's Selective Way," 53–57.

5 Snyder, *Riprap and Cold Mountain Poems*, 46.

6 I have been unable to locate the source of this line in Chan or Zen literature. Its current fame seems to come entirely from its use here. Miriam Levering has suggested to me that it may be Ray misremembering the

forty-sixth koan in the *Wu men guan* collection: "Master Shishuang said, 'You are at the top of the hundred-foot high pole. How will you make a step further?' Another Zen Master of Ancient Times said, 'One who sits on top of the hundred-foot pole has not quite attained true enlightenment. Make another step forward from the top of the pole and throw one's own body into the 100,000 universes.'" Private communication; text found at T.48, no. 2005, 298, c12–14.

7 *Taiping guang ji*, 48. Originally from the fourth-century collection *Biographies of Gods and Transcendents* (Shen xian zhuan).

8 *Yasen Kanna* has been translated a number of times into English. For a scholarly translation and commentary, see Shaw and Schiffer, "*Yasen Kana*." Hakuin's first account of the hermit actually occurs in his commentary to HS 79; Hakuin, *Hakuin Oshō Zenshū*, 4: 108–20.

9 One might compare Ray's list of fidgety activities with a similar list from Gary Snyder's poem "Three Worlds, Three Realms, Six Roads," found in *Mountains and Rivers Without End* (22–26). The poem consists quite simply of things he has done at six different locations of his life, including "Things to Do Around a Lookout." Though the list itself is not that different from Ray's, Snyder relates it with a simple naturalness and good humor that conveys a sense of serenity.

10 Giles, "upside down like fools," 180–81.

11 I am most concerned here with the rhetorical techniques and images that Snyder uses to convey Buddhist ideas in specific poems. For a discussion of the impact of Zen Buddhism on his larger literary concerns and his conception of translation, see Stalling, *Poetics of Emptiness*, chapter 3.

12 Snyder, *Riprap and Cold Mountain Poems*, 3.

13 My discussion here is influenced in part by the thoughtful analysis found in Jody Norton, "The Importance of Nothing," 63–65.

14 Snyder, *Riprap and Cold Mountain Poems*, 22.

15 Snyder, *Axe Handles*, 43–45.

16 Snyder, *Axe Handles*, 5–6, 24–25, 39–40. Snyder may be evoking the bucolic "can-do" spirit of Tao Qian here.

17 Yoshikawa, *An Introduction to Sung Poetry*, 24–28.

18 *Quan Song ci*, 287. The Chinese "lyric" *(ci)* is a form of verse quite different from *shi*. Each lyric is composed to the metrical patterns of a specific tune and is titled according to the name of that tune. Some *ci* were meant to be sung, others to be chanted or recited.

19 Snyder, *danger on peaks*, 50–51.

20 Snyder, *Mountains and Rivers Without End*, 10–21.

21 Hirshfield, *Given Sugar, Given Salt*, 53.

22 Hirshfield, *Lives of the Heart*, 15.

23 Hirshfield, *Lives of the Heart*, 22.

24 Hirshfield, *Lives of the Heart*, 61.

25 The Three Poisons are desire, anger, and ignorance.

26 The refuge meant here is that of the Three Jewels of Buddhism: Buddha, teachings, and monastic order.

27 See for example, Hirshfield, "To Opinion," *After*, 41–42.

28 Hirshfield, *Given Sugar, Given Salt*, 18.

29 Hirshfield, *After*, 61; part of "Seventeen Pebbles."

30 *Zhenzhou Linji Huizhao chanshi yulu*, T. 47, no. 1985, 497, c27.

31 Miyazawa, *Miyazawa Kenji shi shū*, 19–20. Translation is my own.

32 See, for example, the first essay in *Nine Gates*, "Poetry and the Mind of Concentration," and the poem "Inspiration" in *The October Palace*, 47. In this stance she participates in a form of Zen poetics that conceivably could trace its origins to Yan Yu's thirteenth-century *Canglang's Remarks on Poetry* (Canglang shihua). The theoretical assumptions of this tradition are fascinating, but deserve much greater attention than I can grant them here.

33 Japanese Buddhist traditions probably moved most forcefully towards a more sympathetic view of animal life, in spite of continuing ambivalence. See Ambros, *Bones of Contention*, for a recent discussion of this issue, as well as of differences between modern and premodern views on animal sentience within the Japanese Buddhist tradition.

34 Hirshfield, *After*, 68.

35 Hirshfield, "A Small-Sized Mystery," *Come, Thief*, 76.

36 Hirshfield, *After*, 46.

GLOSSARY

baihua wenxue yundong 白話文學運動 vernacular literature movement
Bankei Yōtaku (Japanese) 盤珪永琢 Zen master (1622–93)
ben xing 本性 original nature
Benji 本寂 Chan monk
bianwen 變文 transformation texts
biyu 比喻 metaphor, figurative language
Bo Ya 伯牙 mythical musician
bu ju 卜居 plot-divination
bu ke ren 不可忍 cannot bear

Canglang shihua 滄浪詩話 *Canglang's Remarks on Poetry*
Cao Cao 曹操 warlord (155–220)
Caoshan 曹山 mountain, site of Buddhist monastery
chan 禪 meditation, *dhyāna*
Chang'an 長安 city
Changsha 長沙 city
chi 癡 foolish
Chongwen zongmu 崇文總目 *General Catalogue of Distinguished Letters*
Chu ci 楚辭 *Songs of Chu*
chu jia 出家 leaving the home, becoming a monk
chuan 穿 to bore through, to wear through
ci 詞 song lyrics
cui 啐 urging one [to drink]

Dagui 大溈 mountain, site of Buddhist monastery
Dali 大曆 era (766–779)
Danqiu 丹丘 district

Daode jing 道德經 *Classic of the Way and Its Power*
Daoqiao 道翹 Buddhist monk
Daoxuan 道宣 Buddhist monk and author (596–667)
Dazhi 大智 Chan master, teacher of Guishan Lingyou
Dengtu zi haose fu 登徒子好色賦 *Master Dengtu the Lecher*
Dingling Wei 丁令威 mythical Daoist sage
dongtian 洞天 grotto heaven
Du Fu 杜甫 poet (712–770)
Du Guangting 杜光庭 Daoist master (850–933)
Dui Hanshan zi shi 對寒山子詩 *Reply to Master Hanshan's Poems*
Dunhuang 敦煌 city and site of famous cave complex

fang 方 square, method, direction
fangbian 方便 skillful means
fannao 煩惱 *kleśa*
Fenggan 豐干 Buddhist monk and companion to Hanshan
Fo Guang da ci dian 佛光大辭典 *Buddha's Light Comprehensive Dictionary*
fo xing 佛性 Buddha nature
fugui 富貴 wealth and high position
furong 芙蓉 lotus

gu 蠱 type of poisonous beast
guan 觀 to observe
Guanyin 觀音 bodhisattva
gui 歸 to return
Guishan Lingyou 溈山靈佑 Chan master (771–854)
Guoqing 國清 Buddhist monastery

Hakuin Ekaku (Japanese) 白隱慧鶴 Zen master (1686–1768)
Han E 韓娥 legendary singer
Hanshan 寒山 legendary poet; mountain
Hanyan 寒巖 mountain; alternate name for Hanshan
Hanyu da cidian 漢語大詞典 *Comprehensive Dictionary of the Chinese Language*
Hong Mai 洪邁 author (1123–1202)
Hongzhi Zhengjue 宏智正覺 Chan master (1091–1157)
Hu Shi 胡適 scholar (1891–1962)
Huangbo Xiyun 黃檗希運 Chan master (d. ca. 850)

huatou 話頭 word-head, Zen meditation technique
Huayan 華嚴 Buddhist school
Huineng 惠能 Chan master (638–713)

ji 寄 to lodge
ji 迹 track, path
jiashu 價數 price

Kanzan shi sendai kimon 寒山詩闡提記聞 *Notes on the Lectures on Cold Mountain's Poems at Icchantika Cave*
kaozheng 考證 evidential scholarship
ke chen 客塵 objective dust, *akasmāt*
Ku shu fu 枯樹賦 *Barren Tree Rhapsody*
ku si 苦死 bitter death

laiqu 來去 coming and going
Laozi 老子 philosophical text
Letan 泐潭 place
Li Bai 李白 poet (701–762)
Li He 李褐 Daoist adept
Li Shangyin 李商隱 poet (ca. 813–858)
Lian 蓮 lotus
Liaodong 遼東 district
Lie nü zhuan 列女傳 *Biographies of Virtuous Women*
Liezi 列子 Daoist philosopher
lingchuang 靈牀 altar, spirit platform
Linji lu 臨濟錄 *The Linji Record*
Linji Yixuan 臨濟義玄 Chan master (d. 866)
Linjiang xian 臨江仙 "Transcendent by the River"
Liu Bei 劉備 warlord (161–223)
Liu Chen 劉晨 character in tale
liubo 六博 gambling game
long 龍 dragon
Longshu 龍樹 Chinese name for Nāgārjuna
lou 露 exposure
lun 倫 associates
Luoyang 洛陽 city

Lüqiu Yin 閭丘胤 official; supposed author of Hanshan collection preface
lüshi 律詩 regulated verse

Manqing 曼卿 *See* Shi Yannian
Mao Chang 毛萇 commentator (fl. Han dynasty)
Mao Heng 毛亨 commentator (fl. Han dynasty)
Mazu Daoyi 馬祖道一 Chan master (709–788)
Mei Yaochen 梅堯臣 Chinese poet (1002–1060)
Mi Heng 禰衡 Chinese poet (fl. 190s)
Miyan 祕演 Buddhist monk (fl. 1050s)
Miyazawa Kenji (Japanese) 宮沢賢治 poet (1896–1933)
mofa 末法 latter days of the Law

na kan 那堪 how can I stand?
nai he dang nai he 奈何當奈何 O what to do?
Nanyue Huairang 南嶽懷讓 Chan master (677–744)
niao ji 鳥迹 path of birds

Ouyang Xiu 歐陽修 statesman and writer (1007–1072)

pan 判 judgment
panjiao 判教 division of the doctrines
Penglai 蓬萊 Isle of the Immortals
Piling 毘陵 district

Qi 齊 ancient state
qi gou 乞狗 offer to a dog, begging dog
qin 琴 zither
qing jing jiaorong 情景交融 fusion of emotion and scene
qiong 窮 run out, seek to its source
quan 權 provisional

Rinzai (Japanese) *See* Linji Yixuan
rou 肉 flesh, meat
rou yan 肉眼 eye of flesh
Ruan Zhao 阮肇 character in tale
Ruizong 睿宗 Tang dynasty emperor (r. 710–712)
Rulin wai shi 儒林外史 *An Unofficial History of Scholars*

Shao 韶 ancient state

Shen xian zhuan 神仙傳 *Biographies of Gods and Transcendents*

Shenxiu 神秀 Chan master (606?–706)

shi 實 actual

shi 事 affairs

shi 詩 poetry

Shi shuo xin yu 世說新語 *Tales of the World: New Series*

Shi Yannian 石延年 recluse (d. 1041)

Shide 拾得 Buddhist monk and companion to Hanshan

Shifeng 始豐 district

Shijing 詩經 *Classic of Poetry*

Shishuang 石霜 Chan master

Shitou Xiqian 石頭希遷 Chan master (700–790)

shiye 事業 career

shou ji 受記 receive the designation

shou yang jue 受殃抉 receive calamity and gouging

Shouning Daowan 壽寧道完 Chan master (fl. late Song)

Shu 蜀 province

Si ku tiyao bianzheng 四庫提要辨證 *Evidential Analysis of the Catalogue of the Four Treasuries*

siliang 思量 to ponder

Song gao seng zhuan 宋高僧傳 *Biographies of Eminent Monks Compiled in the Song Dynasty*

Song Yu 宋玉 legendary poet

Su Shi 蘇軾 statesman and writer (1037–1101)

Taiping guang ji 太平廣記 *Comprehensive Records of the Taiping Era*

Taizhou 台州 district

Tang wen 湯問 *Tang Asked*

Tangxing 唐興 district

Tao Qian 陶潛 poet (365–427)

tariki (Japanese) 他力 [dependency on] another's strength

Tianshi dao 天師道 Celestial Masters sect

Tiantai 天台 mountain

tianyuan shi 田園詩 field and garden poetry

Tongbo guan 桐伯觀 Tongbo Tabernacle [Daoist temple]

Urashima Tarō (Japanese) 浦島太郎 hero of early tale

Wang Fanzhi 王梵志 mythical Buddhist poet
Wang Wei 王維 poet (ca. 699–ca. 761)
Wang Zhang 王長 Daoist adept
wanglai 往來 going and coming
Wei Shu 韋述 author
weiji 維基 *Yijing* hexagram
Wen xuan 文選 *Selections of Refined Literature*
Wu Chi-yu (Wu Qiyu) 吳其昱 scholar
wu fang 無妨 no obstructions
wu fang 無方 not have square features
Wu Jingzi 吳敬梓 novelist (1701–1754)
wushi 無事 without affairs, independent of samsara
Wutai 五台 mountain
wuwei 無為 actions independent of causes and conditions

xian 仙 Transcendent [Daoist immortal]
Xian zhuan shiyi 仙傳拾遺 *Addenda to Biographies of Transcendents*
xiang 象 image, phenomenon
xiang 相 marks
Xiantian 先天 era (712–713)
Xiantong 咸通 era (860–874)
Xianyang 咸陽 city
Xianzong 憲宗 Tang dynasty emperor (r. 805–820)
xiaoyao you 逍遙遊 roaming at will [Daoist value]
xin di 心地 ground of mind
Xin Tang shu 新唐書 *New Tang History*
Xu gao seng zhuan 續高僧傳 *Biographies of Eminent Monks Continued*
Xu Lingfu 徐靈府 Daoist adept (fl. early ninth century)
xunjiu 尋究 to seek

Yan Yu 嚴羽 critic (1191–1241)
Yang Xiu 楊脩 Chinese minister
***Yasen kanna* (Japanese)** 夜船閑話 *A Chat in a Boat in the Evening*
Yijing 易經 *The Book of Changes*
ying 影 reflection, shadow
Yingwu fu 鸚鵡賦 *Rhapsody on a Parrot*
yiyang 抑揚 melismatic singing
Yong 雍 district

you 遊 to wander, to ramble
youwei 有為 purposive action, good works
yu 愚 fool, foolish
Yu Jiaxi 余嘉錫 scholar (1884–1955)
Yu Xin 庾信 poet (513–581)
yuan 源 water source
Yuan ren lun 原人論 *Inquiry into the Origin of Humanity*
Yuanhe 元和 era (806–820)
yuchi 愚癡 foolish
Yue nü ci 越女詞 *Lyrics for the Girls of Yue*
yuefu 樂府 music bureau

zan 讚 eulogy
Zanning 贊寧 Buddhist monk and author (919–1001)
zao ci 遭刺 suffer injury, receive criticism
Zen (Japanese) *See* chan
Zhang Daoling 張道陵 Daoist adept (34–156)
Zhanran Yuancheng 湛然圓澄 Chan master (1561–1626)
Zhao hun 招魂 *Summons of the Soul*
Zhao Sheng 趙昇 Daoist adept
zhen yuan 真源 true source
Zheng Xuan 鄭玄 commentator (127–200)
zhenru 真如 True Suchness, *bhūtatathatā*
zhi 智 wisdom, *prajñā*
Zhiyan 智巖 Buddhist monk
Zhiyi 智顗 Buddhist monk and philosopher (538–597)
zhiyin 知音 understanding friend
zhong 終 at the end
zhong 中 within
Zhongzi Qi 鍾子期 legendary friend of Bo Yi
Zhu li guan 竹里館 "Lodge within the Bamboo"
Zhuangzi 莊子 philosopher
Zhuge Liang 諸葛亮 strategist (181–234)
zhuo 著 put on clothes
zhuzhang 拄杖 abbot's staff
Zongmi 宗密 Buddhist monk and author (780–841)
zuan 鑽 bore through

BIBLIOGRAPHY

Abbreviations

CLEAR	*Chinese Literature: Essays, Articles, Reviews*
JAOS	*The Journal of the American Oriental Society*
SBCK	*Sibu congkan*

Citations to the Taishō Tripitaka are as follows:
T = volume number; no. = number of text.

Ambros, Barbara R. *Bones of Contention: Animals and Religion in Contemporary Japan*. Honolulu: University of Hawai'i Press, 2012.

Barrett, T. H. "Hanshan's Place in History." In *Poems of Hanshan,* translated by Peter Hobson, 115–37. Walnut Creek, CA: AltaMira Press, 2003.

Blofeld, John, trans. *The Zen Teaching of Huang Po: On the Transmission of Mind*. New York: Grove Press, 1958.

Bokenkamp, Stephen R. "Chinese Metaphor Again: Reading—and Understanding—Imagery in the Chinese Poetic Tradition." *JAOS* 109, no. 2 (1989): 211–21.

———. "Review of Robert G. Henricks, *The Poetry of Han-shan*." *CLEAR* 13 (1991): 137–45.

Cartelli, Mary Anne. *The Five-Colored Clouds of Mount Wutai: Poems from Dunhuang*. Leiden: Brill, 2012.

Chen Yaodong. *Hanshan shi ji banben yanjiu* (Research on the Editions of Hanshan's Poetry). Beijing: Shijie Zhishi, 2007.

Cold Mountain: Han Shan. Directed by Mike Hazard and Deb Wallwork. The Center for International Education, 2009. Film.

Da ban niepan jing (Nirvāṇa Sūtra). T. 12, no. 374.

Da fangguang fo huayan jing (Avataṃsaka Sūtra). T. 9, no. 278.

Dai Cheng and Shen Jianwen. "Qiong er gui yin, ji er gui fo de Hanshan zi" (Master Hanshan: A Hermit in Poverty and a Convert to Buddhism in Solitude). *Huaiyin shifan xueyuan xuebao: Zhexue shehui kexue ban* 23, no. 5 (2001): 672–76.

———. "You dao ru fo yi dao yi fo de Hanshanzi" (Master Hanshan: From Daoist to Buddhist and Yet Both Daoist and Buddhist). *Huanggang shifan xueyuan xuebao* 21, no. 5 (2001): 89–93.

Faure, Bernard. *The Rhetoric of Immediacy: A Cultural Critique of Chan/Zen Buddhism*. Princeton: Princeton University Press, 1991.

———. "Space and Place in Chinese Religious Traditions." *History of Religions* 26, no. 4 (1987): 337–56.

Fayuan zhulin (The Jeweled Forest of the Garden of the Dharma). T. 53, no. 2122.

Gernet, Jacques. *Buddhism in Chinese Society: An Economic History from the Fifth to the Tenth Centuries.* Translated by Franciscus Verellen. New York: Columbia University Press, 1995.

Giamo, Ben. *Kerouac, The Word and the Way: Prose Artist as Spiritual Quester.* Carbondale: Southern Illinois University Press, 2000.

Giles, Todd. "upside down like fools': Jack Kerouac's 'Desolation Blues' and the Struggle for Enlightenment." *Texas Studies in Literature and Language* 53, no. 2 (2011): 179–206.

Graham, William T., Jr. "Mi Heng's 'Rhapsody on a Parrot.'" *Harvard Journal of Asiatic Studies* 39, no. 1 (1979): 39–54.

Gregory, Peter N., trans. *Inquiry into the Origin of Humanity: An Annotated Translation of Tsung-mi's* Yüan jen lun *with a Modern Commentary.* Honolulu: University of Hawai'i Press, 1995.

Gu lie nü zhuan (Biographies of Virtuous Women). Shanghai: Shangwu yinshu guan, 1936.

Hakuin, *Hakuin Oshō Zenshū* (His Eminence Hakuin: Complete Works). Tokyo: Ryūginsha, 1935.

Hanshan zi shi ji (Master Hanshan's poetry collection). SBCK ed.

He Shanmeng. *Yinyi shiren: Hanshan zhuan* (Reclusive Poet: A Biography of Hanshan). Hangzhou: Zhejiang renmin, 2006.

He, Yuemin. "Gary Snyder's Selective Way to Cold Mountain: Domesticating Han Shan." In *The Emergence of Buddhist American Literature,* edited by John Whalen-Bridge and Gary Storhoff, 45–62. Albany: State University of New York Press, 2009.

Heine, Steven. *Opening a Mountain: Kōans of the Zen Masters.* Oxford: Oxford University Press, 2001.

———. *Shifting Shape, Shaping Text: Philosophy and Folklore in the Fox Kōan.* Honolulu: University of Hawai'i Press, 1999.

Heine, Steven, and Dale S. Wright, eds. *Zen Ritual: Studies of Zen Buddhist Theory in Practice.* New York: Oxford University Press, 2008.

Henricks, Robert G., trans. *The Poetry of Han-shan: A Complete, Annotated Translation of Cold Mountain.* Albany: State University of New York Press, 1990.

Hirshfield, Jane. *After.* New York: HarperCollins, 2006.

———. *Come, Thief.* New York: Knopf, 2011.

———. *Given Sugar, Given Salt.* New York: HarperCollins, 2001.

———. *The Lives of the Heart.* New York: HarperCollins, 1997.

———. *Nine Gates: Entering the Mind of Poetry.* New York: HarperCollins, 1997.

———. *The October Palace.* New York: HarperCollins, 1994.

Hong Mai. *Rongzhai suibi* (Miscellaneous Notes from Rongzhai). Shanghai: Guji, 1978.

Hongzhi chanshi guang lu (Comprehensive Record of Chan Master Hongzhi). T. 48, no. 2001.

Hu Anjiang. *Hanshan shi: Wenben lüxing yu jingdian jian'gou* (Hanshan's Poems: Travels of a Literary Text and the Construction of a Classic). Beijing: Qinghua daxue chubanshe, 2011.

Huangbo Duanji chanshi Wanling lu (The Wanling Record of Chan Master Huangbo Duanji). T. 48, no. 2012b.

Huangbo Shan Duanji chanshi chuan xin fao yao (Essentials of the Dharma from the Mind Transmission of Chan Master Duanji of Huangbo Mountain). T. 48, no. 2012a.

Idema, Wilt L. "Skulls and Skeletons in Art and on Stage." In *Conflict and Accommodation in Early Modern East Asia: Essays in Honour of Erik Zürcher*, edited by Leonard Blussé and Harriet T. Zurndorfer, 191–215. Leiden: E. J. Brill, 1993.

Iritani Sensuke and Matsumura Takashi, eds. *Kanzan shi* (Hanshan's Poems). *Zen no goroku*, vol. 13. Tokyo: Chikuma Shoten, 1970.

Iriya Yoshitaka, ed. *Kanzan* (Hanshan). *Chūgoku shijin senshū,* vol. 5. Tokyo: Iwanami Shoten, 1958.

Jingang boreboluomi jing (Diamond Sūtra). T. 8, no. 235.

Jingde chuan deng lu (Transmission of the Lamp Records from the Jingde Era). T. 51, no. 2076.

Johnston, P. J. "Dharma Bums: The Beat Generation and the Making of Countercultural Pilgrimage." *Buddhist-Christian Studies* 33 (2013): 165–79.

Jones, James T. *A Map of* Mexico City Blues*: Jack Kerouac as Poet*. Carbondale, IL: Southern Illinois University Press, 1992.

Kerouac, Jack. *The Dharma Bums*. New York: Penguin, 1976.

Khoroche, Peter, trans. *Once the Buddha Was a Monkey: Ārya Śūra's Jātakamālā*. Chicago: University of Chicago Press, 1989.

Kieschnick, John. *The Eminent Monk: Buddhist Ideals in Medieval Chinese Hagiography*. Honolulu: University of Hawai'i Press, 1997.

LaFleur, William R. *The Karma of Words: Buddhism and the Literary Arts in Medieval Japan*. Berkeley: University of California Press, 1983.

Lenfestey, James P. *A Cartload of Scrolls: 100 Poems in the Manner of the T'ang Dynasty Hermit Poet Han-Shan*. Duluth: Holy Cow! Press, 2007.

Liezi yi zhu (Liezi Translated and Annotated). Edited and translated by Yan Jie and Yan Beiming. Beijing: Zhonghua, 1987.

Liuzu dashi fabao tan jing (The Platform Sūtra). T. 48, no. 2008.

Longshu pusa zhuan (Biography of the Bodhisattva Nagārjuna). T. 50, no. 2047a.

Luo Shijin. "Hanshan de shenfen yu tongsu shi xushu jiaose zhuanhuan" (The Status of Hanshan and the Change in Roles Described in his Vernacular Poems). *Jianghai xuekan* 2 (2005): 189–93.

Mair, Victor H. "Script and Word in Medieval Vernacular Sinitic." (Review of Henricks). *JAOS* 112, no. 2 (1992): 269–78.

———. *Tun-huang Popular Narratives*. Cambridge: Cambridge University Press, 1983.

McRae, John R. "Religion as Revolution in Chinese Historiography: Hu Shih (1891–1962) on Shen-hui (684–758)." *Cahiers d'Extrême-Asie* 12 (2001): 59–102.

———. *Seeing through Zen: Encounter, Transformation, and Genealogy in Chinese Chan Buddhism*. Berkeley: University of California Press, 2003.

Miao fa lian hua jing (Lotus Sūtra). T. 9, no. 262.

Miller, Stephen D. *The Wind from Vulture Peak: The Buddhification of Japanese Waka in the Heian Period*. With the assistance of Patrick Donnelly. Ithaca: East Asia Program, Cornell University, 2013.

Miyazawa Kenji. *Miyawawa Kenji shi shū* (The Collected Poems of Miyazawa Kenji). Edited by Amazawa Taijirō. Tokyo: Shinchōsha, 1991.

Mollier, Christine. *Buddhism Face to Face: Scripture, Ritual, and Iconographic Exchange in Medieval China*. Honolulu: University of Hawai'i Press, 2008.

Norton, Jody. "The Importance of Nothing: Absence and Its Origins in the Poetry of Gary Snyder." *Contemporary Literature* 28, no. 1 (1987): 41–66.

Nugent, Christopher M. B. *Manifest in Words, Written on Paper: Producing and Circulating Poetry in Tang Dynasty China*. Cambridge, MA: Harvard University Asia Center, 2010.

Ouyang Xiu. *Ouyang Wenzhong gong wen ji* (Anthology of the Writings of Ouyang, the Literary and Loyal Duke). Shanghai: Shangwu yinshu guan, 1929.

Owen, Stephen. "Deadwood: The Barren Tree from Yü Hsin to Han Yü." *CLEAR* 1, no. 2 (1979): 157–79.

———. *The Making of Early Chinese Classical Poetry*. Cambridge, MA: Harvard University Asia Center, 2006.

———. "Poetry and Its Historical Ground." *CLEAR* 12 (1990): 107–118.

———. *The Poetry of the Early T'ang*. New Haven, CT: Yale University Press, 1977.

———. *Traditional Chinese Poetry and Poetics: Omen of the World*. Madison, WI: University of Wisconsin Press, 1985.

Pandey, Rajyashree. *Writing and Renunciation in Medieval Japan: The Works of the Poet-Priest Kamo no Chōmei*. Ann Arbor: The Center for Japanese Studies, University of Michigan, 1998.

Poceski, Mario. *Ordinary Mind as the Way: The Hongzhou School and the Growth of Chan Buddhism*. Oxford: Oxford University Press, 2007.

Pulleyblank, E. G. "Linguistic Evidence for the Date of Han-Shan." In *Studies in Chinese Poetry and Poetics,* vol. 1, edited by Ronald C. Miao, 163–95. San Francisco: Chinese Materials Center, 1978.

Qian Xuelie. "Hanshan zi chan yue shi qianxi" (A Brief Analysis of Master Hanshan's Poems Describing the Pleasure of Meditation). *Zhongguo renmin daxue xue bao* 3 (1998): 97–101.

Quan Song ci (Complete Song Dynasty Lyrics). Edited by Tang Guizhang. Beijing: Zhonghua, 1965.

Quan Tang shi (Complete Tang Poems). Beijing: Zhonghua, 1960.

Ramanujan, A. K., Velcheru Narayama Rao, and David Shulman, trans. *When God Is a Customer: Telugu Courtesan Songs by Kṣetrayya and Others*. Berkeley: University of California Press, 1994.

Red Pine (Bill Porter), trans. *The Collected Songs of Cold Mountain*. 2nd ed. Port Townsend, WA: Copper Canyon Press, 2000.

Saussy, Haun. *Great Walls of Discourse and Other Adventures in Cultural China*. Cambridge, MA: Harvard University Asia Center, 2001.

Seager, Richard Hughes. *Buddhism in America*. Revised ed. New York: Columbia University Press, 2012.

Sharf, Robert H. *Coming to Terms with Chinese Buddhism: A Reading of the* Treasure Store Treatise. Honolulu: University of Hawai'i Press, 2002.

———. "The Zen of Japanese Nationalism." In *Curators of the Buddha: The Study of Buddhism under Colonialism,* edited by Donald S. Lopez, Jr., 107–60. Chicago: The University of Chicago Press, 1995.

Shaw, R. D. M., and W. Schiffer. "*Yasen Kanna*: A Chat on a Boat in the Evening by Hakuin Zenji." *Monumenta Nipponica* 13, nos. 1–2 (1957): 101–27.

Shaw, Sarah, trans. *The Jātakas: Birth Stories of the Bodhisatta.* Delhi: Penguin Books, 2006.

Shishuo xinyu jiaojian (Tales of the World, New Series, Collated and Annotated). Edited by Xu Zhen'e. Beijing: Zhonghua, 1987.

Snyder, Gary. *Axe Handles.* Washington, DC: Shoemaker and Hoard, 1983.

———. *danger on peaks.* Washington, DC: Shoemaker and Hoard, 2004.

———. *Mountains and Rivers Without End.* Berkeley: Counterpoint, 2013.

———. *Riprap and Cold Mountain Poems.* Washington, DC: Shoemaker and Hoard, 2004.

Spring, Madeline K. *Animal Allegories in T'ang China.* New Haven: American Oriental Society, 1993.

Stalling, Jonathan. *Poetics of Emptiness: Transformations of Asian Thought in American Poetry.* New York: Fordham University Press, 2010.

Sun Changwu. *Chan si yu shi qing* (Chan Thought and Poetic Feeling). 2nd ed. Beijing: Zhonghua, 2006.

Taiping guang ji (Comprehensive Records of the Taiping Era). Shanghai: Guji, 1990.

Takeda, Arata. "Blumenreiche Handelswege: Ost-westliche Streifzüge auf den Spuren der Fabel *Der Skorpion und der Frosch*" (Flowery Trade Routes: East-West Incursions on the Trail of the Fable *The Scorpion and the Frog*). *Deutsche Vierteljahrsschrift für Literaturwissenschaft und Geistesgeschichte* 85, no. 1 (2011): 124–52.

Tan, Joan Qionglin. *Han Shan, Chan Buddhism and Gary Snyder's Ecopoetic Way.* Eastbourne: Sussex Academic Press, 2009.

Teiser, Stephen F. *The Ghost Festival in Medieval China.* Princeton: Princeton University Press, 1988.

Tian, Xiaofei. *Beacon Fire and Shooting Star: The Literary Culture of the Liang (502–557).* Cambridge: Harvard University Asia Center, 2008.

Watson, Burton, trans. *Cold Mountain: 100 Poems by the T'ang Poet Han-shan.* New York: Columbia University Press, 1970.

Weimojie suo shuo jing (Vimalakīrti Sūtra). T. 14, no. 475.

Wu Chi-yu [Wu Qiyu]. "A Study of Han-shan." *T'oung pao* 45, nos. 4–5 (1957): 392–450.

Wu deng hui yuan (A Digest of the Five "Lamp Records"). T. 80X, no. 1565.

Wu jia zheng tong zan (Eulogies for the Orthodox Lines of the Five Houses). T. 78X, no. 1554.

Wu men guan (The Gateless Barrier). T. 48, no. 2005.

Xian Qin Han Wei Jin Nanbei Chao shi (Poems of the Pre-Qin, Qin, Han, Wei, Jin, and Southern and Northern Dynasties). Edited by Lu Qinli. Beijing: Zhonghua, 1983.

Xian yu jing (Sūtra of the Wise and Foolish). T. 4, no. 202.

Xiang Chu. "Tang dai de baihua shi pai" (The Vernacular Poetry Faction during the Tang Dynasty). *Jiangxi shehui kexue* 2 (2004): 36–41.

———, ed. *Hanshan shi zhu fu Shide shi zhu* (Hanshan's Poems Annotated, with Annotations of Shide's Poems). Beijing: Zhonghua shuju, 2000.

———, ed. *Wang Fanzhi shi jiaozhu* (Wang Fanzhi's Poems Collated and Annotated). Shanghai: Guji, 2010.

Xiangfa jueyi jing (Sūtra Resolving Doubts Concerning the False Dharma). T. 85, no. 2870.

Yampolsky, Philip B., trans. *Zen Master Hakuin: Selected Writings*. New York: Columbia University Press, 1971.

Yoshikawa, Kōjirō. *An Introduction to Sung Poetry*. Translated by Burton Watson. Cambridge, MA: Harvard University Press, 1967.

Yü, Chün-fang. *Kuan-yin: The Chinese Transformation of Avalokiteśvara*. New York: Columbia University Press, 2001.

Zanning. *Song gao seng zhuan* (Biographies of Eminent Monks Compiled in the Song Dynasty). T. 50, no. 2061.

Zeitlin, Judith T. "Disappearing Verses: Writing on Walls and Anxieties of Loss." In *Writing and Materiality in China: Essays in Honor of Patrick Hanan*, edited by Judith T. Zeitlin and Lydia H. Liu, 73–132. Cambridge: Harvard University Asia Center, 2003.

Zhang Tianjian. "Lüe lun Hanshan de shengnian bian yi yu shenshi" (A Brief Discussion of the Debates Concerning Hanshan's Birth Year and his Era). *Chengdu daxue xuebao: sheke ban* 3 (2004): 43–44.

Zhanran Yuancheng chanshi yulu (Record of the Conversations of Chan Master Zhanran Yuancheng). T. 72X, no. 1444.

Zhenzhou Linji Huizhao chanshi yulu (Record of the Conversations of the Chan Master Linji Huizhao of Zhenzhou). T. 47, no. 1985.

Zhuangzi ji shi (Zhuangzi with Collected Explanations). Edited by Guo Qingfan and Wang Xiaoyu. Beijing: Zhonghua, 1961.

INDEX

C

D

I

J

K

L

M

N

O

P

Q

R

S

X

Y

Z